AF559930

# HOTEL
# PLANNING MANAGEMENT

# HOTEL PLANNING MANAGEMENT

M. C. METTI

ANMOL PUBLICATIONS PVT. LTD.
NEW DELHI - 110 002 (INDIA)

**ANMOL PUBLICATIONS PVT. LTD.**

*H.O.:* 4374/4B, Ansari Road, Darya Ganj,
New Delhi-110 002 (India)
Ph.: 23278000, 23261597

*B.O.:* No. 1015, Ist Main Road, BSK IIIrd Stage
IIIrd Phase, IIIrd Block
Bangalore - 560 085 (India)
Visit us at: www.anmolpublications.com

*Hotel Planning Management*

ISBN 978-81-261-3246-1

PRINTED IN INDIA

Printed at Mehra Offset Press, Delhi.

# Contents

# Preface

Strategic management is that set of managerial decisions and actions that determines the long-run performance of a corporation. It includes environmental scanning, strategy formulation, strategy implementation and evaluation and control.

An organization's strategy must be appropriate for its resources, environmental circumstances, and core objectives. The process involves matching the company's internal resources and capabilities (eg quality management)] to the external business environment the organization faces. Strategy formulation involves, doing a situation analysis: both internal and external; both micro-environmental and macro-environmental. Concurrent with this assessment, objectives are set. This involves crafting vision statements (long term view of a possible future), mission statements (the role that the organization gives itself in society), overall corporate objectives (both financial and strategic), strategic business unit objectives (both financial and strategic), and tactical objectives. These objectives should, in the light of the situation analysis, suggest a strategic plan. The plan provides the details of how to achieve these objectives.

This three-step strategy formulation process is sometimes referred to as determining where you are now, determining where you want to go, and then determining how to get there. These three questions are the essence of strategic planning. SWOT Analysis: I/O Economics for the external factors and RBV for the internal factors.

This book Hotel Management and Planning discuses all the core elements of Planning in business and as well it gives a basic idea about the hotel managerial problems that we face everyday while performing the administrative functions.

Author

## Chapter 1

# Business Planning

Business planning is often conducted when:

- Starting a new venture (organization, product or service)
- Expanding a current organization, product or service
- Buying a current organization, product or service
- Working to improve the management of a current organization, product or service

There are a wide variety of formats for a business plan. The particular format and amount of content included in a plan depends on the complexity of the organization, product or service and on the demands of those who will use the business plan to make a decision, eg, an investor, funder, management, Board of Directors, etc.

Overall, the contents of a business plan typically aim to:

1. Describe the venture (new or current organization, product or service), often including its primary features, advantages and benefits
2. What the organization wants to do with it (buy it, expand it, etc.)
3. Justification that the plans are credible (eg, results of research that indicate the need for what the organization wants to do)
4. Marketing plans, including research results about how the venture will be marketed (eg, who the customers will be, any specific groups (or targets) of

customers, why they need the venture (benefits they seek from the venture), how they will use the venture, what they will be willing to pay, how the venture will be advertised and promoted, etc.)

5. Staffing plans, including what expertise will be needed to build (sometimes included in business plans) and provide the venture on an ongoing basis
6. Management plans, including how the expertise will be organized, coordinated and led
7. Financial plans, including costs to build the venture (sometimes included in business plans), costs to operate the venture, expected revenue, budgets for each of the first several years into the future, when the venture might break-even (begin making more money overall than it has cost), etc.

Business planning is usually conducted when starting a new organization or a new major venture, for example, new product, service or programme. Essentially, a business plan is a combination of a marketing plan, strategic plan, operational/ management plan and a financial plan. Far more important than the plan document, is the planning process itself.

Business planning usually includes a thorough examination of the idea for a new product/service, if there's really a market for it, who the competitors are, how the idea is uniquely positioned to be competitive and noticeable, how the idea will be produced to a product/service, how much it will cost, how it will be promoted, what overall goals must be accomplished, how the development and ongoing operations will be managed and what resources are needed (including money). As noted above, a business plan is a combination of a marketing plan, financial plan, strategic plan and a operational/management plan. Here are a variety of perspectives.

To start, you need to plan your strategy very well. Your restaurant has to focus on some key elements that'll set it apart from the thousands of other eateries out there. These could be location, cuisine, decoration or even—good luck with this one—price. Maybe it's located where there's a lot of traffic, or across the hall from a gym, or near a bookstore, or outside a theater. Maybe there are no fish tacos in your town, or no good Italian restaurants. Maybe there are no cafes near the river with outside seating. You have to know why you're different. In short, don't try to please everybody generally; find your niche market, and please those people very well.

By differentiating your restaurant, you make marketing it much easier. Marketing is critical to restaurant success, but marketing can be expensive. And in most cases, the most effective restaurant marketing depends on repeat business and word-of-mouth. Think about how you choose a restaurant yourself—do you look through your Entertainment book or other coupon source? Do you research with a Zagat guide or online reviews? Or do you ask for recommendations from friends? Ask yourself how people will describe your restaurant and why they'll recommend it. If you can't put that short conversation into easy words, you're in trouble.

Also, if you have a choice, don't start a low-priced restaurant. Low-priced restaurants are much harder to market than mid- to high-priced restaurants. Fast-food franchises are everywhere, and they have a huge corner on that market. People believe in cheap food when they see strong branding and lots of customers. You don't want to be the dive on the corner that can't attract business.

Unless you're already partnered with an investor, you should assume you won't be. In general, restaurants aren't targets for professional investors because they're so risky. The few exceptions include celebrities who back restaurants that capitalize on their names, and well-known chefs and successful restaurant owners opening new venues.

Not having access to startup financing doesn't mean you shouldn't start the business. It means you should carefully decide whether you're going to start slowly, minding expenses, or borrow enough money to start big. Your borrowing options include commercial bank loans, which require assets you can stake as collateral, and SBA loans, which require less collateral than bank loans but still require you to put up 30 percent of the starting costs to qualify for the guaranteed loan. When in doubt about loans go straight to your favourite bank and ask for advice.

Be sure to count your startup costs well. You don't want to get into a bind where you've spent half of what you thought you needed and you've run out of money. You'll probably have to rent a location and spend a few months fixing it up, and you may need employees some employees to help out during the fix-up period, too. Unless you're moving into an existing restaurant, you'll need to buy kitchen equipment, tables and chairs, cash registers, phone systems and décor to establish ambience. And then you need to budget for what's called "working capital" for the startup period when your spending exceeds your sales. Some say you need at least six months of expenses ready to go; others recommend having 12 months covered.

Your sales forecast is also important. We like to build a sales forecast based on unit sales, meaning meals and drinks, not just gross sales amounts. That helps us break the sales forecast into components I can count. How many tables do you have? How many meals will you serve on Friday night when the place is almost full? What does an average meal cost? How many drinks come with the meals? Then calculate unit sales, average revenue per unit and average cost per unit.

Then comes your expense forecast. With meals and drinks already priced out, your remaining operating expenses are mainly people, rent and other fixed costs. Estimate those per month, and match them to your sales forecast.

When all the costs are tallied, you'll get a good picture of the cash flow and how much money you'll need to keep the restaurant operational. During the early months of startup, your cash flow probably won't cover all your expenses, so you'll want your plan to include how you'll cover the difference.

Finally, as you get started, remember that business plans continually go out of date, and good business plans are never done. You should take an hour or so every month to review the difference between what you planned and what actually happened, and update your plan accordingly.

A business plan is often the entry-level requirement to getting government money, investor capital or bank loans. Although, you may have a complete picture of the business in your head, investors and bankers need to see if you really have an understanding of the business and have thought it through.

Preparing a plan is a long and daunting task but in the end the business owner often sees things from a new perspective and has mitigated any risks. The business plan is not just for banks and investors but also supplies you with a blueprint of succeeding in business. The plan provides you with the direction of your company and is a guidepost for your employees too.

The primary job of a business owner is to manage and run a business. The term manage implies the task of planning and execution. Are you considering bringing in an outside expert to help with your business plan? The idea is appealing to some because planning is daunting and there are experts out there—if you can afford them. However, it's not nearly as simple as you'd like.

Critical fact: your business plan isn't a stand-alone document; it's you, your business and your promise. You have to know every date, every deadline, every last word, and every number in your plan. Investors invest in people, not plans. They buy the jockey more than the horse. Expert help can't change this fundamental principle. It must be your plan, yours down to your bones, and it must not be the consultant's plan.

If you work within the framework that the business plan is yours, then there are some things that outside help can do for your plan and your planning process. If you have the money to spend, and you find the right person or resource, here the benefits of hiring outside help:

- A professional plan review. Does your plan cover the most obvious points? Does it have any obvious logical holes? Is it easy to read and is it easy to find the most important information? Ask an expert to review it.

- Help with the financials. You don't have to be an MBA or accountant to plan your business, but some of the underlying math and financial principles can be daunting. The ideal is doing it yourself with an expert looking on and coaching.
- General planning coaching. An outside expert can facilitate your thinking and planning by guiding discussion towards key issues, drawing out definitions, highlighting and focusing on important points.
- Industry-specific coaching. Don't reinvent wheels when you can leverage off of an expert's experience.
- Contacts and introductions. Be careful with this one, however, because you're swimming in shark-infested waters here (and I'm referring to the consultants as sharks, not just the investors). There are good consultants who deliver on promises, but there are far more bad consultants who make promises. A consultant can get you an investor no matter how good the plan, because the investor wants (or doesn't want) you, not your plan.

Please be sure to avoid the common problems with outside planning consulting. Some of these come up far too often:

- Misunderstanding the deliverables. Don't pay for vague promises. Business-plan review, coaching and help with the financials are credible deliverables, but getting your plan financed isn't credible because that depends on you, not your plan.
- Wanting a turnkey business plan. That just won't work. If a consultant wants to go away without you and come back with a plan, you go away first.
- Not checking references. Always ask for references of previous clients and talk to those people.

- Paying in advance. Some consultants need to ask a fair payment up front, but not the whole thing.

The worst element of outside consulting is the consultants who let you think that paying their fees will get you investment, when in fact they're just going to give you advice. This happens too frequently and it's the clients' fault too, not just the consultants. You should immediately mistrust somebody who promises open doors and contacts as part of the job. The promise isn't credible unless the consultants very carefully filter their prospective clients and take only those whose background, track record, team and business proposition are likely to succeed. Otherwise, they're making false promises because the investors invest in the people, not the plan.

Writing a business plan is one of the least favourite activities of the majority of small business owners. The traditional rule of credit is if you want to grow and operate your business you will need a business plan to find capital. This is quickly changing as more and more business owners learn about business plan-free financing.

Change has swept through industries, society and careers. Over the last few years, change and its companion, information technology, is altering the face of small business lending.

The relationship-based banking in the small loans and credit market is becoming irrelevant. The decision of loan approval is determined by a computerized credit scoring programme unless a business requires a loan or credit product over $100,000.

## MARKET PLANNING

A product is nothing without a market. Regardless of how novel a product or service is, there must be a way to turn the need it satisfies into revenues. Each hotel, club, restaurant and casino has different needs for handling common issues such as modeling volume driven relationships, multiple templates for different planning needs (e.g. owned vs. franchised locations), and deployment to disparate and multiple locations.

Your operation needs the flexibility to meet these divisional challenges while maintaining consistency across your business. Business Objects Planning for Hospitality delivers on both counts:

- Reduce operating expenses, improve staffing levels, and optimize revenues - all while shortening cycle time
- Track the key business drivers for your diverse operations, food and beverage, room occupancy and operations

Though time-consuming, multi-layered, and complex budgeting is a critical component of planning and controlling your day-to-day hospitality and leisure operations. To ensure more timely and accurate budgets, hotels, restaurants, casinos, and food service operators need to streamline and formalize the budgeting process-and produce detailed, yet flexible budgets that are fully aligned with strategic goals.

Business Objects solutions create budgets, sales forecasts, and payroll plans that automatically incorporate data from your long-range plans, source systems, and end users so you can move into action faster.

Whether you are running a single hotel, restaurant, or casino-or a worldwide chain of properties-you need access to timely and accurate information to make the right decisions. Incomplete or out of- date data can hamstring employees, hamper decision making, and compromise enterprise performance. With a comprehensive reporting solution, hospitality and leisure organizations like yours can ensure that the right information gets to the right people at the right time enabling management teams to make smart decisions that improve performance.

## ORGANISATION PLANNING

Planning is also a management function, concerned with defining goals for future organizational performance and deciding on the tasks and resources to be used in order to attain those goals. To meet the goals, managers will invest significant resources for training and incentives to motivate employees.

Planning is the process of setting objectives and determining how to accomplish them. Simply it is the act of thinking before doing. It accesses us in predicting about the future. So, it serves as the standard for the function of controlling if there is any deviation.

In most organizations 'strategic planning' is an annual process, typically covering just the year ahead. Occasionally, a few organizations may look at a practical plan which stretches three or more years ahead.

To be most effective, the plan has to be formalized, usually in written form, as a formal 'marketing plan'. The essence of the process is that it moves from the general to the specific; from the overall objectives of the organization down to the individual action plan for a part of one marketing programme. It is also an iterative process, so that the draft output of each stage is checked to see what impact it has on the earlier stages - and is amended accordingly.

**The Corporate Plan**

The starting point for the marketing plan, and the context within which it is set, is the corporate plan. In most marketing-oriented organizations the contents of the corporate plan will closely match those of the marketing plan itself; but it will also include the plans for the disposition of the other internal resources of the organization. Thus, the corporate plan is likely to contain three main components:

The first category is intimately involved with the customers. In marketing terms, although there are many other factors to take into account, the most important definition of where the company 'is' revolves around where it is in the market (and hence where it is with its consumers). The same is largely true of the second stage as well; since, no matter how much its managers may wish otherwise, where the company can realistically expect to go is totally in the hands of its customers. It is only at the third stage that the 4 Ps come into play as vehicles for moving the company to reach its objectives.

**Corporate Objectives**

The overall objectives of commercial organizations are conventionally supposed to be financial. However, other aims are also possible. Many companies choose long-term growth (which may be quite different to revenue maximization in the short term). Almost all have an implicit, and very powerful, aim of survival.

One of the best known 'alternatives', that of 'satisfying' (rather than profit maximization), came from Herbert Simon: "In one way or another, they incorporate the notions of bounded rationality: the need to search for decision alternatives, the replacement of optimization by targets and satisfying [minimal] goals, and mechanisms of learning and adaptation."

Pfeffer and Salancik said that: "We prefer to view organizations as coalitions altering their purposes and domains to accommodate new interests, sloughing off parts of themselves to avoid some interests, and when necessary, becoming involved in activities far afield from their stated central purposes. Organizations are social instruments of tremendous power and energy, and the critical issue becomes who will control this energy and for what purpose."

If we accept the traditional assumption, as to the financial basis of the objectives behind the corporate plan, these objectives are ideally meant to be quantified in numerical and, in particular, financial terms.

In the most general terms, though, the 'objectives' behind a strategy address two questions: ''Where' do we want to be?' and ''When' do we expect to be there?'

***Short Term Forecasting***

This is the type of forecasting you will recognise. It is normally based upon a projection of historical trends, usually focused on sales volumes. There are many sophisticated techniques, increasingly using large amounts of computing power, but in essence all of these try to separate out the four main components:

1. Long term trends probably represent the most important information you are trying to extract from the mass of data before you.
2. Medium term cycles are supposed to result from regular economic ups and downs which used to be encapsulated in a 5 year 'business cycle' which, unfortunately, became unpredictable in the 1980s. The much quoted 'Kondratieff Cycles' are much longer, if they exist at all, being of the order of 25 - 50 years; and hence do not normally enter into shorter term forecasts.
3. Seasonal is the pattern within a single year, a pattern which most suppliers who are affected by it know well.
4. Random fluctuations, which do not fit regular patterns, afflict all products and services, and make computer analysis a very difficult proposition.

The end result of all these patterns superimposed may appear very confusing indeed. Despite all the sophistication on offer, therefore, by far the best advice is to keep it as simple as possible. The human eye is much better at resolving the complications shown above than the most powerful computer. Thus, the best approach to forecasting (and certainly the best check on any more sophisticated technique) is 'eyeballing' the sales charts! With some practise you should be able to sort out the main features of what is happening - and that is better than most computer models achieve.

The evidence is that the sophistication adds little or nothing to the accuracy (though it does to the image of the forecasters, and the prices they charge). Worst of all, such unnecessary complexity hinders your understanding of what is going on under the covers of the computer (and hides the fact that most forecasts are really based on human judgement). In any case, even if historical trends are accurately analysed, there is no guarantee that the future will be the same as the past. It is much better that you surface all the assumptions, and make your own judgements in full knowledge of what is involved.

Two very simple techniques to use (if nothing else but as a check on the forecasts others are trying to sell to you);

- Eyeballing - the technique I mentioned above is the first, and best, method. It merely requires you to plot historical results graphically; and then look for the patterns. Trust your own judgement - until you are proved wrong.
- Exponential Smoothing - this is the mathematical technique which reportedly gives the best results; probably because it is so simple, and consequently easily understood. Indeed, it is a very impressive title for a simple, but useful, mathematical technique; which can quite easily be handled manually. It just allows greater weight to be given to recent periods. Instead of, for example, the average trend over the whole of the last year being calculated, the sales data for each of the months is given a weighting, depending on how recent that month was. It simply takes the previous forecast, and adds on the latest 'actual' sales figure; except that it does this in a fixed proportion, which is chosen to reflect the weighting to be given to the latest period. The general form is; Ft+1 = Ft + aEt where Ft+1 is the new forecast you are calculating, Ft is the previous one and Et is the deviation (or 'error') of the actual performance recorded against that previous period forecast; and 'a' is the weighting to be given to the most recent events. Exponential smoothing will not, in this simple form, allow for seasonality; though more sophisticated (but less easily understood) versions can do this.

### *Long Term Forecasting*

This tends to be qualitative (as compared with the quantitative, numeric, focus of short term forecasts). It is even more dependent on judgement; and most of the more complicated approaches to it (such as Delphi, or Jury methods) aim to reduce the risks implicit in the judgement by spreading the process over panels of experts. It does not, in the final analysis, absolve the manager from backing his or her own judgement (which is probably better informed, in terms of the specific situation, than that of the 'experts').

Of all the techniques the most useful involves developing complementary scenarios, which allow for the uncertainties involved; as well as expanding the viewpoint of all the managers involved in the process. Unfortunately, in the form most often described it can also be the most complex and sophisticated of these techniques - and in this form perhaps only the very large corporate planning team at Shell have used it really effectively. A much simplified approach, based on the version which Shell recommend for their line managers who are not part of their corporate planning group, is more practical for most organisations. In this simplified version of the form originally described by Shell the four steps to this process are:

1. Identify the important variables - what (in the whole of the external environment, not just the marketing environment) are the most important factors which will determine the future of the organisation.
2. Brainstorm to find the possible outcomes - work through the different outcomes which different alternatives for these variables may lead to.
3. Link these together in a series of alternative scenarios - start to build six or seven scenarios ('stories' about the future of the organisation, or more importantly its market) which are able to contain these different alternatives.
4. Refine these scenarios - then work on the scenarios until they are condensed to two or three meaningful alternative (but complementary) descriptions of the future.

**Corporate Mission**

Behind the corporate objectives, which in themselves offer the main context for the marketing plan, will lie the "corporate mission; which in turn provides the context for these corporate objectives. This 'corporate mission' can be thought of as a definition of what the organization is; of what it does.

This definition should not be too narrow, or it will constrict the development of the organization; a too rigorous concentration on the view that 'We are in the business of making meat-scales', as IBM was during the early 1900s, might have limited its subsequent development into other areas. On the other hand, it should not be too wide or it will become meaningless; 'We want to make a profit' is not too helpful in developing specific plans.

Abell suggested that the definition should cover three dimensions: 'customer groups' to be served, 'customer needs' to be served, and 'technologies' to be utilized.

Thus, the definition of IBM's 'corporate mission' in the 1940s might well have been: 'We are in the business of handling accounting information [customer need] for the larger US organizations [customer group] by means of punched cards [technology].' Fortunately, as the name itself (International Business Machines) indicates, IBM already had a wider perspective (and its corporate mission was virtually defined by its name).

**Corporate Vision**

Perhaps the most important factor in successful marketing is the 'corporate vision'. Surprisingly, it is largely neglected by marketing textbooks; although not by the popular exponents of corporate strategy - indeed, it was perhaps the main theme of the book by Peters and Waterman, in the form of their 'Superordinate Goals'. Theodore Levitt said: "Nothing drives progress like the imagination. The idea precedes the deed."

If the organization in general, and its chief executive in particular, has a strong vision of where its future lies, then there is a good chance that the organization will achieve a strong position in its markets (and attain that future). This will be not least because its strategies will be consistent; and will be supported by its staff at all levels. In this context, all of IBM's marketing activities were underpinned by its philosophy of 'customer service'; a vision originally promoted by the charismatic Watson dynasty.

Henry Mintzberg explained: "... in some cases, in addition to the mission there is the `sense of mission', that is, a feeling that the group has banded together to create something new and exciting. This is common in new organizations".

What a worthwhile vision consists of is, however, usually open to debate; hence the reason why such visions tend to be associated with strong, charismatic leaders. But the vision must be relevant. The message for the marketer is that, to be most effective, the marketing strategies must be converted into a powerful long-term vision; if such a vision does not already exist.

**Marketing Audit**

The first formal step in the marketing planning process is that of conducting the marketing audit. Ideally, at the time of producing the marketing plan, this should only involve bringing together the source material which has already been collected throughout the year - as part of the normal work of the marketing department.

The emphasis at this stage is on obtaining a complete and accurate picture. In a single organization, however, it is likely that only a few aspects will be sufficiently important to have any significant impact on the marketing plan; but all may need to be reviewed to determine just which 'are' the few.

In this context some factors related to the customer, which should be included in the material collected for the audit, may be:

- Who are the customers?
- What are their key characteristics?
- What differentiates them from other members of the population?
- What are their needs and wants?
- What do they expect the 'product' to do?
- What are their special requirements and perceptions?
- What do they think of the organization and its products or services?

- What are their attitudes?
- Are their buying intentions?

A 'traditional' - albeit product-based - format for a 'brand reference book' (or, indeed, a 'marketing facts book') was suggested by Godley more than three decades ago:

1. Financial data —Facts for this section will come from management accounting, costing and finance sections.
2. Product data —From production, research and development.
3. Sales and distribution data - Sales, packaging, distribution sections.
4. Advertising, sales promotion, merchandising data - Information from these departments.
5. Market data and miscellany - From market research, who would in most cases act as a source for this information.

His sources of data, however, assume the resources of a very large organization. In most organizations they would be obtained from a much smaller set of people (and not a few of them would be generated by the marketing manager alone). It is apparent that a marketing audit can be a complex process, but the aim is simple: 'it is only to identify those existing (external and internal) factors which will have a significant impact on the future plans of the company'.

It is clear that the basic material to be input to the marketing audit should be comprehensive. Accordingly, the best approach is to accumulate this material continuously, as and when it becomes available; since this avoids the otherwise heavy workload involved in collecting it as part of the regular, typically annual, planning process itself - when time is usually at a premium. Even so, the first task of this 'annual' process should be to check that the material held in the current 'facts book' or 'facts files' actually 'is' comprehensive and accurate, and can form a sound basis for the marketing audit itself.

The structure of the facts book will be designed to match the specific needs of the organization, but one simple format - suggested by Malcolm McDonald - may be applicable in many cases. This splits the material into three groups:

1. 'Review of the marketing environment'. A study of the organization's markets, customers, competitors and the overall economic, political, cultural and technical environment; covering developing trends, as well as the current situation.
2. 'Review of the detailed marketing activity'. A study of the company's marketing mix; in terms of the 4 Ps - product, price, promotion and place.
3. 'Review of the marketing system'. A study of the marketing organization, marketing research systems and the current marketing objectives and strategies.

The last of these is too frequently ignored. The marketing system itself needs to be regularly questioned, because the validity of the whole marketing plan is reliant upon the accuracy of the input from this system, and 'garbage in, garbage out' applies with a vengeance.

**Analysis**

The analysis of this material will, no doubt, require significant effort. In the first instance it is a matter of selection, of sorting the wheat from the chaff. What is important, and will need to be taken into account in the marketing plan that will eventually emerge from the overall process, will be different for each product or service in each situation. One of the most important skills to be learned in marketing is that of being able to concentrate on just what is important.

It is important to say not just what happened but why. The process of marketing planning encompasses all of the marketing skills. However, a number of these may be particularly relevant at this stage:

- 'Positioning'. The starting point of the marketing plan must be the consumer. It is a matter of definition that his or her needs should drive the whole marketing process. The techniques of positioning and segmentation therefore usually offer the best starting point for what has to be achieved by the whole planning process.

- 'Portfolio planning'. In addition, the coordinated planning of the individual products and services can contribute towards the balanced portfolio.
- '80:20 rule'. To achieve the maximum impact, the marketing plan must be clear, concise and simple. It needs to concentrate on the 20 per cent of products or services, and on the 20 per cent of customers, which will account for 80 per cent of the volume and 80 per cent of the 'profit'.
- '4 Ps'. The 4 Ps can sometimes divert attention from the customer, but the framework they offer can be very useful in building the action plans.

**Marketing Objectives**

It is only at this stage (of deciding the marketing objectives) that the active part of the marketing planning process begins'.

This next stage in marketing planning is indeed the key to the whole marketing process. The marketing objectives state just where the company intends to be; at some specific time in the future. James Quinn succinctly defined objectives in general as: "Goals (or objectives) state 'what' is to be achieved and 'when' results are to be accomplished, but they do not state 'how' the results are to be achieved".

They typically relate to what products (or services) will be where in what markets (and must be realistically based on customer behaviour in those markets). They are essentially about the match between those 'products' and 'markets'. Objectives for pricing, distribution, advertising and so on are at a lower level, and should not be confused with marketing objectives. They are part of the marketing strategy needed to achieve marketing objectives.

To be most effective, objectives should be capable of measurement and therefore 'quantifiable'. This measurement may be in terms of sales volume, money value, market share, percentage penetration of distribution outlets and so on. An example of such a measurable marketing objective might be 'to enter the market with product Y and capture 10 per cent of the market by value within one year'. As it is quantified it can, within limits, be unequivocally monitored; and corrective action taken as necessary.

The marketing objectives must usually be based, above all, on the organization's financial objectives; converting these financial measurements into the related marketing measurements.

It is conventionally assumed that marketing objectives will be designed to maximize volume or profit (or to optimize the utilization of resources in the non-profit sector), by creating demand or rejuvenating existing demand, say; although the various sub-objectives may indicate many different routes to achieving such optimization. However, as Kotler suggested (in the earlier edition of his book), there may be a number of other objectives:

1. Synchromarketing - The aim may be to 'redistribute' existing sales (which are already at optimum levels) so that they occur at times, or in places, which the supplier prefers. Thus, for example, organizations which have highly seasonal sales (which make inefficient use of resources) may want to increase non-seasonal sales. Walls achieved this by balancing its summer sales of ice-cream with pies and sausages, demand for which peaks in winter. The suppliers of central-heating oil offer special deals for those customers willing to restock their tanks in summer.
2. Demarketing' - Demand may sometimes exceed supply. In these circumstances the emphasis will be on rationing scarce supplies. Occasionally the supplier, rather than bring on-stream expensive new plant, may seek to persuade customers to buy less

(or be less dissatisfied with the scarcity). Some suppliers of electrical energy (electricity generators in Europe and the USA) have heavily advertised energy conservation measures to achieve this end (otherwise, the cost of meeting the peak winter loads would be very high - and unprofitable).

3. Counter-marketing - In what is usually a public-sector activity, there may be an objective of stopping consumption completely. The anti-tobacco and anti-drug campaigns are the most obvious examples; but McDonald's campaigns to stop its customers dropping litter, or the brewers' campaigns to stop drinking and driving, fall into this category.

In this case, the intended strategy, decided upon traditionally or incrementally, is overtaken by events in two main ways. One, which will probably be recognised by the organisation, is that of unrealised strategy; where it proves impossible to implement the chosen strategy·in practice.

Less obvious is the emergent strategy which is decided by events in the external environment; and, thus, forced upon the organisation. This may not necessarily be recognised, in its totality, by the organisation - since many of its implications may be hidden. As markets become more complex, however, such emergent strategies are becoming more common.

Many organizations see both these processes in terms of failure - they have been forced, usually by unpredictable events, to abandon their own strategy. There is, accordingly, a tendency for these unwelcome facts to be ignored until they are so obvious that they cannot be avoided. This is a major error. Such deviations must be recognised (probably through one or other form of environmental analysis coupled with networking) as soon as possible- so that the organisation can react in good time.

A much more powerful approach is, though, to be proactive; so seize upon these deviations as the basis for future developments. What needs to be recognised is that emergent strategies are the most powerful of all. They must, by definition, be dierctly derived from the needs of the market - where even successful deliberate strategies may not ideally match market needs but may achieve their targets by sheer force (especially where conviction marketing lies behind them). Emergent strategies are, thus, likely to be vigorous ones.

There are two main approaches to capitalising on such emergent strategies. The first of these, favoured in the West, is the umbrella strategy. This is a form of very positive delegation, in that the overall strategies, the umbrella, are very general in nature - and allow the lower level managers, who are closest to the external environment, the freedom to react to these changes.

A much more direct, and hence even more powerful, approach is that favoured by the Japanese corporations. They integrate emergent strategies with their own. Indeed it is arguable that, in terms of marketing, to a large extent they use emergent strategies instead of their own deliberate strategies. This is evidenced as much by an attitude of mind as by any other feature. They deliberately go out to look for symptoms of such emergent trends which can be detected in the performance of their own products. More than that, though, they often deliberately launch a range of products rather than a single one to see which is most successful. It is almost as if they deliberately seek out the emergent strategies by offering the best environment for them to develop - the very reverse of the Western approach which seeks to avoid them! The Japanese then go on to build on these emergent strategies with a number of very effective tools - most of which are designed to overcome the major problem which accompanies emergent strategies, that they emerge on the scene much later than deliberate ones (and are likely to be visible to all the competitors at the same time) so that time is the essence. Thus, time management techniques (including parallel development along with flexible manufacturing and JIT) which have been developed by the Japanese offer them a significant competitive advantage in handling such emergent strategies.

There are numerous definitions of what strategy is, but again James Quinn again gave a succinct general definition: "A strategy is a 'pattern' or 'plan' that 'integrates' an organization's 'major' goals, policies and action sequences into a 'cohesive' whole"

He went on to explain his view of the role of 'policies', with which strategy is most often confused: "Policies are rules or guidelines that express the 'limits' within which action should occur.

In principle, these strategies describe how the objectives will be achieved. The 4 Ps are a useful framework for deciding how the company's resources will be manipulated (strategically) to achieve the objectives. It should be noted, however, that they are not the only framework, and may divert attention from the real issues. The focus of the strategies must be the objectives to be achieved - not the process of planning itself. Only if it fits the needs of these objectives should you choose, as we have done, to use the framework of the 4 Ps.

The strategy statement can take the form of a purely verbal description of the strategic options which have been chosen. Alternatively, and perhaps more positively, it might include a structured list of the major options chosen.

One aspect of strategy which is often overlooked is that of 'timing'. Exactly when it is the best time for each element of the strategy to be implemented is often critical. Taking the right action at the wrong time can sometimes be almost as bad as taking the wrong action at the right time. Timing is, therefore, an essential part of any plan; and should normally appear as a schedule of planned activities.

Having completed this crucial stage of the planning process, you will need to re-check the feasibility of your objectives and strategies in terms of the market share, sales, costs, profits and so on which these demand in practice. As in the rest of the marketing discipline, you will need to employ judgement, experience, market research or anything else which helps you to look at your conclusions from all possible angles.

At this stage, you will need to develop your overall marketing strategies into detailed plans and programmes. Although these detailed plans may cover each of the 4 Ps, the focus will vary, depending upon your organization's specific strategies. A product-oriented company will focus its plans for the 4 Ps around each of its products. A market or geographically oriented company will concentrate on each market or geographical area. Each will base its plans upon the detailed needs of its customers, and on the strategies chosen to satisfy these needs.

Again, the most important element is, indeed, that of the detailed plans; which spell out exactly what programmes and individual activities will take place over the period of the plan (usually over the next year). Without these specified - and preferably quantified - activities the plan cannot be monitored, even in terms of success in meeting its objectives.

It is these programmes and activities which will then constitute the 'marketing' of the organization over the period. As a result, these detailed marketing programmes are the most important, practical outcome of the whole planning process.

## STRATEGIC PLANNING IN HOTEL MANAGEMENT

Strategic planning involves defining objectives and developing strategies to reach those objectives. It may employ methods like SWOT analysis to help clarify objectives and strategies. Strategic planning uses "the big picture" to pursue large scale, long term objectives. This is in contradistinction to "tactical" planning, which has to focuss on short term, smaller objectives. "Long range" planning typically projects current activities and programs onto a model of the external world, thereby predicting likely results. "Strategic" planning tries to "create" more desirable future results by (a) influencing the outside world or (b) adapting current programs and actions so as to have more favourable outcomes in the external environment.

Within business, strategic planning may provide overall direction strategic management to a company or give specific direction in such areas as:

- Financial strategies
- Human resource/organizational development strategies
- Information technology deployments
- Marketing strategy

We want to do Strategic Planning to:

- Have the capability to obtain the desired objective
- Fit well both with the external environment and with an organization's resources and core competencies - it should appear feasible and appropriate
- Have the capability of providing an organization with a sustainable competitive advantage - ideally through uniqueness and sustainability
- Prove dynamic, flexible, and able to adapt to changing situations
- Suffice on its own - specifically providing favorable outcomes without the need for cross-subsidization

Most strategic planning methodologies depend on a three-step process (sometimes called the STP process):

- Situation - evaluate the current situation and how it came about
- Target - define goals and/or objectives (sometimes called ideal state)
- Path - map a possible route to the goals/objectives

An alternative approach is called Draw-See-Think

- Draw - what is the ideal image or the desired end state?
- See - what is today's situation? What is the gap from ideal and why?
- Think - what specific actions must be taken to close the gap between today's situation and the ideal state?

- Plan - what resources are required to execute the activities?

In general terms, strategic planning can proceed incrementally or revolutionarily.

Strategic planning as a set of logical and creative steps

1. Clarification of objective (end-state) to be pursued. The following terms have been used in the literature: desired end states, plans, policies, goals, objectives, strategies, tactics and actions. Definitions vary, overlap and fail to achieve clarity. The following concept has been found useful. The items listed above may be organized in a hierarchy of means and ends and numbered as follows: Top Rank Objective (TRO), Second Rank Objective, Third Rank Objective, etc. From any rank, the objective in a lower rank answers to the question "How?" and the objective in a higher rank answers to the question "Why?" The exception is the Top Rank Objective (TRO): there is no answer to the "Why?" question. That is how the TRO is defined. An example may help to clarify the concept presented above.
2. Information gathering and analysis. This includes an external assessment (such as environmental scanning), and an internal resource assessment. Morphological analysis may be applied to both internal resource assessments and external assessments. SWOT (Strengths, Weaknesses, Opportunities, Threats) Analysis may be used to assess those aspects of the organization and the environment that are important to achieving the objective of the strategic plan.
3. Evaluation of the feasibility of the objective in view of the SWOTs.
4. Strategy-development. This is a creative step that answers these four questions: How can we use the Strengths, stop the Weaknesses, exploit the Opportunities and defend against the Threats in pursuit of the selected objetive.

5. Developing Action Programs for the more attractive strategies, covering: Name of the strategy, Benefits to be expected from implementing this programme, Actions: What will be done? Responsible persons: Who will be in charge of the programme? Timing: When will the programme start? When will it be completed? Location(s): Where will the programme be implemented? Resources: What will be needed: people, money, information, other resources? Control System: How will progress be measured and reported? Rewards for performance, if any. Contingency plans: What will be done if results fall short?

**Strategy as Revolution**

- Identify the unquestioned beliefs in the organization and challenge them - look for opportunities to re-write the rules of the environment
- Look for major discontinuities in technology, and embrace such changes wholeheartedly - do not waste time making small incremental adjustments - stand by to create a completely new business model at any time
  - More a mind-set than a formal technique
  - Not rule or ritual-oriented, not reductionist, not reactive, not autocratic

Theorists frequently make the distinction between strategy and tactics. Strategy involves planning how to get where one wants to go. Tactics can potentially comprise the implementation of such over-arching plans. They deal with specific actions by particular people or by particular groups. Some theorists see it as a mistake to separate strategy and tactics. Constantinos Markides describes strategy formation and implementation (tactics) as an on-going, never-ending, integrated process requiring continuous re-assessment and reformation. He sees strategic planning as both planned and emergent - dynamic and interactive. J. Moncrieff also stresses strategy dynamics - he recognizes strategy as partially deliberate and partially unplanned.

The unplanned element comes from two sources:

1. Emergent strategies - resulting from the emergence of opportunities and threats in the environment
2. Strategies in action - ad hoc actions by many people from all parts of an organization

Strategic plans typically look 5 or more years into the future. They differ in this respect from tactical plans (sometimes referred to as functional plans), which look 2 to 4 years into the future; and from operational plans [such as budgets] which have an annual scope.

Finally, strategic planning is not what you think you want to do but a thing that you have to do.

## SITUATIONAL ANALYSIS

When developing Corporate strategies, analysis of the company and environment as it is at the moment and how it will be in the future, is very necessary, this is called the analysis phase of strategic planning. The analysis has to be executed at an internal level as well as an external level to identify all opportunities and threats of the new strategy.

One aspect of internal analysis that has been underestimated through the last decades in developing corporate strategies is the field of corporate cultures. Consultants, when developing corporate strategies, are mostly focused on tangible internal and external factors when analyzing the company and did not really take the cultural, often intangible and invisible, aspects into account.

### Identifying Cultures

When creating new corporate strategies, or adjusting existing ones, as said in the introduction, the business consultant most generally starts by analyzing the following aspects of an organization:

1. Visionary aspects such as goals and objectives.
2. Situational aspects such as financial information, company structure and systems and the business which the company is operating in.

3. External aspects concerning the environment, market findings, competitors and rules and legislations that apply to the region the company is in.
4. Technical aspects that concern the amount of risk involved in the new strategy, the time span the strategy has to be enrolled in and resources and inputs required.

The one aspect that is not often thought of is the cultural aspect of a company. With culture we mean:

"Culture is a series of values, standard interpretations, insights and ways of thinking that is shared by members of an organization and is passed on to new members of this organization."

This is hardly plausible when thinking of the resistance and problems a group of employees can cause if they oppose to-be-employed or already-employed strategies. The relation between culture and strategy has been described thoroughly by Kono :

"The product-market strategy defines the work which employees have to do. If the work requires a high level of competence and new skills, this revitalizes the culture. The strategy also affects the financial performance and the level of salaries and incentives which are available to employees. On the other hand, the effective implementation of new strategies depends on the creativity of the employees and their willingness to change."

Kono precisely describes the relation that the company culture and the company strategy have with each other, they are interdependent. So it is key to analyze the company culture as well as possible, to be able to adjust the 'to be developed' strategy the best way possible to avoid conflicts and maximize compatibility.

**Perspectives**

To analyze the culture of a company, one has to use some kind of perspective to look at the artifacts (visible or not) that are active within the company and describe its culture. Basically two important schools with their perspectives can be distinguished:

- Ethnographical versus clinical analysis
- Functionalistic versus Interpretionistic analysis

This approach towards analyzing corporate cultures has been developed by Schein and makes the distinction between the following two ways of looking at artifacts within a company:

- Ethnographical – Focused on concrete data to understand the culture, which is mostly used for scientific research. Researchers who use this ethnographical way of analysis start with some predefined assumptions and try to find proof for these assumptions when investigating the organization.
- Clinical – Focused on cultural processes that are active within the organization and how these processes can be adjusted or modified to achieve a certain goal. Hereby looking at indicators such as artifacts, values and assumptions.

**Functionalistic Versus Interpretionistic Approach**

- The functionalistic approach towards analyzing culture is concerned with merely the same aspects as the clinical approach and is aimed at analyzing current cultural signals that can possibly be extracted to be used in other organizations
- The interpretionistic approach is more interested in the processes that form the coherence between employees in the same company. The interpretionistic approach thus is more aimed at communicational processes between employees in contrary to the more 'describing' way of the functionalistic approach.

**Visible Artifacts**

Visible artifacts include the following and can be experienced and analysed fairly easy because of the extrovert character they have. Visible artifacts include:

- Rituals and ceremonies
- Organization Stories
- Symbols
- Business Language

The business language of a company is the use of language employees speak, common used words and textual expressions that characterize the companies culture.

**Invisible Artifacts**

Next to visible artifacts, a company's culture also thrives on processes and events that are not that easily seen by outside consultants or even in-house employees.

These include:

- Value (personal and cultural)
- Assumptions
- Perspectives
- Attitudes
- Feelings

When looking at these invisible artifacts, one can state that these are of great value when creating a new corporate strategy, the attitudes and feelings that employees have towards for example radical changes can make or break your corporate strategy. The company's strategy also depends on the external / internal focus and needs from the environment of the company.

**Culture Types**

When setting the external versus internal strategic focus against the environmental needs (flexibility versus stability) The following figure emerges: to be very externally oriented when it comes to the strategic focus. Companies that hold this culture are flexible and able to respond to outside needs and changes fast and adequately. Employees are stimulated to be innovative. Examples of these companies today are mainly in the services-sector such as online marketplaces like eBay or online communities such as Hyves in the Netherlands.

- Mission Culture: The mission culture is externally oriented like the adjustment based entrepreneurial culture, but is not subject to quick environmental and external changes. Companies that have the mission culture are focused on reaching targets that have been set earlier in order to be competitive. A company such as Iriver (Korea), which is a company that produces mp3 players, is a good example. Iriver is very externally focused, and copies existing mp3 player models like the Apple iPod, but is also very focused on internal targets to guarantee low prices.
- Clan Culture: The clan culture is focused at flexibility when it comes to external needs, but this is reached through excellence of the employees, which makes the strategic focus internally focused. Examples of companies who fit the clan culture are Baan and IBM who are mainly considering the wellbeing of their employees as top priority and have the intention not to fire a single employee from the company perspective.
- Bureaucratic Culture: The bureaucratic culture is internally focused and operates in a market that is not demanding high flexibility. Examples are some government institutions or insurance companies.

  When a company's culture is analyzed, by using one of the perspectives used before, artifacts will make clear in what part of the quadrant (or very possibly also a combination of more than one) a company is in according to their culture. This information can be valuable to adjust the corporate strategy too but it can also be valuable to identify the current culture and change it according to for example changing needs from the external environment.

## CHANGING CULTURES AND STRATEGY

When a corporate strategy is developed, or an existing strategy is altered, the previous sections prove that the culture aspect of an organization is important because it can oppose new strategies when culture and strategy do not fit together.

When a culture does not match the strategy that is going to be deployed (which for some reason cannot be altered to the culture because of a changing external environment for example), some tactics to change this culture are available.

**Approaches**

1. The All-Out attack: The all out approach of implementing a new culture consists of removing all the cultural and strategic plans that are active at the moment and turn it all around. This is mainly done when a big conglomerate acquires another company and wants to enroll their own culture and strategic goals.
2. The inside venture approach: This tactic is based on the power of internal rewards and innovation. A company encourages employees to be innovative and come up with new ideas, and reward their employees with their own project team when the idea is feasible enough. This leads to a better external focus (employees are more focused on customer needs) and results in a company that is very flexible to the environmental needs.
3. Strategic alliance or Alliances: Include efforts such as joint ventures with other companies.
4. Organizational and Personnel management approach: When changing a corporate culture, expanding of the organizational (which formulates and regulates the strategies) and personnel departments is advisory.

**Resistance**

When situations change, especially not for the better, people generally resist this. When changing a culture, resistance will most probably also occur, resistance which most of the time is the result of the organizational climate, the shared meaning of employees about the way things go around in the company. Afterall, humans are creatures of habit and generally resist organisational change.

The existence of subcultures can also be a great cause of resistance and opposition against new plans. Subcultures, as the name says, are cultures with other assumptions and beliefs when compared to the general companywide culture. Subcultures can be horizontal (within the same hierarchical layer) or vertical (from manager to work floor employees) which in general can even cause more problems when changes are at hand.

**Measurements**

- A status ladder system: A skill based method of paying your employees, derived from Japan, which pays employees according to the knowledge and capabilities they have instead of the jobs they perform.
- Salary Reduction
- Job Transfers
- Early retirements
- Less recruiting

These measurements are mainly meant to keep employees at the company, even though the new corporate strategy will change things inside the company.

## THE EXTERNAL ENVIRONMENT

The element of the environment that has the most immediate impact, and one which dominated management activities in the 1980s and 1990s - competitive strategy. Following the widely accepted frameworks developed by Michael Porter, this initially concentrates on the competitive features of different industry types, and in particular the entry barriers to them. The main part, however, revolves around competitive responses and strategies, especially between leaders and followers.

However, Pfeffer and Salancik made the following comment:

"The key to organizational survival is the ability to acquire and maintain resources. This problem would be simplified if organizations were in complete control of all the components necessary for their operation. However, no organization is completely self-contained. Organizations are embedded in an environment composed of other organizations. They depend on those organizations for the many resources they themselves require. Organizations are linked to environments by federations, associations, customer-supplier relationships, competitive relationships and a socio-legal apparatus defining and controlling the nature and limits of those relationships."

Most organizations, however, seem (at least formally) to ignore this dimension of their business. If they are well managed, they devote immense efforts to optimizing the internal factors which are within their control; but they barely notice what is happening outside, and make little attempt to formally manage that side of their activities, except for some marketing responses. A major element of that outside environment is made up from the factors which are now grouped under the global heading of 'marketing'. Beyond this, however, there is a whole range of social and political factors which may have even greater impact. Not least is the impact of government regulation, which may make or break whole sectors of industry.

**Theoretical Frameworks**

As is frequently the case in marketing, a number of alternative frameworks for studying the wider environment are offered, the most conventional of which describes it in terms of an ' - onion :

This is a useful approach, since it distinguishes between three different degrees of interaction:

- Organization (or internal environment) -This includes those activities, contained totally - within - the organization itself, which make up the daily life of most organizations.
- Marketing environment -This is the area of the external environment which has the most immediate impact on organizations, and is generally recognized by them (and is the subject of much of this book).

- External environment -This is often not recognized as a force impinging on organizations; and yet, as we have seen, it may well contain the - major - factors which determine the performance of that organization.

These external factors are most often grouped as the - STEP - factors (Social, Technological, Economic and Political). They can have dramatic effects on organizations. The (political) results of legislation, for example, determine the boundaries of the actions of most organizations, and yet they are often 'taken as read', and are a relatively unnoticed element of organizational performance.

Cultural traditions are not easily overturned, but over the years they can change quite significantly - without the organizations involved noticing. From the 1970s to the Millennium, for example, the role of woman in society - and, in particular, woman's role at work - changed dramatically; and this was of considerable significance to those supplying services to women. No longer could they assume that the average woman was the stereotypical housewife. The women's magazine industry, as one example, was changed out of all recognition.

Over the past two decades there have been major changes in a number of areas of the overall sociocultural environment. The 'Information Revolution' in particular had a measurable impact on the patterns of employment; with economists pointing to a degree of 'structural unemployment' caused by its progress. It is arguable, indeed, that the social effects of this particular 'revolution' will dominate many of the changes in society over the coming two decades.

Related to this particular 'technological' driver, there have been a number of predictions made about how society will change. One of the earlier ones, and also one of the most influential, was that by Daniel Bell, concerning the development of the - post-industrial society -

As early as the 1970s he specified five dimensions, or components, of this:

1. Economic sector: the change from a goods-producing to a service economy
2. Occupational distribution: the pre-eminence of the professional and technical class
3. Axial principle: the centrality of theoretical knowledge as the source of innovation and of policy formulation for the society
4. Future orientation: the control of technology and technological assessment
5. Decision making: the creation of a new 'intellectual technology'.

As with many such 'forecasts', the pace of change has been slower than Daniel Bell expected. However, Bell recognized that his 'forecast' was based as much on hope and desire as on rational projection. In the context of his fifth element, for instance, he added:

"The goal of the new intellectual technology is neither more or less to realize a social alchemist's dream, the dream of `ordering' the mass of society... That this dream - as utopian, in its way, as the dreams of a perfect `commonwealth' - has faltered is laid, on the part of its believers, to the known human resistance.

From the point of view of the marketer, perhaps the most important predicted change is that from a materialist society to a post-materialist one. It is only fair to report that 'post-materialism' is taking longer to arrive than its most ardent supporters would wish.

Some changes are, however, totally predictable. The most obvious, and possibly the most important, are those resulting from demography. The 'baby boom' of the 1960s, and the subsequent dramatic decline in birth rates, have produced very different cohorts of population; with accompanying (totally predictable) changes in earnings and consumption.

The impact of changing technology is also a major factor in the development of the external environment. The 'Information Revolution' already mentioned is just one example of changes driven by technology.

The direct impact of new technology on organizations may be obvious. Even then, 'marketing myopia' -where they are so involved in short-term problems that they cannot see wider perspectives which will determine the future - may blind them to the obvious. Less apparent, though, are the social or 'structural' changes generated by such new technology. The 'Information Revolution' is having its wider impact, for one example, by allowing much smaller organizations to achieve 'economies of scale'. In the larger organizations it is having a different effect by encouraging horizontal communications (via electronic mail) to take over from the traditional vertical (hierarchical) organization; and in the process is creating new structures which are close to those of Japanese companies.

Peter Senker identified four main 'drivers' in the field of technology:

1. Information technology
2. New materials
3. Environmental issues
4. Biotechnology

Some of the 'theory' of marketing is also shared with other academic disciplines - or at least appears to be! Thus, although the 'market' is clearly at the heart of marketing, it has also become central to economic theory; and, indeed, to the basic philosophies of 'capitalism'. The way in which each of these two disciplines approaches the concept of the market could not, however, be more different.

The population in general, and the business community in particular, have uncritically accepted the basic tentets of economics as the given fundamentals of business life. Put simply, it is widely believed that economic theory accurately describes what happens in the wider business world. The reality (at least as described by marketing theory - and, even more clearly, by marketing practice) is often very different.

In the earliest days there was very little practical difference between economics and any theory of business management; or of 'marketing' as then practised, in a society which had few surpluses to exchange. Adam Smith wrote his justifiably renowned - Wealth of Nations - as a treatise to be studied as much by businessmen as by government.

Even in the Victorian period, 'neoclassical' economics, as developed by Alfred Marshall for example, was still spending much of its time trying to describe practical business processes, albeit in more scientific terms. The 'laws of supply and demand', which now lie at the heart of modern micro-economics, represented a practical attempt to describe how prices were set at a time when almost all major markets were commodity markets, and the one variable which the seller could control was price.

At that time the political debate, led by Karl Marx, revolved around the ownership of the capital involved (and hence, most importantly, ownership of the profit), together with the associated division of wealth and income. 'Capitalism' was about just that - about who owned the capital. It too, in its own perverse way, was firmly based on conventional economic theory. Even so, business economics, or the related 'micro-economics', remained closely linked to actual business activities through the first half of the twentieth century.

Economists, however, increasingly focused on the need to create a body of theory which would justify their claim that economics was a legitimate academic discipline. At this time 'macro-economics', that element which described the factors pertaining to the economy as a whole (and was clearly the responsibility of government rather than business), was split off as a separate subject - particularly after the pioneering work of Lord Keynes became generally accepted - to become the part of economics which received the most publicity.

The debate about whether the government should control demand or supply was won, in the 1970s, by the latter view (now espoused by many governments).

Over the same period, the political basis of capitalism has also shifted. As described above, the key factor had been seen to be the ownership of capital; the prime need was for 'profit' to stimulate the 'entrepreneur' to innovate, and improve business efficiency. Indeed, it had previously been widely believed that the strength of the capitalist West derived from that profit motive, which by itself led to enterprises almost automatically being better managed; for the good of all involved.

Unfortunately, by the 1970s, after the development of the global money markets, and after Kenneth Galbraith's very influential teachings, it had become clear that, at least in terms of routine operations, ownership of capital had largely become divorced from the management of most large organizations.

The political theme then became that of the 'market'. The great benefit of 'capitalism', it thus emerged, was that the 'market' was the best (and only 'natural') mechanism for allocating resources; for deciding how demand could be met. 'The discipline of the market' or the 'virtue of market-led economies', then became the central theme of 'capitalist' governments; and is now espoused almost as enthusiastically by the governments of the former communist bloc.

Modern micro-economics experiences no theoretical problem in describing the activities of the ' - perfect firm - '. This 'ideal' organization is involved in perfect competition, where price is the one dominant factor (and this, above all, is the element manipulated in the many economic equations which are used to describe that firm). All decisions are taken rationally, based upon maximization of monetary outcomes (profit), where all the relationships are exactly known; and can be plotted upon definitive graphs.

In the 1990s the 'transaction cost' approach explored the relationships between economic theory and business management, by looking at the difference in `transaction costs' between the alternatives considered, as the reason for the logical choice made. This field of theory has, in particular, concentrated upon business structure - including the `make' or `buy in' decision. Here it argued, with some success, that the firm's decision as to whether to `make' a component itself or buy it from a supplier is (or at least should be) taken on `cost' grounds (though the definition of `cost' was complex than normal). Transaction costs however further got complicated and therefore a number of ERP solutions cropped up to reslove them to a great extent.

Whatever the approach, micro-economics finds considerable difficulty in dealing with ' - imperfect competition - ', since no generally agreed model for representing this state of affairs has yet emerged. Worst of all, particularly in the current climate of uncertainty, it cannot easily handle the 'fuzzy' relationships which do not fit neatly into the exact equations. Finally, as Kenneth Galbraith and others so succinctly observed, management decision-making is often anything but rational; and is frequently not designed to achieve the simple monetary outcomes which are the staple diet of economics - and instead reflect rather more complex motivations.

Marketing, which has grown as a business function over this period (while economics has waned, in terms of its comparable use as a business management tool), thrives on precisely these elements, which are the stuff of real business life. Thus, the aim of every brand manager is to make competition ever - more - imperfect (aiming for the 'ideal' brand which holds a monopoly over its customers, who will stridently demand Carlsberg beer and reject any alternatives). In this environment the 'intangible' (and often seemingly irrational) needs and wants of the customer predominate. The tools of marketing are frequently the 'creative' tools which address the 'fuzzy' areas; of formulating the most attractive product or service, and of developing the most effective promotions. Having to compete on price, as the micro-economists would ideally wish for, is usually seen as defeat by such marketers.

Thus, there are many disadvantages to adopting the pure economic view-point. On the other hand, there still remain some clear advantages to investigating such an economic perspective. In particular, economics has benefited from almost a century of concentrated academic activity; developing a rigorous, logical, framework. It is the rigidity of thinking imposed by this framework which has often now detached it from real life. But the very strength of this body of academic theory means that economics can offer a useful reference framework with which to compare many marketing decisions.

The boundaries within which organizations can operate are frequently set by legislation; from the ingredients they can legally put into their products to the buildings that their employees are allowed to work in. Pressure groups campaign directly to change legislation, but also work indirectly to change the public's buying habits.

Organizations themselves may well join pressure groups, to force government to protect their entrenched positions, and are often very successful.

It might be thought that only the larger organizations are the direct targets of pressure groups or have the resources to be involved in pressure groups themselves; but it is just as important that the smaller organizations understand the political machinations which are taking place around them, and which have a major, albeit relatively unseen, impact.

Most aspects of marketing transactions will be covered by one or other form of legislation; not least that of contract law. The marketing manager or sales manager, then, must be well aware of those aspects that most directly affect them; and this will vary from industry to industry, and from country to country. The chemicals industry, for instance, is driven by legislation on safety, whereas financial services providers in the UK look to the Financial Services Act. Most managers, however, should at least understand exactly what their own contract means; and, even more importantly, what the implications are when others insist that their own contractual terms are followed instead.

The laws which affect your business need to be handled expertly, by specialists, for two main reasons:

- Specificity - there is a vast array of laws, only some of which affect individual industries or organizations in specific countries

- Currency - more importantly, laws change, often quite rapidly

The pressure group which has had the most direct impact on organizations in recent years has been that of the consumer movement; to which has now been added the environmental lobby and the green movement. The motivation of these movements has been sincere, no matter how annoying they may have been to the producers that they have targeted. They have aimed to benefit the consumer - high ideals, which are in stark contrast with those of some of the rather more self-interested industrial pressure groups.

These movements are often closer to the average consumer than the supplier. What they urge often makes very good marketing sense; and their views are often a sound guide to what future legislation may bring.

A concept which has recently emerged is that there are a number of different groups which can claim an interest or 'stake' (Gareth Morgan actually referred to them as 'multiple stakeholders') in the organization. Using a now more usual terminology, Lusch and Lusch define the 'public' of an organization as 'any group which has an actual or potential interest or impact on an organization's ability to achieve its objectives'.

Traditionally, especially in the view of economists, only the owners (the 'stockholders') have been legitimately entitled to an interest in what the organization does. More recently it has been recognized that employees' interests should also be taken into account.

The power of the financial stakeholders should not, however, be under-estimated. It is often seen in its most active form (at least by the defenders) when acquisitions or mergers take place (not infrequently on an 'unfriendly' basis). The rationale for mergers and acquisitions is not always financial. It is, indeed, often for reasons related to marketing; in the diplomatic terms which accompany such manoeuvres, 'to obtain some synergy from complementary marketing assets', or in more forthright terms, 'to try and increase monopolistic control over customers'.

Strategic planning is a very important business activity. It is practiced widely. In spite of that, it is not done well. All strategic planning and decision processes must start with agreed upon objectives (desired end states). In practice and in the literature, this is a murky area.

The following terms have been used in Strategic Planning: desired end states, plans, policies, goals, objectives, strategies, tactics and actions. Definitions vary, overlap and fail to achieve clarity.

Differences between a current situation and a future aspirational state can appear as a deficiency or as a gap. Objectives and goal management serve to eliminate this gap. Some writers distinguish between goals (inexactly formulated aims that lack specificity) and objectives (aims formulated exactly and quantitatively as to time-frames and magnitude of effect). For example, a gambler might have the ambiguous goal: "I want to get lucky tonight". Converting this into an objective, it might become: "I want to make $100 at the blackjack table by 8 o'clock tonight." Not all authors make this distinction, preferring to use the two terms interchangeably.

In the financial arena, or when talking statistically, one often refers to goals as "targets". People typically have several goals at the same time. "Goal congruency" refers to how well the goals combine with each other. Does goal A appear compatible with goal B? Do they fit together to form a unified strategy? "Goal hierarchy" consists of the nesting of one or more goals within other goal(s).

One approach recommends having short-term goals, medium-term goals, and long-term goals. In this model, one can expect to attain short-term goals fairly easily: they stand just slightly above one's reach. At the other extreme, long-term goals appear very difficult, almost impossible to attain. Strategic management jargon sometimes refers to "Big Hairy Audacious Goals" (BHAGs) in this context.) Using one goal as a stepping-stone to the next involves goal sequencing. A person or group starts by attaining the easy short-term goals, then steps up to the medium-term, then to the long-term goals.

Goal sequencing can create a "goal stairway".In an organizational setting, the organization may co-ordinate goals so that they do not conflict with each other. The goals of one part of the organization should mesh compatibly with those of other parts of the organization.

Individuals within organizations will typically have personal goals. Although individuals often have goals that oppose organizational goals (such as having as high a salary as possible), if personal goals diverge too incompatibly from organizational goals they may result in limited progress towards the mere organizational goals.

Organizations sometimes summarize goals and objectives into a mission statement and / or a vision statement:

- A Definition of Vision in a dictionary: 'An Image of the future we seek to create'.

A vision statement describes in graphic terms where the goal-setters want to see themselves in the future. It may describe how they see events unfolding over 10 or 20 years if everything goes exactly as hoped.

- A definition of Mission in a dictionary: purpose, reason for being; also, an inner calling to pursue an activity or perform a service.

Many people mistake vision statement for mission statement. The Vision describes a future identity and the Mission describes how it will be achieved. A Mission statement may define the purpose or broader goal for being in existence or in the business. It serves as an ongoing guide without time frame. The mission can remain the same for decades if crafted well. Vision is more specific in terms of objective and future state. Vision is related to some form of achievement if successful.

For example, "We help transport goods and people efficiently and cost effectively without damaging environment" is a mission statement. Ford's brief but powerful slogan "Quality is Job 1" could count as a mission statement. "We will be one amongst the top three transporters of goods and people in North America by 2010" is a vision statement. It is very concrete and unambiguous goal.

Mission and Values go hand in hand. To make the mission statement effective, it needs to be aligned with the prevailing culture of its stakeholders, organization, market and political sphere. A lofty mission statement means nothing if it is not in congruence with the values practiced by the organization. A statement of values provides guiding principles when ethical issues related to realizing the Vision, and undertaking the Mission, arise.

A mission statement can resemble a vision statement in a few companies, but that can be a grave mistake. It can confuse people. The vision statement can galvanize the people to achieve defined objectives, even if they are stretch objectives, provided the vision is SMART (Specific, Measurable, Achievable, Realistic and Timebound). A mission statement provides a path to realize the vision in line with its values. These statements have a direct bearing on the bottomline and success of the organization.

Features of an effective vision statement may include:

- Clarity and lack of ambiguity
- Paint a vivid and clear picture, not ambiguous
- Describing a bright future (hope)
- Memorable and engaging expression
- Realistic aspirations, achievable
- Alignment with organizational values and culture, Rational
- Time bound if it talks of achieving any goal or objective

In order to become really effective, an organizational vision statement must (the theory states) become assimilated into the organization's culture. Leaders have the responsibility of communicating the vision regularly, creating narratives that illustrate the vision, acting as role-models by embodying the vision, creating short-term objectives compatible with the vision, and encouraging others to craft their own personal vision compatible with the organization's overall vision.

In general, strategic plans can fail for two types of reasons: inappropriate strategy and poor implementation.

Inappropriate strategies may arise due to:

- Failure to define end states (objectives) correctly
- Incomplete SWOT analysis with respect to the desired end state(s)
- Lack of creativity in identifying possible strategies
- Strategies incapable of obtaining the desired objective
- Poor fit between the external environment and organizational resources - infeasibility

Poor implementation of a strategy may happen due to:

- Over-estimation of resources and abilities
- Under-estimation of time, personnel, or financial requirements
- Failure to coordinate
- Ineffective attempts to gain the support of others or resistance
- Failure to follow the plan
- Loss of senior management focus and continued sponsorship

## CONDUCTING STRATEGIC PLANNING

Many managers spend most of their time "fighting fires" in the workplace. — their time is spent realizing and reacting to problems. For these managers — and probably for many of us — it can be very difficult to stand back and take a hard look at what we want to accomplish and how we want to accomplish it. We're too buy doing what we think is making progress. However, one of the major differences between new and experienced managers is the skill to see the broad perspective, to take the long view on what we want to do and how we're going to do it. One of the best ways to develop this skill is through ongoing experience in strategic planning.

The following guidelines may help you to get the most out of your strategic planning experience.

1. The real benefit of the strategic planning process is the process, not the plan document.
2. There is no "perfect" plan. There's doing your best at strategic thinking and implementation, and learning from what you're doing to enhance what you're doing the next time around.
3. The strategic planning process is usually not an experience. It's like the management process itself — it's a series of small moves that together keep the organization doing things right as it heads in the right direction.
4. In planning, things usually aren't as bad as you fear nor as good as you'd like.
5. Start simple, but start!

You may want to consider using a facilitator from outside of your organization if:

1. Your organization has not conducted strategic planning before.
2. For a variety of reasons, previous strategic planning was not deemed to be successful.
3. There appears to be a wide range of ideas and/or concerns among organization members about strategic planning and current organizational issues to be addressed in the plan.
4. There is no one in the organization whom members feel has sufficient facilitation skills.
5. No one in the organization feels committed to facilitating strategic planning for the organization.
6. Leaders believe that an inside facilitator will either inhibit participation from others or will not have the opportunity to fully participate in planning themselves.

7. Leaders want an objective voice, i.e., someone who is not likely to have strong predispositions about the organization's strategic issues and ideas.

Strategic planning should be conducted by a planning team.

Consider the following guidelines when developing the team.

1. The chief executive and board chair should be included in the planning group, and should drive development and implementation of the plan.
2. Establish clear guidelines for membership, for example, those directly involved in planning, those who will provide key information to the process, those who will review the plan document, those who will authorize the document, etc.
3. A primary responsibility of a board of directors is strategic planning to effectively lead the organization. Therefore, insist that the board be strongly involved in planning, often including assigning a planning committee (often, the same as the executive committee).
4. Ask if the board membership is representative of the organization's clientele and community, and if they are not, the organization may want to involve more representation in planning. If the board chair or chief executive balks at including more of the board members in planning, then the chief executive and/or board chair needs to seriously consider how serious the organization is about strategic planning!
5. Always include in the group, at least one person who ultimately has authority to make strategic decisions, for example, to select which goals will be achieved and how.
6. Ensure that as many stakeholders as possible are involved in the planning process.

7. Involve at least those who are responsible for composing and implementing the plan.
8. Involve someone to administrate the process, including arranging meetings, helping to record key information, helping with flipcharts, monitoring status of prework, etc.
9. Consider having the above administrator record the major steps in the planning process to help the organization conduct its own planning when the plan is next updated.
10. Different types of members may be needed more at different times in the planning process, for example, strong board involvement in determining the organization's strategic direction (mission, vision, and values), and then more staff involvement in determining the organization's strategic analysis to determine its current issues and goals, and then primarily the staff to determine the strategies needed to address the issues and meet the goals.
11. In general, where there's any doubt about whether a certain someone should be involved in planning, it's best to involve them. It's worse to exclude someone useful then it is to have one or two extra people in planning — this is true in particular with organizations where board members often do not have extensive expertise about the organization and its products or services.
12. Therefore, an organization may be better off to involve board and staff planners as much as possible in all phases of planning. Mixing the board and staff during planning helps board members understand the day-to-day issues of the organization, and helps the staff to understand the top-level issues of the organization.

## PLANNING MEETINGS

1. New planners usually want to know how many meetings will be needed and what is needed for each

meeting, i.e., they want a procedure for strategic planning. The number of meetings depends on whether the organization has done planning before, how many strategic issues and goals the organization faces, whether the culture of the organization prefers short or long meetings, and how much time the organization is willing to commit to strategic planning.

2. Attempt to complete strategic planning in at most two to three months, or momentum will be lost and the planning effort may fall apart.

## SCHEDULING OF MEETINGS

1. Have each meeting at most two to three weeks apart when planning. It's too easy to lose momentum otherwise.
2. The most important factor in accomplishing complete attendance to planning meetings is evidence of strong support from executives. Therefore, ensure that executives a) issue clear direction that they strongly support and value the strategic planning process, and b) are visibly involved in the planning process.

One example of a brief planning process is the following which includes four planning meetings and develops a top-level strategic plan which is later translated into a yearly operating plan by the staff:

1. Planning starts with a half-day or all-day board retreat and includes introductions by the board chair and/or chief executive, their explanations of the organization's benefits from strategic planning and the organization's commitment to the planning process, the facilitator's overview of the planning process, and the board chairs and/or chief executive's explanation of who will be involved in the planning process. In the retreat, the organization may then begin the next step in planning, whether this be visiting their mission, vision, values, etc. or

identifying current issues and goals to which strategies will need to be developed. (Goals are often reworded issues.) Planners are asked to think about strategies before the next meeting.

2. The next meeting focuses on finalizing strategies to deal with each issue. Before the next meeting, a subcommittee is charged to draft the planning document, which includes updated mission, vision, and values, and also finalized strategic issues, goals, strategies. This document is distributed before the next meeting.
3. In the next meeting, planners exchange feedback about the content and format of the planning document. Feedback is incorporated in the document and it is distributed before the next meeting.
4. The next meeting does not require entire attention to the plan, e.g., the document is authorized by the board during a regular board meeting.
5. Note that in the above example, various subcommittees might be charged to gather additional information and distribute it before the next planning meeting.
6. Note, too, that the staff may take this document and establish a yearly operating plan which details what strategies will be implemented over the next year, who will do them, and by when.
7. No matter how serious organizations are about strategic planning, they usually have strong concerns about being able to find time to attend frequent meetings. This concern can be addressed by ensuring meetings are well managed, having short meetings as needed rather than having fewer but longer meetings, and having realistic expectations from the planning project.

A frequent complaint about the strategic planning process is that it produces a document that ends up collecting dust on a shelf – the organization ignores the precious information depicted in the document.

The following guidelines will help ensure that the plan is implemented.

*(Note that reference to boards of directors is in regard to organizations that are corporations.)*

1. When conducting the planning process, involve the people who will be responsible for implementing the plan. Use a cross-functional team (representatives from each of the major organization's products or service) to ensure the plan is realistic and collaborative.
2. Ensure the plan is realistic. Continue asking planning participants "Is this realistic? Can you really do this?"
3. Organize the overall strategic plan into smaller action plans, often including an action plan (or work plan) for each committee on the board.
4. In the overall planning document, specify who is doing what and by when (action plans are often referenced in the implementation section of the overall strategic plan). Some organizations may elect to include the action plans in a separate document from the strategic plan, which would include only the mission, vision, values, key issues and goals, and strategies. This approach carries some risk that the board will lose focus on the action plans.
5. In an implementation section in the plan, specify and clarify the plan's implementation roles and responsibilities. Be sure to detail particularly the first 90 days of the implementation of the plan. Build in regular reviews of status of the implementation of the plan.
6. Translate the strategic plan's actions into job descriptions and personnel performance reviews.
7. Communicate the role of follow-ups to the plan. If people know the action plans will be regularly reviewed, implementers tend to do their jobs before they're checked on.

8. Be sure to document and distribute the plan, including inviting review input from all.
9. Be sure that one internal person has ultimate responsibility that the plan is enacted in a timely fashion.
10. The chief executive's support of the plan is a major driver to the plan's implementation. Integrate the plan's goals and objectives into the chief executive's performance reviews.
11. Place huge emphasis on feedback to the board's executive committee from the planning participants.

    Consider all or some of the following to ensure the plan is implemented.

12. Have designated rotating "checkers" to verify, e.g., every quarter, if each implementer completed their assigned tasks.
13. Have pairs of people be responsible for tasks. Have each partner commit to helping the other to finish the other's tasks on time.

A frequent complaint about strategic plans is that they are merely "to-do" lists of what to accomplish over the next few years. Or, others complain that strategic planning never seems to come in handy when the organization is faced with having to make a difficult, major decision. Or, other complains that strategic planning really doesn't help the organization face the future. These complaints arise because organizations fail to conduct a thorough strategic analysis as part of their strategic planning process. Instead, planners decide to plan only from what they know now. This makes the planning process much less strategic and a lot more guesswork. Strategic analysis is the heart of the strategic planning process and should not be ignored.

**PHASES IN PLANNING**

Whether the system is an organization, department, business, project, etc., the basic planning process typically includes similar nature of activities carried out in similar sequence. The phases are carried out carefully or — in some cases — intuitively, for example, when planning a very small, straightforward effort. The complexity of the various phases (and their duplication throughout the system) depend on the scope of the system. For example, in a large corporation, the following phases would be carried out in the corporate offices, in each division, in each department, in each group, etc.

During planning, planners have in mind (consciously or unconsciously) some overall purpose or result that the plan is to achieve. For example, during strategic planning, it's critical to reference the mission, or overall purpose, of the organization.

For example, during strategic planning, planners often conduct a "SWOT analysis". (SWOT is an acronym for considering the organization's strengths and weaknesses, and the opportunities and threats faced by the organization.) During this analysis, planners also can use a variety of assessments, or methods to "measure" the health of systems.

Based on the analysis and alignment to the overall mission of the system, planners establish a set of goals that build on strengths to take advantage of opportunities, while building up weaknesses and warding off threats. The particular strategies (or methods to reach the goals) chosen depend on matters of affordability, practicality and efficiency. Objectives are selected to be timely and indicative of progress toward goals. Responsibilities are assigned, including for implementation of the plan, and for achieving various goals and objectives. Ideally, deadlines are set for meeting each responsibility.

The above information is organized and written in a document which is distributed around the system.

This critical step is often ignored — which can eventually undermine the success of many of your future planning efforts. The purpose of a plan is to address a current problem or pursue a development goal. It seems simplistic to assert that you should acknowledge if the problem was solved or the goal met. However, this step in the planning process is often ignored in lieu of moving on the next problem to solve or goal to pursue. Skipping this step can cultivate apathy and skepticism -- even cynicism -- in your organization. Don't skip this step.

A common failure in many kinds of planning is that the plan is never really implemented. Instead, all focus is on writing a plan document. Too often, the plan sits collecting dust on a shelf. Therefore, most of the following guidelines help to ensure that the planning process is carried out completely and is implemented completely -- or, deviations from the intended plan are recognized and managed accordingly.

Going back to the reference to systems, it's critical that all parts of the system continue to exchange feedback in order to function effectively. This is true no matter what type of system. When planning, get input from everyone who will responsible to carry out parts of the plan, along with representative from groups who will be effected by the plan. Of course, people also should be involved in they will be responsible to review and authorize the plan.

New managers, in particular, often forget that others don't know what these managers know. Even if managers do communicate their intentions and plans verbally, chances are great that others won't completely hear or understand what the manager wants done. Also, as plans change, it's extremely difficult to remember who is supposed to be doing what and according to which version of the plan. Key stakeholders (employees, management, board members, funders, investor, customers, clients, etc.) may request copies of various types of plans. Therefore, it's critical to write plans down and communicate them widely.

For example, it's difficult to know what someone should be doing if they are to pursue the goal to "work harder". It's easier to recognize "Write a paper". It's difficult to know what the scope of "Writing a paper" really is. It's easier to appreciate that effort if the goal is "Write a 30-page paper". If I'm to take responsibility for pursuit of a goal, the goal should be acceptable to me. For example, I'm not likely to follow the directions of someone telling me to write a 30-page paper when I also have to five other papers to write. However, if you involve me in setting the goal so I can change my other commitments or modify the goal, I'm much more likely to accept pursuit of the goal as well.

Even if I do accept responsibility to pursue a goal that is specific and measurable, the goal won't be useful to me or others if, for example, the goal is to "Write a 30-page paper in the next 10 seconds". It may mean more to others if I commit to a realistic goal to "Write a 30-page paper in one week". However, it'll mean more to others (particularly if they are planning to help me or guide me to reach the goal) if I specify that I will write one page a day for 30 days, rather than including the possibility that I will write all 30 pages in last day of the 30-day period.

The goal should stretch the performer's capabilities. For example, I might be more interested in writing a 30-page paper if the topic of the paper or the way that I write it will extend my capabilities. I'm more inclined to write the paper if the paper will contribute to an effort in such a way that I might be rewarded for my effort.

Plans should specify who is responsible for achieving each result, including goals and objectives. Dates should be set for completion of each result, as well. Responsible parties should regularly review status of the plan. Be sure to have someone of authority "sign off" on the plan, including putting their signature on the plan to indicate they agree with and support its contents. Include responsibilities in policies, procedures, job descriptions, performance review processes, etc.

During the planning process, regularly collect feedback from participants. Do they agree with the planning process? If not, what don't they like and how could it be done better? In large, ongoing planning processes (such as strategic planning, business planning, project planning, etc.), it's critical to collect this kind of feedback regularly.

During regular reviews of implementation of the plan, assess if goals are being achieved or not. If not, were goals realistic? Do responsible parties have the resources necessary to achieve the goals and objectives? Should goals be changed? Should more priority be placed on achieving the goals? What needs to be done?

Finally, take 10 minutes to write down how the planning process could have been done better. File it away and read it the next time you conduct the planning process.

Far too often, primary emphasis is placed on the plan document. This is extremely unfortunate because the real treasure of planning is the planning process itself. During planning, panners learn a great deal from ongoing analysis, reflection, discussion, debates and dialogue around issues and goals in the system. Perhaps there is no better example of misplaced priorities in planning than in business ethics. Far too often, people put emphasis on written codes of ethics and codes of conduct. While these documents certainly are important, at least as important is conducting ongoing communications around these documents. The ongoing communications are what sensitize people to understanding and following the values and behaviors suggested in the codes.

A prominent example of this type of potential problem is when planners don't prefer the "top down" or "bottom up", "linear" type of planning (for example, going from general to specific along the process of an environmental scan, SWOT analysis, mission/vision/values, issues and goals, strategies, objectives, timelines, etc.) There are other ways to conduct planning.

## SYSTEMS THINKING

Systems thinking is an approach to analysis that is based on the belief that the component parts of a system will act differently when isolated from its environment or other parts of the system, and argues against Descartes's reductionist view. It includes viewing systems in a holistic manner, rather than through purely reductionist techniques. Systems thinking is about gaining insights into the whole by understanding the linkages and interactions between the elements that comprise the whole "system", consistent with systems philosophy. Systems Thinking recognizes that all human activity systems are open systems; therefore, they are affected by the environment in which they exist. Systems Thinking recognizes that in complex systems, events are separated by distance and time; therefore, small catalytic events can cause large changes in the system. Systems thinking acknowledges that a change in one area of a system can adversely affect another area of the system; thus, it promotes organizational communication at all levels in order to avoid the silo effect.

Systems thinkers consider that:

- A "system" is a dynamic and complex whole, interacting as a structured functional unit
- Information flows between the different elements that compose the system
- A system is a community situated within an environment
- Information flows from and to the surrounding environment via semi-permeable membranes or boundaries
- Systems are often composed of entities seeking equilibrium, but can exhibit oscillating, chaotic, or exponential growth/decay behaviour

Systems thinkers are particularly interested in studying systems because changing a system frequently leads to counterintuitive system responses. For example feedback loops may operate to either keep the organization in check or unbalance it.

Traditional decision making tends to involve linear cause and effect relationships. By taking a systems approach, we can see the whole complex of bidirectional interrelationships. Instead of analysing a problem in terms of an input and an output, for example, we look at the whole system of inputs, processes, outputs, feedback, and controls. This larger picture will typically provide more useful results than traditional methods.

System thinking also helps us integrate the temporal dimension of any decision. Instead of looking at discrete "snapshots" at points in time, a systems methodology will allow us to see change as a continuous process.

Systems Thinking is a world view based on the perspective of the systems sciences, which seeks to understand interconnectedness, complexity and wholeness of components of systems in specific relationship to each other. Systems thinking is not only constructivist, rather systems thinking embraces the values of reductionist science by understanding the parts, and the constructivist perspectives which seek to understand wholes, and more so, the understanding of the complex relationships that enable 'parts' to become 'wholes'.

A system is any set (group) of interdependent or temporally interacting parts. Parts are generally systems themselves and are composed of other parts, just as systems are generally parts or holons of other systems.

Systems thinking techniques may be used to study any kind of system — natural, scientific, human, or conceptual.

Systems thinking often involves considering a "system" in different ways:

Rather than trying to improve the braking system on a car by looking in great detail at the composition of the brake pads (reductionist), the boundary of the braking system may be extended to include not only the components of the car, but the driver, the road and the weather, and considering the interactions between them.

Looking at something as a series of conceptual systems according to multiple viewpoints. A supermarket could be considered as a "profit making system" from the perspective of management, an "employment system" from the perspective of the staff, and a "shopping system" — or perhaps an "entertainment system" — from the perspective of the customers. As a result of such thinking, new insights may be gained into how the supermarket works, why it has problems, or how changes made to one such system may impact on the others.

Systems thinking uses a variety of techniques that may be divided into:

- Hard systems - involving simulations, often using computers and the techniques of operations research. Useful for problems that can justifiably be quantified. However it cannot easily take into account unquantifiable variables (opinions, culture, politics, etc), and may treat people as being passive, rather than having complex motivations.
- Soft systems - Used to tackle systems that cannot easily be quantified, especially those involving people holding multiple and conflicting frames of reference. Useful for understanding motivations, viewpoints, and interactions and addressing qualitative as well as quantitative dimensions of problem situations. Soft systems are a field that utilizes foundation methodological work developed by Peter Checkland, Brian Wilson and their colleagues at Lancaster University. Morphological analysis is a complementary method for structuring and analysing non-quantifiable problem complexes.
- Evolutionary systems - the development of Evolutionary Systems Design by Bela H. Banathy integrates critical systems inquiry and soft systems methodologies to create a meta-methodology applicable to the design of complex social systems. These systems, similar to dynamic systems are understood as open, complex systems, but further accounts for their potential capacity to evolve over time. Banathy uniquely integrated the multidisciplinary perspectives of systems research (including chaos, complexity, cybernetics), cultural anthropology, evolutionary theory, and others.

## BUSINESS CONTINUITY PLANNING

Business Continuity Planning (BCP) is an interdisciplinary peer mentoring methodology used to create and validate an exercised logistical plan for how an organization will recover and restore partially or completely interrupted critical function(s) within a predetermined time after a disaster or extended disruption.

BCP may be a part of an organizational learning effort that helps reduce operational risk associated with lax information management controls. This process may be integrated with improving information security and corporate reputation risk management practices.

British Standards Institute is planning to release a new independent standard for BCP — BS 25999. The draft of standard had been put up for public comments and the final standard is expected in early 2007. This standard would reduce the reliance on Information Security oriented standards which dealt with BCP marginally.

A completed BCP cycle results in a formal printed manual available for reference before, during, and after disruptions have occurred. Its purpose is to reduce adverse stakeholder impacts determined by both the disruption's scope and duration. Measureable Business Impact Analysis (BIA) "zones" include civil, economic, natural, technical, secondary and subsequent.

Business Continuity Planning is not a new concept; plans for disasters, like Noah's Ark, are evidenced from the beginning of human history. Prior to January 1, 2000, governments anticipated computer failures, called the Y2k problem, in important public utility infrastructures like banking, power, telecommunication, health and financial industries. Since 1983, regulatory agencies like the American Bankers Association and Banking Administration Institute (BAI) required their supporting members to exercise operational continuity practices (later supported by more formal BCP manuals) that protect the public interests. Newer regulations were often based on formalized standards defined under ISO/IEC 17799 or BS 7799.

Both regulatory and global business focus on BCP arguably waned after the problem-free Y2K rollover. This lax attitude unequivocally ended September 11th 2001, when simultaneous terrorist attacks devastated downtown New York City and changed the 'worst case scenario' paradigm for business continuity planning.

BCP methodology is scalable for an organization of any size and complexity. Even though the methodology has roots in regulated industries, any type of organization may create a BCP manual, and arguably every organization should have one in order to ensure the organization's longevity. Evidence that firms do not invest enough time and resources into BCP preparations are evident in disaster survival statistics. Fires permanently close 44% of the business affected. In the 1993 World Trade Center bombing, 150 businesses out of 350 affected failed to survive the event. Conversely, the firms affected by the Sept 11 attacks with well-developed and tested BCP manuals were back in business within days.

A BCP manual for a small organization may be simply a printed manual stored safely away from the primary work location, containing the names, addresses, and phone numbers for crisis management staff, general staff members, clients, and vendors along with the location of the offsite data backup storage media, copies of insurance contracts, and other critical materials necessary for organizational survival. At its most complex, a BCP manual may outline a secondary work site, technical requirements and readiness, regulatory reporting requirements, work recovery measures, the means to reestablish physical records, the means to establish a new supply chain, or the means to establish new production centers. Firms should ensure that their BCP manual is realistic and easy to use during a crisis. As such, BCP sits along side crisis management and disaster recovery planning and is a part of an organization's overall risk management.

The development of a BCP manual has five main phases:

1. Analysis
2. Solution design
3. Implementation
4. Testing and organization acceptance
5. Maintenance

Much of the BCP material on the internet is sponsored by consultancies who offer fee-based services for BCP solution development, however basic tutorials are freely available on the internet for properly motivated organizations.

The analysis phase in the development of a BCP manual consists of an impact analysis, threat analysis, and impact scenarios with the resulting BCP plan requirement documentation. An impact analysis results in the differentiation between critical and non-critical organization functions. A function may be considered critical if the implications for stakeholders of damage to the organization resulting are regarded as unacceptable. Perceptions of the acceptability of disruption may be modified by the cost of establishing and maintaining appropriate business or technical recovery solutions. A function may also be considered critical if dictated by law. Next, the impact analysis results in the recovery requirements for each critical function. Recovery requirements consist of the following information:

- The time frame in which the critical function must be resumed after the disaster
- The business requirements for recovery of the critical function, and/or
- The technical requirements for recovery of the critical function

The organizations also banned face-to-face contact between opposing team members during business and non-business hours. With such a split, organizations increased their resiliency against the threat of government-ordered quarantine measures if one person in a team contracted or was exposed to the disease. Damage from flooding also has a unique characteristic. If an office environment is flooded with non-salinated and contamination-free water (e.g.m, in the event of a pipe burst), equipment can be thoroughly dried and may still be functional.

After defining potential threats, documenting the impact scenarios that form the basis of the business recovery plan is recommended. In general, planning for the most wide-reaching disaster or disturbance is preferable to planning for a smaller scale problem, as almost all smaller scale problems are partial elements of larger disasters. A typical impact scenario like 'Building Loss' will most likely encompass all critical business functions, and the worst potential outcome from any potential threat. A business continuity plan may also document additional impact scenarios if an organization has more than one building. Other more specific impact scenarios - for example a scenario for the temporary or permanent loss of a specific floor in a building - may also be documented.

After the completion of the analysis phase, the business and technical plan requirements are documented in order to commence the implementation phase. For an office-based, IT intensive business, the plan requirements may cover the following elements which may be classed as ICE (In Case of Emergency) Data:

- The numbers and types of desks, whether dedicated or shared, required outside of the primary business location in the secondary location
- The individuals involved in the recovery effort along with their contact and technical details
- The applications and application data required from the secondary location desks for critical business functions
- The manual workaround solutions
- The maximum outage allowed for the applications
- The peripheral requirements like printers, copier, fax machine, calculators, paper, pens etc.

Other business environments, such as production, distribution, warehousing etc will need to cover these elements, but are likely to have additional issues to manage following a disruptive event.

The goal of the solution design phase is to identify the most cost effective disaster recovery solution that meets two main requirements from the impact analysis stage. For IT applications, this is commonly expressed as:

1. The minimum application and application data requirements
2. The time frame in which the minimum application and application data must be available

Disaster recovery plans may also be required outside the IT applications domain, for example in preservation of information in hard copy format, or restoration of embedded technology in process plant. This BCP phase overlaps with Disaster recovery planning methodology. The solution phase determines:

- The crisis management command structure
- The location of a secondary work site (where necessary)
- Telecommunication architecture between primary and secondary work sites
- Data replication methodology between primary and secondary work sites
- The application and software required at the secondary work site, and
- The type of physical data requirements at the secondary work site.

The implementation phase, quite simply, is the execution of the design elements identified in the solution design phase. Work package testing may take place during the implementation of the solution, however; work package testing does not take the place of organizational testing.

The purpose of testing is to achieve organizational acceptance that the business continuity solution satisfies the organization's recovery requirements. Plans may fail to meet expectations due to insufficient or inaccurate recovery requirements, solution design flaws, or solution implementation errors. Testing may include:

- Crisis command team call-out testing
- Technical swing test from primary to secondary work locations

- Technical swing test from secondary to primary work locations
- Application test
- Business process test

At minimum, testing is generally conducted on a biannual or annual schedule. Problems identified in the initial testing phase may be rolled up into the maintenance phase and retested during the next test cycle.

Maintenance of a BCP manual is broken down into three periodic activities. The first activity is the confirmation of information in the manual. The second activity is the testing and verification of technical solutions established for recovery operations. The third activity is the testing and verification of documented organization recovery procedures. A biannual or annual maintenance cycle is typical.

All organizations change over time, therefore a BCP manual must change to stay relevant to the organization. Once data accuracy is verified, normally a call tree test is conducted to evaluate the notification plan's efficiency as well as the accuracy of the contact data. Some types of changes that should be identified and updated in the manual include:

- Staffing changes
- Staffing persona
- Changes to important clients and their contact details
- Changes to important vendors/suppliers and their contact details
- Departmental changes like new, closed or fundamentally changed departments.

## RISK MANAGEMENT

Risk Management is the process of measuring, or assessing, risk and developing strategies to manage it. Strategies include transferring the risk to another party, avoiding the risk, reducing the negative effect of the risk, and accepting some or all of the consequences of a particular risk.

Traditional risk management focuses on risks stemming from physical or legal causes (e.g. natural disasters or fires, accidents, death, and lawsuits). Financial risk management, on the other hand, focuses on risks that can be managed using traded financial instruments.

In ideal risk management, a prioritization process is followed whereby the risks with the greatest loss and the greatest probability of occurring are handled first, and risks with lower probability of occurrence and lower loss are handled later. In practice the process can be very difficult, and balancing between risks with a high probability of occurrence but lower loss vs. a risk with high loss but lower probability of occurrence can often be mishandled.

Intangible risk management identifies a new type of risk - a risk that has a 100% probability of occurring but is ignored by the organization due to a lack of identification ability. For example, knowledge risk occurs when deficient knowledge is applied. Relationship risk occurs when collaboration ineffectiveness occurs. Process-engagement risk occurs when operational ineffectiveness occurs. These risks directly reduce the productivity of knowledge workers, decrease cost effectiveness, profitability, service, quality, reputation, brand value, and earnings quality. Intangible risk management allows risk management to create immediate value from the identification and reduction of risks that reduce productivity.

Risk management also faces difficulties allocating resources. This is the idea of opportunity cost. Resources spent on risk management could have been spent on more profitable activities. Again, ideal risk management minimizes spending while maximizing the reduction of the negative effects of risks.

Establishing the context includes planning the remainder of the process and mapping out the scope of the exercise, the identity and objectives of stakeholders, the basis upon which risks will be evaluated and defining a framework for the process, and agenda for identification and analysis of risk involved in the process.

After establishing the context, the next step in the process of managing risk is to identify potential risks. Risks are about events that, when triggered, cause problems. Hence, risk identification can start with the source of problems, or with the problem itself.

- Source analysis- Risk sources may be internal or external to the system that is the target of risk management. Examples of risk sources are: stakeholders of a project, employees of a company or the weather over an airport.
- Problem analysis -Risks are related to identified threats. For example: the threat of losing money, the threat of abuse of privacy information or the threat of accidents and casualties. The threats may exist with various entities, most important with shareholder, customers and legislative bodies such as the government.

When either source or problem is known, the events that a source may trigger or the events that can lead to a problem can be investigated. For example: stakeholders withdrawing during a project may endanger funding of the project; privacy information may be stolen by employees even within a closed network; lightning striking a Boeing 747 during takeoff may make all people onboard immediate casualties.

The chosen method of identifying risks may depend on culture, industry practice and compliance. The identification methods are formed by templates or the development of templates for identifying source, problem or event. Common risk identification methods are:

- Objectives-based Risk Identification- Organizations and project teams have objectives. Any event that may endanger achieving an objective partly or completely is identified as risk. Objective-based risk identification is at the basis of COSO's Enterprise Risk Management - Integrated Framework
- Scenario-based Risk Identification In scenario analysis different scenarios are created. The scenarios may be

the alternative ways to achieve an objective, or an analysis of the interaction of forces in, for example, a market or battle. Any event that triggers an undesired scenario alternative is identified as risk.

- Taxonomy-based Risk Identification The taxonomy in taxonomy-based risk identification is a breakdown of possible risk sources. Based on the taxonomy and knowledge of best practices, a questionnaire is compiled. The answers to the questions reveal risks.

Once risks have been identified, they must then be assessed as to their potential severity of loss and to the probability of occurrence. These quantities can be either simple to measure, in the case of the value of a lost building, or impossible to know for sure in the case of the probability of an unlikely event occurring. Therefore, in the assessment process it is critical to make the best educated guesses possible in order to properly prioritize the implementation of the Risk Management Plan.

The fundamental difficulty in risk assessment is determining the rate of occurrence since statistical information is not available on all kinds of past incidents. Furthermore, evaluating the severity of the consequences (impact) is often quite difficult for immaterial assets. Asset valuation is another question that needs to be addressed. Thus, best educated opinions and available statistics are the primary sources of information. Nevertheless, risk assessment should produce such information for the management of the organization that the primary risks are easy to understand and that the risk management decisions may be prioritized. Thus, there have been several theories and attempts to quantify risks. Numerous different risk formulae exist, but perhaps the most widely accepted formula for risk quantification is: Rate of occurrence multiplied by the impact of the event equals risk.

Later research has shown that the financial benefits of risk management are less dependent on the formula used but are more dependent on the frequency and how risk assessment is performed.

In business it is imperative to be able to present the findings of risk assessments in financial terms. Robert Courtney Jr. proposed a formula for presenting risks in financial terms. The Courtney formula was accepted as the official risk analysis method for the US governmental agencies. The formula proposes calculation of ALE (Annualised Loss Expectancy) and compares the expected loss value to the security control implementation costs.

Once risks have been identified and assessed, all techniques to manage the risk fall into one or more of these four major categories:

- Tolerate (aka Retention)
- Treat (aka Mitigation)
- Terminate (aka Elimination)
- Transfer (aka Buying Insurance)

Ideal use of these strategies may not be possible. Some of them may involve trade-offs that are not acceptable to the organization or person making the risk management decisions.

**Risk Avoidance**

Includes not performing an activity that could carry risk. An example would be not buying a property or business in order to not take on the liability that comes with it. Another would be not flying in order to not take the risk that the airplane were to be hijacked. Avoidance may seem the answer to all risks, but avoiding risks also means losing out on the potential gain that accepting (retaining) the risk may have allowed. Not entering a business to avoid the risk of loss also avoids the possibility of earning profits.

**Risk Reduction**

Involves methods that reduce the severity of the loss. Examples include sprinklers designed to put out a fire to reduce the risk of loss by fire. This method may cause a greater loss by water damage and therefore may not be suitable. Halon fire suppression systems may mitigate that risk, but the cost may be prohibitive as a strategy.

Modern software development methodologies reduce risk by developing and delivering software incrementally. Early methodologies suffered from the fact that they only delivered software in the final phase of development; any problems encountered in earlier phases meant costly rework and often jeopardized the whole project. By developing in increments, software projects can limit effort wasted to a single increment. A current trend in software development, spearheaded by the Extreme Programming community, is to reduce the size of increments to the smallest size possible, sometimes as little as one week is allocated to an increment.

### Risk Retention

Involves accepting the loss when it occurs. True self insurance falls in this category. Risk retention is a viable strategy for small risks where the cost of insuring against the risk would be greater over time than the total losses sustained. All risks that are not avoided or transferred are retained by default. This includes risks that are so large or catastrophic that they either cannot be insured against or the premiums would be infeasible. War is an example since most property and risks are not insured against war, so the loss attributed by war is retained by the insured. Also any amounts of potential loss (risk) over the amount insured is retained risk. This may also be acceptable if the chance of a very large loss is small or if the cost to insure for greater coverage amounts is so great it would hinder the goals of the organization too much.

### Risk Transfer

Means causing another party to accept the risk, typically by contract or by hedging. Insurance is one type of risk transfer that uses contracts. Other times it may involve contract language that transfers a risk to another party without the payment of an insurance premium. Liability among construction or other contractors is very often transferred this way. On the other hand, taking offsetting positions in derivatives is typically how firms use hedging to financially manage risk.

Some ways of managing risk fall into multiple categories. Risk retention pools are technically retaining the risk for the group, but spreading it over the whole group involves transfer among individual members of the group. This is different from traditional insurance, in that no premium is exchanged between members of the group up front, but instead losses are assessed to all members of the group.

## CREATING THE PLAN

Decide on the combination of methods to be used for each risk. Each risk management decision should be recorded and approved by the appropriate level of management. For example, a risk concerning the image of the organization should have top management decision behind it whereas IT management would have the authority to decide on computer virus risks.

The Risk Management Plan should propose applicable and effective security controls for managing the risks. For example, an observed high risk of computer viruses could be mitigated by acquiring and implementing anti virus software. A good Risk Management Plan should contain a schedule for control implementation and responsible persons for those actions. The risk management concept is old but is still not very effectively measured

## IMPLEMENTATION

Follow all of the planned methods for mitigating the effect of the risks. Purchase insurance policies for the risks that have been decided to be transferred to an insurer, avoid all risks that can be avoided without sacrificing the entity's goals, reduce others, and retain the rest.

Initial Risk Management Plans will never be perfect. Practice, experience, and actual loss results will necessitate changes in the plan and contribute information to allow possible different decisions to be made in dealing with the risks being faced.

Risk analysis results and management plans should be updated periodically. There are two primary reasons for this:

1. To evaluate whether the previously selected security controls are still applicable and effective, and
2. To evaluate the possible risk level changes in the business environment. For example, information risks are a good example of rapidly changing business environment.

If risks are improperly assessed and prioritized, time can be wasted in dealing with risk of losses that are not likely to occur. Spending too much time assessing and managing unlikely risks can divert resources that could be used more profitably. Unlikely events do occur but if the risk is unlikely enough to occur it may be better to simply retain the risk and deal with the result if the loss does in fact occur.

Prioritizing too highly the Risk management processes could keep an organization from ever completing a project or even getting started. This is especially true if other work is suspended until the risk management process is considered complete.

It is also important to keep in mind the distinction between risk and uncertainty. Risk can be measured by Impacts x Probability.

As applied to corporate finance, risk management is a technique for measuring, monitoring and controlling the financial or operational risk on a firm's balance sheet.

The Basel II framework breaks risks into market risk (price risk), credit risk and operational risk and also specifies methods for calculating capital requirements for each of these components.

In Enterprise Risk Management, a risk is defined as a possible event or circumstance that can have negative influences on the Enterprise in question. Its impact can be on the very existence, the resources (human and capital), the products and services, or the customers of the Enterprise, as well as external impacts on Society, Markets or the Environment.

In addition, every probable risk can have a pre-formulated plan to deal with its possible consequences (to ensure contingency if the risk becomes a liability).

From the information above and the average cost per employee over time, or Cost Accrual Ratio, a project manager can estimate

- The cost associated with the risk if it arises, estimated by multiplying employee costs per unit time by the estimated time lost (cost impact, C where C = Cost Accrual Ratio S)
- The probable increase in time associated with a risk (schedule variance due to risk, Rs where Rs = PS):
  - Sorting on this value puts the highest risks to the schedule first. This is intended to cause the greatest risks to the project to be attempted first so that risk is minimized as quickly as possible.
  - This is slightly misleading as schedule variances with a large P and small S and vice versa are not equivalent. (The risk of the RMS Titanic sinking vs. the passengers' meals being served at slightly the wrong time).
- The probable increase in cost associated with a risk (cost variance due to risk, Rc where Rc = P*C = P*CAR*S = P*S*CAR)
  - Sorting on this value puts the highest risks to the budget first.

Risk in a project or process can be due either to Special Cause Variation or Common Cause Variation and requires appropriate treatment. That is to re-iterate the concern about extremal cases not being equivalent in the list immediately above.

## RISK MANAGEMENT ACTIVITIES AS APPLIED TO PROJECT MANAGEMENT

In project management, risk management includes the following activities:

- Planning how risk management will be held in the particular project. Plan should include risk management tasks, responsibilities, activities and budget.
- Assigning a risk officer - a team member other than a project manager who is responsible for foreseeing potential project problems. Typical characteristic of risk officer is a healthy skepticism.
- Maintaining live project risk database. Each risk should have the following attributes: opening date, title, short description, probability and importance. Optionally a risk may have an assigned person responsible for its resolution and a date by which the risk must be resolved.
- Creating anonymous risk reporting channel. Each team member should have possibility to report risk that he foresees in the project.
- Preparing mitigation plans for risks that are chosen to be mitigated. The purpose of the mitigation plan is to describe how this particular risk will be handled – what, when, by who and how will be done to avoid it or minimize consequences if it becomes a liability.
- Summarizing planned and faced risks, effectiveness of mitigation activities and effort spend for the risk management

Risk management is simply a practice of systematically selecting cost effective approaches for minimising the effect of threat realization to the organization. All risks can never be fully avoided or mitigated simply because of financial and practical limitations. Therefore all organizations have to accept some level of residual risks.

Whereas risk management tends to be pre-emptive, Business Continuity Planning (BCP) was invented to deal with the consequences of realised residual risks. The necessity to have BCP in place arises because even very unlikely events will occur if given enough time. Risk management and BCP are often mistakenly seen as rivals or overlapping practices. In fact these processes are so tightly tied together that such separation seems artificial. For example, the risk management process creates important inputs for the BCP (assets, impact assessments, cost estimates etc). Risk management also proposes applicable controls for the observed risks. Therefore, risk management covers several areas that are vital for the BCP process. However, the BCP process goes beyond risk management's pre-emptive approach and moves on from the assumption that the disaster will realise at some point.

**Financial Risk Management**

Financial risk management is the practice of creating value in a firm by using financial instruments to manage exposure to risk. Similar to general risk management, financial risk management requires identifying the sources of risk, measuring risk, and plans to address them. As a specialization of risk management, financial risk management focuses on when and how to hedge using financial instruments to manage costly exposures to risk.

In the banking sector worldwide, Basel Accord are generally adopted by internationally active banks to tracking, reporting and exposing operational, credit and market risks.

Finance theory (i.e. financial economics) prescribes that a firm should take on a project when it increases shareholder value. Finance theory also shows that firm managers cannot create value for shareholders, also called its investors, by taking on project that shareholders could do for themselves at the same cost. When applied to financial risk management, this implies that firm managers should not hedge risks that investors can hedge for themselves at the same cost. This notion is captured by the hedging irrelevance proposition: In a perfect market, the firm cannot create value by hedging a risk when the price of bearing that risk within the firm is the same as the price of bearing it outside of the firm. In practice, financial markets are not likely to be perfect markets. This suggests that firm managers likely have many opportunities to create value for shareholders using financial risk management. The trick is to determine which risks are cheaper for the firm to manage than the shareholders. A general rule of thumb, however, is that market risks that result in unique risks for the firm are the best candidates for financial risk management.

## Chapter 2

# Important Management Areas in Planning

The purpose of a Management Plan is to identify values, threats (real and potential) to those values, and uses that are consistent with maintaining ecological character while sustaining the livelihoods of local communities.

The 5 key steps in the Management Planning process are:

1. Identifying priority values
2. Identifying threats to the priority values
3. Identifying the sources of those threats
4. Developing management strategies and recommending actions to manage those threats, including goals for each priority value
5. Monitoring & review – allowing changes and adaptation to new needs and ways of thinking.

Community-based management planning:

1. Undertake a desktop assessment and prepare a Background Paper
2. Guided by the Background Paper, establish a Community Reference Group (CRG) and Scientific and Technical Advisory Group (STAG)
3. Consult with the CRG and STAG on the Background Paper via a facilitated workshop
4. Undertake a values, condition and threat assessment (desktop and/or on-ground) and prepare an Issues Paper

5. Develop a Communication Strategy to disseminate information in the Issues Paper to raise broad awareness in the community
6. Consult with the CRG and STAG on the Issues Paper and Communication Strategy, via focus groups and a facilitated workshop
7. Implement the Communication Strategy
8. Develop the Draft Management Plan in consultation with the STAG and following feedback from the CRG and broader community (through the Communications Strategy)
9. Consult with the CRG and STAG on the Draft Management Plan, via a facilitated workshop
10. Public release of the Draft Management Plan

Two critical components of the management planning process are:

- Values Mapping - a tool for building management partnerships
- Issues Paper

## VALUES MAPPING – A TOOL FOR BUILDING MANAGEMENT PARTNERSHIPS

The Values Mapping process uses identification strategies from business marketing and consensus-building strategies from Alternative Dispute Resolution, as a tool for bringing together the diversity of interests in a range of aspects of planning for sustainable living.

The Values Mapping process involves:

- Background research directed to understanding the issues, the language relevant to the area and its issues, and the history of the issues
- Identifying the key players – their interests and roles in management of the area
- Designing the process so that it is accessible and meaningful to all who need to be involved

- Establishing 'buy in' – encouraging participation and building trust
- Mapping values - reporting on the outcomes

Four key activities in Values Mapping

1. Telephone Survey: People with an interest in the area, whether for conservation reasons or as recreational or commercial users, are asked to complete a telephone survey addressing the values of the area and management issues.
2. Focus Group Sessions: A series of information gathering sessions (usually of 1--1½ hours duration) with interest groups (e.g. farmers & graziers, commercial fishers, recreational fishers, other recreational users, scientific researchers, government staff with management responsibilities in the area, and community conservation representatives).

These focus group sessions are directed to gathering and confirming local and technical knowledge of the area – what places are special, what makes them special, what are the threats to those values and what management actions are possible.

3. Field Trip: A field trip, which all participants are strongly encouraged to attend, looks at key sites and the management issues of concern for retaining those values, helps all participants gain a shared understanding of the area and the differing values it holds for people in the area.
4. Facilitated Workshop: A professionally facilitated Values Mapping workshop, which brings together the knowledge and experience of the different sectors with an interest in the area, shares values and concerns, and seeks to find common ground which will help achieve the best possible future management for the area.

Both the focus group sessions and the Values Mapping workshop use topographical or other suitable maps of the area, with overlays to depict visually the areas valued and the management issues of concern.

**Issues Paper**

The objectives of an Issues Paper (focused on shorebirds, as opposed to broader natural, social and economic values) should be to:

- Review the status of knowledge on shorebirds and their habitat.
- Investigate and identify threats to important shorebird habitat, rank threats and identify sites/habitats with the highest level of threat.
- Investigate and identify options for mitigating threats and prioritise these options.
- Recommend opportunities for collaborative approaches to manage threats among local stakeholder groups.

A Shorebird Issues Paper developed for the Clarence Estuary in NSW took the following approach to meeting the objectives stated above:

Review the status of knowledge on shorebirds and their habitat

To review the status of knowledge on shorebirds and their habitat it is necessary to evaluate the data and identify gaps in the data/data collection.

Data evaluation – things to consider:

- Survey duration – the period over which surveys were undertaken.
- Survey frequency – the number of survey periods (individual surveys).
- Survey effort – the number of survey days/survey period.
- Methods used – general indication of how data were collected.

- Number of personnel – number of counters involved in the survey.
- Number of sites sampled – the number of sites listed in the data and sites within the area sampled.
- Survey coverage – general appraisal of the area surveyed.
- Data presentation – notes on the manner in which data are presented. This information is important for assessing the utility of data in identifying important roost and feeding sites.

Potential gaps – things to consider:

- Temporal coverage of surveys to document use of the site during northwards and southwards migration.
- Number of high tide surveys that encompass the entire site.
- Number of low tide surveys that encompass the entire site.
- Management of data i.e. specific information for each site sampled.
- Nocturnal surveys to identify night roost and feeding sites.
- Accessibility of information on methods and timing.
- Use of standard site names.

**Assessing the importance of habitat**

Things to consider in assessing (and comparing) the importance of habitat:

Roost Sites

- Maximum spring/summer counts,
- Average spring/summer counts,
- Species diversity and occurrence of threatened species between sites/locations

Note: This provides a broad indication of the relative importance of known roost sites, however, there are important issues such as nocturnal habitat use, nesting and feeding sites and roost function (i.e. spring, neap or staging; spring tide roosts given a higher ranking than either neap roosts or staging areas).

Investigate and identify threats to important shorebird habitat, rank threats and identify sites/habitats with the highest level of threat.

Threats to shorebirds and their habitat can be broadly categorised as:

- Habitat Loss – removal of habitat through reclamation and in severe cases erosion.
- Habitat Modification – changes in the characteristics of habitat that reduces its utility for shorebirds.
- Habitat Disturbance – activities that often result in disturbance to roosting and foraging birds (including. sources of disturbance i.e. location of infrastructure and types of disturbance i.e. activities that may affect shorebirds)
- Habitat Pollution – accumulation of pollutants in body fat that reduces life span and potentially reproductive ability and abundance of food.
- Mortality – death of individuals through hunting by humans for food, recreation or site protection.

To rank threats, their occurrence and proximity to shorebird habitat was assessed and a matrix developed to allow comparisons among sites.

The method adopted to rank threats included:

- Each threat was given a score of 1, 5 or 10 depending on its proximity to a site.
- A score of 10 was given to threats that occur on-site, 5 for threats within 100m of a site and 1 for threats within 1km of a site.
- A score of 20 was given to sites approved for development. Such a high score was deemed necessary to reflect the strong likelihood that the site would be removed once the development proceeds.

- Threat scores were then added together to give a combined threat score. Sites were then ranked from highest to lowest based on the total threat score.
- The higher the score the greater level of threat experienced.
- A general indication of which threats are most prevalent was obtained by adding threats across sites to obtain a total threat score.
- Comparing the importance of each site to the threat scores gave an indication of where conflicts between habitat values and threats exist.

**Investigate and Identify Options for Mitigating Threats**

Options for managing threats to shorebirds/their habitat were broadly categorised as follows:

- Further research to clearly identify threats
- Community awareness and involvement
- Improved environmental planning and regulation
- Habitat conservation and remediation.
- On-ground works

**Further Information**

Clarence Estuary Shorebird Issues Paper

## THE ENTREPRENEUR PLAN

This is otherwise known as business plan. It is a written explanation of the company's business model for the venture in question. Business plans are developed for ventures in both business and government.

Business plans are used internally for management and planning and are also used to convince outsiders such as banks or venture capitalists to invest money into a venture.

Business plans are noted for often quickly becoming out of date. One common belief within business circles is that the actual plan may have little value, but what is more important is the process of planning, through which the manager gains a greater understanding of the business and of the options available.

Business plan is prepared for customers for they need to know whether the product serves the purpose or not and the utility of the product, for government because it is necessary to know for government whether the legal economical and subsidy concerns are met or the like. Business plans can be divided roughly into four separate types. They require very different amounts of labour and not always with proportionately different results.

- The Miniplan: A miniplan, better known as the Executive Summary, may consist of one to 10 pages and should include at least cursory attention to such key matters as business concept, financing needs, marketing plan and financial statements, especially cash flow, income projection and balance sheet. It's a great way to quickly test a business concept or measure the interest of a potential partner or minor investor. It can also serve as a valuable prelude to a full-length plan later on.
- The Working Plan: A working plan is a tool to be used to operate the business. It has to be long on detail but may be short on presentation. As with a miniplan, one can probably afford a somewhat higher degree of candor and informality when preparing a working plan.
- The Presentation Plan: If a working plan is twisted to boost the amount of attention paid to its looks, it will become a presentation plan. This plan is suitable for showing to bankers, investors and others outside the company.
- The Electronic Plan: The majority of business plans are composed on a computer of some kind, then printed out and presented in hard copy. But more and more business information that once was transferred between parties only on paper is now sent

electronically. An electronic plan can be handy for presentations to a group using a computer-driven overhead projector, for example, or for satisfying the demands of a discriminating investor who wants to be able to delve deeply into the underpinnings of complex spreadsheets.

A solid strategic plan delivers the following benefits:

- You focus your time and energy on activities that are most likely to achieve your goals.
- You know how to allocate resources.
- You put a solid strategy in place to set your business apart from the competition.
- You can communicate your plan to employees, and hold them accountable for results.
- You can track the results of your efforts and make mid-course corrections to get back on track if you need to.
- You can adapt your plan to create a second business plan to raise investment capital or get a business loan.

For an effective business plan, the following steps can be followed:

- Idea Generation
- Environment Scanning
- Feasibility Analysis
- Drawing up a Functional Plan
- Project Report Preparation
- Evaluation, Control & Review

A business plan can be seen as a collection of sub-plans including a marketing plan, financial plan, production plan, and human resource plan.

The business plan has many forms. There is however a format that is typical:

- Executive summary
  - Explains the basic business model
  - Gives rationale for the strategy

- Background
  - Gives short history of company (unless it is a new company)
  - Provides background details such as:
    - Age of company
    - Number of employees
    - Annual sales figures
    - Location of facilities
    - Form of ownership including
    - Sole proprietor
    - Partnership
    - Entrepreneurial startup
    - Private corporate startup
    - Publicly traded corporation
    - Limited liability company
    - Public utility
    - Non-profit organization
  - Background of key personnel including
    - Owners
    - Senior managers
    - Managing partners
    - Head scientists and researchers
- Marketing
  - The macroenvironment
  - The competitive environment
  - The industry
  - The customer priorities
  - Product strategy
  - Pricing strategy
  - Promotion strategy
  - Distribution strategy
- Production and manufacturing
  - Describe all processes
  - Production facility requirements - size, layout, capacity, location
  - Inventory requirements - raw materials inventory, finished goods inventory, warehouse space requirements

  - Equipment requirements
  - Supply chain requirements
  - Fixed cost allocation
- Finance
  - Source of funds
  - Existing loans and liabilities
  - Projected sales and costs
  - Break even analysis
  - Expected return
  - Monthly pro-forma cash flow statement
- Human resources
  - Assign responsibilities
  - Training required
  - Skills required
  - Union issues
  - Compensation
  - Skills availability
  - New hiring

Specialized sections such as product research and development, legal strategies, marketing research, or inter-company collaborations, are added to deal with unique features or characteristics of the business or its markets.

Cost and revenue estimates are central to any business plan for deciding the viability of the planned venture. But costs are often underestimated and revenues overestimated resulting in later cost overruns, revenue shortfalls, and possibly non-viability. During the dot-com bubble 1997-2001 this was a problem for many technology start-ups. However, the problem is not limited to technology or the private sector; public works projects also routinely suffer from cost overruns and/or revenue shortfalls. The main causes of cost overruns and revenue shortfalls are optimism bias and strategic misrepresentation. Reference class forecasting was developed to curb optimism bias and strategic misrepresentation and thus arrive at more accurate cost and revenue estimates in business plans.

## MARKETING PLAN

A Marketing Plan is a written document that details the actions necessary to achieve a specified marketing objective(s). It can be for a product or service, a brand, or a product line. It can cover one year (referred to as an annual marketing plan), or cover up to 5 years.

A marketing plan may be part of an overall business plan. Solid marketing strategy is the foundation of a well-written marketing plan. While a marketing plan contains a list of actions, a marketing plan without a sound strategic foundation is of little use.

There are many formats for marketings plans and every company does it a little differently, but the outline that follows is a very complete format. Using this format will produce a 30 to 40 page plan. Many companies prefer an abridged format that would yield a 10 to 20 page plan.

1. Title page
2. Executive Summary
3. Current Situation - Macroenvironment
   - Economy
   - Legal
   - Government
   - Technology
   - Ecological
   - Sociocultural
   - Supply chain
4. Current Situation - Market Analysis
   - Market definition
   - Market size
   - Market segmentation
   - Industry structure and strategic groupings
   - Porter 5 forces analysis
   - Competition and market share
   - Competitors' strengths and weaknesses
   - Market trends

5. Current Situation - Consumer Analysis
   - Nature of the buying decision
   - Participants
   - Demographics
   - Psychographics
   - Buyer motivation and expectations
   - Loyalty segments
6. Current Situation - Internal
   - Company resources
     - Financial
     - People
     - Time
     - Skills
   - Objectives
     - Mission statement and vision statement
     - Corporate objectives
     - Financial objective
     - Marketing objectives
     - Long term objectives
   - Corporate culture
7. Summary of Situation Analysis
   - External threats
   - External opportunities
   - Internal strengths
   - Internal weaknesses
   - Key success factors in the industry
   - our sustainable competitive advantage
8. Marketing research
   - Information requirements
   - Research methodology
   - Research results
9. Marketing Strategy - Product
   - Product mix
   - Product strengths and weaknesses
     - Perceptual mapping

- Product life cycle management and new product development
- Brand name, brand image, and brand equity
- The augmented product
- Product portfolio analysis
  - B.C.G. Analysis
  - contribution margin analysis
  - G.E. Multi Factoral analysis
  - Quality Function Deployment

10. Marketing Strategy - Market share objectives
    - By products,
    - By customer segments,
    - By geographical markets
11. Marketing Strategy - Price
    - Pricing objectives
    - Pricing method (eg.: cost plus, demand based, or competitor indexing)
    - Pricing strategy (eg.: skimming, or penetration)
    - Discounts and allowances
    - Price elasticity and customer sensitivity
    - Price zoning
    - Break even analysis at various prices
12. Marketing Strategy - promotion
    - Promotional goals
    - Promotional mix
    - Advertising reach, frequency, flights, theme, and media
    - Sales force requirements, techniques, and management
    - Sales promotion
    - Publicity and public relations
    - Electronic promotion (eg.: Web, or telephone)
13. Marketing Strategy - Distribution
    - Geographical coverage
    - Distribution channels

- Physical distribution and logistics
- Electronic distribution

14. Implementation
    - Personnel requirements
        - Assign responsibilities
        - Give incentives
        - Training on selling methods
    - Financial requirements
    - Management information systems requirements
    - Month-by-month agenda
        - PERT or critical path analysis
    - Monitoring results and benchmarks
    - Adjustment mechanism
    - Contingencies (What if's)

15. Financial Summary
    - Assumptions
    - Pro-forma monthly income statement
    - Contribution margin analysis
    - Breakeven analysis
    - Monte Carlo method
    - ISI: Internet Strategic Intelligence

16. Scenarios
    - Prediction of Future Scenarios
    - Plan of Action for each Scenario

17. Appendix
    - Pictures and specifications of the new product
    - Results from research already completed

The final stage of any marketing planning process is to establish targets (or standards) so that progress can be monitored. Accordingly, it is important to put both quantities and timescales into the marketing objectives (for example, to capture 20 per cent by value of the market within two years) and into the corresponding strategies.

Changes in the environment mean that the forecasts often have to be changed. Along with these, the related plans may well also need to be changed. Continuous monitoring of performance, against predetermined targets, represents a most important aspect of this. However, perhaps even more important is the enforced discipline of a regular formal review. Again, as with forecasts, in many cases the best (most realistic) planning cycle will revolve around a quarterly review. Best of all, at least in terms of the quantifiable aspects of the plans, if not the wealth of backing detail, is probably a quarterly rolling review - planning one full year ahead each new quarter. Of course, this does absorb more planning resource; but it also ensures that the plans embody the latest information, and - with attention focused on them so regularly - forces both the plans and their implementation to be realistic.

Plans only have validity if they are actually used to control the progress of a company: their success lies in their implementation, not in the writing.

Most organizations track their sales results; or, in non-profit organizations for example, the number of clients. The more sophisticated track them in terms of 'sales variance' - the deviation from the target figures - which allows a more immediate picture of deviations to become evident. 'Micro-analysis', which is a nicely pseudo-scientific term for the normal management process of investigating detailed problems, then investigates the individual elements (individual products, sales territories, customers and so on) which are failing to meet targets.

Relatively few organizations, however, track market share. In some circumstances this may well be a much more important measure. Sales may still be increasing, in an expanding market, while share is actually decreasing - boding ill for future sales when the market eventually starts to drop. Where such market share is tracked, there may be a number of aspects which will be followed:

- Overall market share
- Segment share - that in the specific, targeted segment
- Relative share -in relation to the market leaders

The key ratio to watch in this area is usually the 'marketing expense to sales ratio'; although this may be broken down into other elements (advertising to sales, sales administration to sales, and so on).

The 'bottom line' of marketing activities should at least in theory, be the net profit (for all except non-profit organizations, where the comparable emphasis may be on remaining within budgeted costs). There are a number of separate performance figures and key ratios which need to be tracked:

- Gross contribution<>net profit
- Gross profit<>return on investment
- Net contribution<>profit on sales

There can be considerable benefit in comparing these figures with those achieved by other organizations (especially those in the same industry); using, for instance, the figures which can be obtained (in the UK) from 'The Centre for Interfirm Comparison'. The most sophisticated use of this approach, however, is typically by those making use of PIMS (Profit Impact of Management Strategies), initiated by the General Electric Company and then developed by Harvard Business School, but now run by the Strategic Planning Institute.

The above performance analyses concentrate on the quantitative measures which are directly related to short-term performance. But there are a number of indirect measures, essentially tracking customer attitudes, which can also indicate the organization's performance in terms of its longer-term marketing strengths and may accordingly be even more important indicators. Some useful measures are:

- Market research - including customer panels (which are used to track changes over time)
- Lost business - the orders which were lost because, for example, the stock was not available or the product did not meet the customer's exact requirements

- Customer complaints - how many customers complain about the products or services, or the organization itself, and about what

A formal, written marketing plan is essential; in that it provides an unambiguous reference point for activities throughout the planning period. However, perhaps the most important benefit of these plans is the planning process itself. This typically offers a unique opportunity, a forum, for 'information-rich' and productively focused discussions between the various managers involved. The plan, together with the associated discussions, then provides an agreed context for their subsequent management activities, even for those not described in the plan itself.

The classic quantification of a marketing plan appears in the form of budgets. Because these are so rigorously quantified, they are particularly important. They should, thus, represent an unequivocal projection of actions and expected results. What is more, they should be capable of being monitored accurately; and, indeed, performance against budget is the main (regular) management review process.

The purpose of a marketing budget is, thus, to pull together all the revenues and costs involved in marketing into one comprehensive document. It is a managerial tool that balances what is needed to be spent against what can be afforded, and helps make choices about priorities. It is then used in monitoring performance in practice.

The marketing budget is usually the most powerful tool by which you think through the relationship between desired results and available means. Its starting point should be the marketing strategies and plans, which have already been formulated in the marketing plan itself; although, in practice, the two will run in parallel and will interact. At the very least, the rigorous, highly quantified, budgets may cause a rethink of some of the more optimistic elements of the plans.

Many budgets are based on history. They are the equivalent of 'time-series' forecasting. It is assumed that next year's budgets should follow some trend that is discernible over recent history. Other alternatives are based on a simple 'percentage of sales' or on 'what the competitors are doing'.

However, there are many other alternatives:

- Affordable - This may be the most common approach to budgeting. Someone, typically the managing director on behalf of the board, decides what is a 'reasonable' promotional budget; what can be afforded. This figure is most often based on historical spending. This approach assumes that promotion is a cost; and sometimes is seen as an avoidable cost.
- Percentage of revenue - This is a variation of 'affordable', but at least it forges a link with sales volume, in that the budget will be set at a certain percentage of revenue, and thus follows trends in sales. However, it does imply that promotion is a result of sales, rather than the other way round.

Both of these methods are seen by many managements to be 'realistic', in that they reflect the reality of the business strategies as those managements see it. On the other hand, neither makes any allowance for change. They do not allow for the development to meet emerging market opportunities and, at the other end of the scale, they continue to pour money into a dying product or service.

- Competitive parity - In this case, the organization relates its budgets to what the competitors are doing: for example, it matches their budgets, or beats them, or spends a proportion of what the brand leader is spending. On the other hand, it assumes that the competitors know best; in which case, the service or product can expect to be nothing more than a follower.
- Zero-based budgeting - In essence, this approach takes the objectives, as set out in the marketing plan, together with the resulting planned activities and then costs them out.

## ENVIRONMENTAL SCANNING

For a company to gain or maintain a sustainable competitive advantage, it must be ever vigilant, watching for changes in the business environment. It must also be agile enough to alter its strategies and plans when the need arises.

**Methods**

There are three ways of scanning the business environment:

- Ad-hoc scanning - Short term, infrequent examinations usually initiated by a crisis
- Regular scanning - Studies done on a regular schedule (say, once a year)
- Continuous scanning - (also called continuous learning) - continuous structured data collection and processing on a broad range of environmental factors

Most commentators feel that in today's turbulent business environment the best scanning method available is continuous scanning. This allows the firm to act quickly, take advantage of opportunities before competitors do, and respond to environmental threats before significant damage is done.

Environmental scanning usually refers just to the macroenvironment, but it can also include industry and competitor analysis, consumer analysis, product innovations, and the company's internal environment. Macroenvironmental scanning involves analysing:

- The Economy
  - GNP or GDP per capital
  - GNP or GDP growth
  - Unemployment rate
  - Inflation rate
  - Consumer and investor confidence
  - Inventory levels
  - Currency exchange rates
  - Merchandise trade balance
  - Financial and political health of trading partners
  - Balance of payments
  - Future trends

- Government
  - Political climate - amount of government activity
  - Political stability and risk
  - Government debt
  - Budget deficit or surplus
  - Corporate and personal tax rates
  - Payroll taxes
  - Import tariffs and quotas
  - Export restrictions
  - Restrictions on international financial flows
- Legal
  - Minimum wage laws
  - Environmental protection laws
  - Worker safety laws
  - Union laws
  - Copyright and patent laws
  - Anti- monopoly laws
  - Sunday closing laws
  - Municipal licences
  - Laws that favour business investment
- Technology
  - Efficiency of infrastructure, including: roads, ports, airports, rolling stock, hospitals, education, healthcare, communication, etc.
  - Industrial productivity
  - New manufacturing processes
  - New products and services of competitors
  - New products and services of supply chain partners
  - Any new technology that could impact the company
  - Cost and accessibility of electrical power
- Ecology
  - Ecological concerns that affect the firms production processes

- Ecological concerns that affect customers' buying habits
- Ecological concerns that affect customers' perception of the company or product

- Socio-Cultural
  - Demographic factors such as:
    - Population size and distribution
    - Age distribution
    - Education levels
    - Income levels
    - Ethnic origins
    - Religious affiliations
  - Attitudes towards:
    - Materialism, capitalism, free enterprise
    - Individualism, role of family, role of government, collectivism
    - Role of church and religion
    - Consumerism
    - Environmentalism
    - importance of work, pride of accomplishment
  - Cultural structures including:
    - Diet and nutrition
    - Housing conditions
- Potential Suppliers
  - Labour supply
    - Quantity of labour available
    - Quality of labour available
    - Stability of labour supply
    - Wage expectations
    - Employee turn-over rate
    - Strikes and labour relations
    - educational facilities
  - Material suppliers
    - Quality, quantity, price, and stability of material inputs
    - Delivery delays
    - Proximity of bulky or heavy material inputs
    - Level of competition among suppliers

- Service Providers
  - Quantity, quality, price, and stability of service facilitators
  - Special requirements

Scanning these macroenvironmental variables for threats and opportunities requires that each issue be rated on two dimensions. It must be rated on its potential impact on the company, and rated on its likeliness of occurrence. Multiplying the potential impact parameter by the likeliness of occurrence parameter gives us a good indication of its importance to the firm.

When an issue is detected, there are generally six (6) ways of responding to them:

- Opposition strategy - try to influence the environmental forces so as to negate their impact - this is only successful where you have some control over the environmental variable in question
- Adaptation strategy - adapt your marketing plan to the new environmental conditions
- Offensive strategy - try to turn the new influence into an advantage - quick response can give you a competitive advantage
- Redeployment strategy - redeploy your assets into another industry
- Contingency strategies - determine a broad range of possible reactions - find substitutes
- Passive strategy - no response - study the situation further

**Market Segment**

Market segmentation is the process in marketing of dividing a market into distinct subsets (segments) that behave in the same way or have similar needs. Because each segment is fairly homogeneous in their needs and attitudes, they are likely to respond similarly to a given marketing strategy. That is, they are likely to have similar feeling and ideas about a marketing mix comprised of a given product or service, sold at a given price, distributed in a certain way, and promoted in a certain way.

Broadly, markets can be divided according to a number of general criteria, such as by industry or public versus private sector. Small segments are often termed niche markets or specialty markets. However, all segments fall into either consumer or industrial markets. Although it has similar objectives and it overlaps with consumer markets in many ways, the process of Industrial market segmentation is quite different.

The process of segmentation is distinct from targeting (choosing which segments to address) and positioning (designing an appropriate marketing mix for each segment). The overall intent is to identify groups of similar customers and potential customers; to prioritise the groups to address; to understand their behaviour; and to respond with appropriate marketing strategies that satisfy the different preferences of each chosen segment.

The requirements for successful segmentation are:

- Homogeneity within the segment
- Heterogeneity between segments
- Segments are measurable and identifiable
- Segments are accessible and actionable
- Segment is large enough to be profitable

These criteria can be summarized by the word SADAM:

- S Substantial: the segment has to be large and profitable enough
- A Accessible: it must be possible to reach it efficiently
- D Differential: it must respond differently to a different marketing mix
- A Actionable: you must have a product for this segment
- M Measurable: size and purchasing power can be measured

Currently a college student studying the marketing mix is introduced to the Four Ps of the Marketing Mix; Product, Place, Promotion, Price.

Product (service) is whatever it may be that is being sold/ marketed.

Price refers to not only the actual price but also price elasticity.

Place has evidently replaced distribution simply by where or what area the marketing campaign is going to cover, as well as what types of distribution channel (retail, wholesale, online, etc) will be used. Today the idea of place is not limited to geographic profiling but also demographics and other categorizing variables. This has only occurred over the last ten years with the expansion of internet use and its ability to target specific types of people and not just people in a geographic area.

Promotion simply refers to what medium will deliver the message and what the overall marketing strategy is offering as a benefit.

The variables used for segmentation include:

- Geographic variables
  - Region of the world or country, East, West, South, North, Central, coastal, hilly, etc.
  - Country size/country size : Metropolitian Cities, small cities, towns.
  - Density of Area Urban, Semi-urban, Rural.
  - climate Hot, Cold, Humid, Rainy.
- Demographic variables
  - Age
  - Gender Male and Female
  - Sexual orientation
  - Family size
  - Family life cycle
  - Education Primary, High School, Secondary, College, Universities.

- Income
- Education
- Religion
- Language
- Occupation
- Socioeconomic status
- Nationality/race

- Psychographic variables
  - Personality
  - Life style
  - Value
  - Attitude
- Behavioural variables
  - Benefit sought
  - Product usage rate
  - Brand loyalty
  - Product end use
  - Readiness-to-buy stage
  - Decision making unit

When numerous variables are combined to give an in-depth understanding of a segment, this is referred to as depth segmentation. When enough information is combined to create a clear picture of a typical member of a segment, this is referred to as a buyer profile. When the profile is limited to demographic variables it is called a demographic profile (typically shortened to "a demographic"). A statistical technique commonly used in determining a profile is cluster analysis.

George Day describes model of segmentation as the top-down approach: You start with the total population and divide it into segments. He also identified an alternative model which he called the bottom-up approach. In this approach, you start with a single customer and build on that profile. This typically requires the use of customer relationship management software or a database of some kind. Profiles of existing customers are created and analysed.

Various demographic, behavioural, and psychographic patterns are built up using techniques such as cluster analysis. This process is sometimes called database marketing or micromarketing. Its use is most appropriate in highly fragmented markets. McKenna claims that this approach treats every customer as a "micromajority". Pine used the bottom-up approach in what he called "segment of one marketing". Through this process mass customization is possible.

Where a monopoly exists, the price of a product is likely to be higher than in a competitive market and the quantity sold less, generating monopoly profits for the seller. These profits can be increased further if the market can be segmented with different prices charged to different segments, charging higher prices to those segments willing and able to pay more and charging less to those whose demand is price elastic. The price discriminator might need to create rate fences that will prevent members of a higher price segment from purchasing at the prices available to members of a lower price segment. This behaviour is rational on the part of the monopolist, but is often seen by competition authorities as an abuse of a monopoly position, whether or not the monopoly itself is sanctioned.

**Competitor analysis**

Competitor analysis in marketing and strategic management is an assessment of the strengths and weaknesses of current and potential competitors.

One common and useful technique is constructing a competitor array. The steps include:

- Define your industry - scope and nature of the industry
- Determine who your competitors are
- Determine who your customers are and what benefits they expect
- Determine what the key success factors are in your industry
- Rank the key success factors by giving each one a weighting - The sum of all the weightings must add up to one.

- Rate each competitor on each of the key success factors - this can best be displayed on a two dimensional matrix - competitors along the top and key success factors down the side.
- Multiply each cell in the matrix by the factor weighting.
- Sum columns for a weighted assessment of the overall strength of each competitor relative to each other.

We can learn a lot about the competitive environment by scanning our competitors' ads. Changes in a competitor's advertising message can reveal new product offerings, new production processes, a new branding strategy, a new positioning strategy, a new segmentation strategy, line extensions and contractions, problems with previous positions, insights from recent marketing or product research, a new strategic direction, a new source of sustainable competitive advantage, or value migrations within the industry. It might also indicate a new pricing strategy such as penetration, price discrimination, price skimming, product bundling, joint product pricing, discounts, or loss leaders.

It may also indicate a new promotion strategy such as push, pull, balanced, short term sales generation, long term image creation, informational, comparative, affective, reminder, new creative objectives, new unique selling proposition, new creative concepts, appeals, tone, and themes, or a new advertising agency. It might also indicate a new distribution strategy, new distribution partners, more extensive distribution, more intensive distribution, a change in geographical focus, or exclusive distribution. Little of this intelligence is definitive : additional information is needed before conclusions should be drawn.

A competitor's media strategy reveals budget allocation, segmentation and targeting strategy, and selectivity and focus. From a tactical perspective, it can also be used to help a manager implement his/her own media plan. By knowing the competitor's media buy, media selection, frequency, reach, continuity, schedules, and flights, the manager can arrange his/her own media plan so that they do not coincide.

Other sources of corporate intelligence include trade shows, patent filings, mutual customers, annual reports, and trade associations.

Some firms hire competitor intelligence professionals to obtain this information.

In addition to analysing current competitors, it is necessary to estimate future competitive threats. The most common sources of new competitors are:

- Companies competing in a related product/market
- Companies using related technologies
- Companies already targeting your prime market segment but with unrelated products
- Companies from other geographical areas and with similar products
- New start-up companies organised by former employees and/or managers of existing companies

The entrance of new competitors is likely when:

- There are high profit margins in the industry
- There is unmet demand (insufficient supply) in the industry
- There are no major barriers to entry
- There is future growth potential
- Competitive rivalry is not intense
- Gaining a competitive advantage over existing firms is feasible

## Demographic Profiles in Marketing

Marketers typically combine several variables to define a demographic profile. A demographic profile (often shortened to "a demographic") provides enough information about the typical member of this group to create a mental picture of this hypothetical aggregate. For example, a marketer might speak of the single, female, middle-class, age 18 to 24 demographic.

Marketing researchers typically have two objectives in this regard: first to determine what segments or subgroups exist in the overall population; and secondly to create a clear and complete picture of the characteristics of a typical member of each of these segments. Once these profiles are constructed, they can be used to develop a marketing strategy and marketing plan. A demographic or demographic profile is a term used in marketing and broadcasting, to describe a demographic grouping or a market segment. This typically involves age bands (as teenagers do not wish to purchase denture fixant), social class bands (as the rich may want different products than middle and poorer classes and may be willing to pay more) and gender (partially because different physical attributes require different hygiene and clothing products, and partially because of the male/female mindsets).

A demographic profile can be used to determine when and where advertising should be placed so as to achieve maximum results. In all such cases, it is important that the advertiser get the most results for their money, and so careful research is done to match the demographic profile of the target market to the demographic profile of the advertising medium.

A good way to figure out the intended demographic of a television show, TV channel, or magazine is to study the ads that accompany it. For example, in the United States the television programme The Price is Right most frequently airs from 11 a.m. to Noon. The commercials on it (besides the use of product placement in the show itself) are often for things like arthritis pain relievers and diapers. This indicates that the target demographics are senior citizens and parents with young children, both of which would be home at that time of day and see that show.

## RESEARCH MARKETING

Research is the search for and retrieval of existing, discovery or creation of new information or knowledge for a specific purpose. Research has many categories, from medical research to literary research. 'Marketing research is a form of business research. and Business-to-Business (B2B)Marketing

Research, or Business Marketing Research, previously known as Industrial Marketing Research.

B2B Marketing Research investigates the markets for products sold by one business to another, rather than to consumers.

Consumer Marketing Research is a form of applied sociology which concentrates on understanding the behaviours, whims and preferences, of consumers in a market-based economy. The field of consumer marketing research as a statistical science was pioneered by Arthur Nielsen with the founding of the ACNielsen Company in 1923.

In addition to marketing research, other forms of business research include:

- Market research is broader in scope and examines all aspects of a business environment. It asks questions about competitors, market structure, government regulations, economic trends, technological advances, and numerous other factors that make up the business environment. Sometimes the term refers more particularly to the financial analysis of companies, industries, or sectors. In this case, financial analysts usually carry out the research and provide the results to investment advisors and potential investors.
- Product research - This looks at what products can be produced with available technology, and what new product innovations near-future technology can develop.
- Advertising research - This attempts to assess the likely impact of an advertising campaign in advance, and also measure the success of a recent campaign..

**Types of Marketing Research**

Marketing research techniques come in many forms, including:

- Test marketing - A small-scale product launch used to determine the likely acceptance of the product when it is introduced into a wider market

- Concept testing - To test the acceptance of a concept by target consumers
- Mystery shopping - An employee or representative of the market research firm anonymously contacts a salesperson and indicates he or she is shopping for a product. The shopper then records the entire experience. This method is often used for quality control or for researching competitors' products.
- Store audit - To measure the sales of a product or product line at a statistically selected store sample in order to determine market share, or to determine whether a retail store provides adequate service
- Demand estimation - To determine the approximate level of demand for the product
- Commercial Eye tracking research - examine advertisements, package designs, websites, etc by analyzing visual behaviour of the consumer
- Sales forecasting - To determine the expected level of sales given the level of demand. With respect to other factors like Advertising expenditure, sales promotion etc.
- Customer satisfaction studies - Exit interviews or surveys that determine a customer's level of satisfaction with the quality of the transaction
- Distribution channel audits - To assess distributors' and retailers' attitudes toward a product, brand, or company
- Price elasticity testing - To determine how sensitive customers are to price changes
- Segmentation research - To determine the demographic, psychographic, and behavioural characteristics of potential buyers
- Consumer decision process research - To determine what motivates people to buy and what decision-making process they use

- Positioning research - How does the target market see the brand relative to competitors? - what does the brand stand for?
- Brand name testing - What do consumers feel about the names of the products?
- Brand equity research - How favorably do consumers view the brand?
- Advertising and promotion research - How effective are ads - do potential customers recall the ad, understand the message, and does the ad influence consumer purchasing behaviour?
- Internet Strategic Intelligence - Searching for customer opinions in the internet: chats, forums, web pages, blogs... where people express freely about their experiences with products, becoming strong "opinion formers"

All of these forms of marketing research can be classified as either problem-identification research or as problem-solving research.

A company collects primary research by gathering original data. Secondary research is conducted on data published previously and usually by someone else. Secondary research costs far less than primary research, but seldom comes in a form that exactly meets the needs of the researcher.

A similar distinction exists between exploratory research and conclusive research. Exploratory research provides insights into and comprehension of an issue or situation. It should draw definitive conclusions only with extreme caution. Conclusive research draws conclusions: the results of the study can be generalized to the whole population.

Exploratory research is conducted to explore a problem to get some basic idea about the solution at the preliminary stages of research. It may serve as the input to conclusive research. Exploratory research information is collected by focus group interviews, reviewing literature or books, discussing with experts, etc. This is unstructured and qualitative in nature.

If a secondary source of data is unable to serve the purpose, a convenience sample of small size can be collected. Conclusive research is conducted to draw some conclusion about the problem. It is primary, structured and quantitative research, and the output of this research is the input to Management information systems (MIS).

**Marketing Research Methods**

Methodologically, marketing research uses four types of research designs, namely:

- Qualitative marketing research - generally used for exploratory purposes - small number of respondents - not generalizable to the whole population - statistical significance and confidence not calculated - examples include focus groups, in-depth interviews, and projective techniques
- Quantitative marketing research - generally used to draw conclusions - tests a specific hypothesis - uses random sampling techniques so as to infer from the sample to the population - involves a large number of respondents - examples include surveys and questionnaires
- Observational techniques - the researcher observes social phenomena in their natural setting - observations can occur cross-sectionally (observations made at one time) or longitudinally (observations occur over several time-periods) - examples include product-use analysis and computer cookie traces
- Experimental techniques - the researcher creates a quasi-artificial environment to try to control spurious factors, then manipulates at least one of the variables - examples include purchase laboratories and test markets

Researchers often use more than one research design. They may start with secondary research to get background information, then conduct a focus group (qualitative research design) to explore the issues. Finally they might do a full nation-wide survey (quantitative research design) in order to devise specific recommendations for the client.

Business to business (b2b) research is inevitably more complicated than consumer research. The researchers need to know what type of multi-faceted approach will answer the objectives, since seldom is it possible to find the answers using just one method. Finding the right respondents is crucial in b2b research since they are often busy, and may not want to participate. Encouraging them to "open up" is yet another skill required of the b2b researcher. Last, but not least, most business research leads to strategic decisions and this means that the business researcher must have expertise in developing strategies that are strongly rooted in the research findings and acceptable to the client.

There are four key factors that make b2b market research special and different to consumer markets:

- The decision making unit is far more complex in b2b markets than in consumer markets
- B2b products and their applications are more complex than consumer products
- B2b marketers address a much smaller number of customers who are very much larger in their consumption of products than is the case in consumer markets
- Personal relationships are of critical importance in b2b markets.

Market research techniques resemble those used in political polling and social science research. Meta-analysis (also called the Schmidt-Hunter technique) refers to a statistical method of combining data from multiple studies or from several types of studies. Conceptualization means the process of converting vague mental images into definable concepts. Operationalization is the process of converting concepts into specific observable behaviours that a researcher can measure. Precision refers to the exactness of any given measure. Reliability refers to the likelihood that a given operationalized construct will yield the same results if re-measured. Validity refers to the extent to which a measure provides data that captures the meaning of the operationalized construct as defined in the study. It asks, "Are we measuring what we intended to measure?"

Applied research sets out to prove a specific hypothesis of value to the clients paying for the research. For example, a cigarette company might commission research that attempts to show that cigarettes are good for one's health. Many researchers have ethical misgivings about doing applied research.

Sugging (or Selling Under the Guise of market research) forms a sales technique in which sales people pretend to conduct marketing research, but with the real purpose of obtaining buyer motivation and buyer decision-making information to be used in a subsequent sales call.

Frugging comprises the practice of soliciting funds under the pretense of being a research organization.

Experimental research designs are used for the controlled testing of causal processes. The general procedure is one or more independent variables are manipulated to determine their effect on a dependent variable. These designs can be used where: 1) There is time priority in a causal relationship (cause precedes effect), 2) There is consistency in a causal relationship (a cause will always lead to the same effect), and 3) The magnitude of the correlation is great. The most common applications of these designs in marketing research and experimental economics are test markets and purchase labs. The techniques are commonly used in other social sciences including sociology and psychology.

One of the most important requirements of experimental research designs is the necessity of eliminating the effects of spurious, intervening, and antecedent variables. In the most basic model, cause (X) leads to effect (Y). But there could be a third variable (Z) that influences (Y), and X might not be the true cause at all. Z is said to be a spurious variable and must be controlled for. The same is true for intervening variables (a variable in between the supposed cause (X) and the effect (Y)), and anteceding variables (a variable prior to the supposed cause (X) that is the true cause). When a third variable is involved and has not been controlled for, the relation is said to be a [zero order] relationship. In most practical applications of experimental research designs there are several causes (X1,X2,X3). In most designs only one of these causes is manipulated at a time.

A true experimental design requires an artificial environment so as to control for all spurious, intervening, and antecedent variables. A purchase laboratory approaches this ideal. Participants are given money, script, or credit to purchase products in a simulated store. Researchers modify one variable at a time (for example; price, packaging, shelf location, size, or competitors' offerings) and determine what effect that has on sales volume. Internet based purchase labs (called virtual purchase labs) are becoming more common.

Simplified versions of the purchase laboratory are often used for pragmatic reasons. An example of this would be to use tachistocopes for testing packaging and shelf location.

Quasi-experimental designs control some, but not all, of the extraneous factors. A test market is an example of this. A new product is typically introduced in a select number of cities. These cities must be representative of the overall national (or international) population. They should also be relatively unpolluted by outside influences (for example : media from other cities). The marketer has some control over the marketing mix variables, but almost no control over the broader business environment variables. Competitors could change their prices during the test. Government could change the level of taxes. New competing products could be introduced. An advertising campaign could be initiated by competitors. Any of these spurious variables could contaminate the test market.

In an attempt to control for extraneous factors, several experimental research designs have been developed, including:

- Classical pretest-post test - The total population of participants is randomly divided into two samples; the control sample, and the experimental sample. Only the experimental sample is exposed to the manipulated variable. The researcher compares the pretest results with the post test results for both samples. Any divergence between the two samples is assumed to be a result of the experiment.
- Solomon four group design - The population is randomly divided into four samples. Two of the groups are experimental samples. Two groups experience no experimental manipulation of variables. Two groups receive a pretest and a post test. Two groups receive only a post test. This is an improvement over the classical design because it controls for the effect of the pretest.
- Factorial design - This is similar to a classical design except additional samples are used. Each group is exposed to a different experimental manipulation.

## PRICING OBJECTIVES

Pricing objectives or goals give direction to the whole pricing process. Determining what your objectives are is the first step in pricing. When deciding on pricing objectives you must consider: 1) the overall financial, marketing, and strategic objectives of the company; 2) the objectives of your product or brand; 3) consumer price elasticity and price points; and 4) the resources you have available.

Some of the more common pricing objectives are:

- Maximize long-run profit
- Maximize short-run profit
- Increase sales volume (quantity)
- Increase dollar sales
- Increase market share
- Obtain a target rate of return on investment (ROI)
- Obtain a target rate of return on sales

- Stabilize market or stabilize market price: an objective to stabilize price means that the marketing manager attempts to keep prices stable in the marketplace and to compete on nonprice considerations. Stabilization of margin is bascially a cost-plus approach in which the manager attemptes to maintain the same margin regradless of changes in cost.
- Company growth
- Maintain price leadership
- Desensitize customers to price
- Discourage new entrants into the industry
- Match competitors prices
- Encourage the exit of marginal firms from the industry
- Survival
- Avoid government investigation or intervention
- Obtain or maintain the loyalty and enthusiasm of distributors and other sales personnel
- Enhance the image of the firm, brand, or product
- Be perceived as "fair" by customers and potential customers
- Create interest and excitement about a product
- Discourage competitors from cutting prices
- Use price to make the product "visible"
- Build store traffic
- Help prepare for the sale of the business (harvesting)
- Social, ethical, or ideological objectives
- Get competitive advantage

# Chapter 3

# Organsation and Marketing

## THE ROLE OF THE MARKET

A market is a social arrangement that allows buyers and sellers to discover information and carry out a voluntary exchange of goods or services. It is one of the two key institutions that organize trade, along with the right to own property. Allowing markets to arrive at a pareto efficient outcome is one of the key components of capitalism.

In everyday usage, the word "market" may refer to the location where goods are traded, sometimes known as a marketplace, or to a street market.

The function of a market requires, at a minimum, that both parties expect to become better off as a result of the transaction. Markets generally rely on price adjustments to provide information to parties engaging in a transaction, so that each may accurately gauge the subsequent change of their welfare. In less sophisticated markets, such as those involving barter, individual buyers and sellers must engage in a more lengthy process of haggling in order to gain the same information. Markets are efficient when the price of a good or service attracts exactly as much demand as the market can currently supply. The chief function of a market, then, is to adjust prices to accommodate fluctuations in supply and demand in order to achieve allocative efficiency. An economic system in which goods and services are exchanged by market functions is called a market **economy**. An alternative economic system in which non-market forces (often government mandates) determine prices are called planned economies or command economies. The attempt to combine socialist ideals with the incentive system of a market is known as market socialism.

Although many markets exist in the traditional sense—such as a flea market—there are various other types of them and various organizational structures to assist their functions.

A market can be organized as an auction, as a shopping center, as a complex institution such as a stock market, and as an informal discussion between two individuals.

In economics, a market that runs under laissez-faire policies is a free market. It is "free" in the sense that the government makes no attempt to intervene through taxes, subsidies, minimum wages, price ceilings, etc. Markets may be distorted by a seller or sellers with monopoly power, or a buyer with monopsony power. Also, the level of organization or negotiation power of buyers, markedly affects the functioning of the market. Markets where price negotiations do not arrive at efficient outcomes for both sides are said to experience market failure.

Most markets are regulated by state wide laws and regulations. While barter markets exist, most markets use currency or some other form of money.

Markets of varying types can spontaneously arise whenever a party has interest in a good or service that some other party can provide. Hence there can be a market for cigarettes in correctional facilities, another for chewing gum in a playground, and yet another for contracts for the future delivery of a commodity.

## MARKET FAILURE

Market failure is a term used to describe a situation in which markets do not efficiently allocate goods and services. To economists, the term would normally be applied to situations where the inefficiency is particularly dramatic, or when it is suggested that non-market institutions (such as public policing and firefighting) would be more efficient and wealth-producing than their private alternatives.

On the other hand, the term "market failure" is also often used to describe situations where market forces do not serve the perceived public interest. In this article, however, the focus is on market failure as defined by mainstream economics. Economists use model-like theorems to explain or understand such cases. The two main reasons that markets fail are:

- The inadequate expression of costs or benefits in prices and thus into microeconomic decision-making in markets.
- Sub-optimal market structures.

The existence of a market failure in a certain economic activity is often used as an argument that the activity in question should not be directed by market forces. This generally leads to a debate on the question of what - if anything - should be used to replace markets. The most common response to a market failure in the present day is to use the government to produce certain goods and services. However, government intervention may cause nonmarket failure by the intevention itself causing externalitites.

## TYPES OF MARKET FAILURES

### Imperfect Competition

In economic theory, imperfect competition, is the competitive situation in any market where the conditions necessary for perfect competition are not satisfied.

Forms of imperfect competition include:

- Monopoly, in which there is only one seller of a good.
- Oligopoly, in which there is a small number of sellers.
- Monopolistic competition, in which there are many sellers producing highly differentiated goods.
- Monopsony, in which there is only one buyer of a good.
- Oligopsony, in which there is a small number of buyers.

There may also be imperfect competition in markets due to buyers or sellers lacking information about prices and the goods being traded.

There may also be imperfect competition due to a time lag in a market. For example, in the 1990s, there was a shortage of computer programmers, but becoming a skilled programmer requires several years of experience. This drove up salaries. Another example is the "jobless recovery". There are many growth opportunities available after a recession, but it takes time for employers to react, leading to high unemployment. High unemployment decreases wages, which makes hiring more attractive, but it takes time for new jobs to be created.

**Market Power**

In economics, market power is the ability of a firm to alter the market price of a good or service. A firm with market power can raise price without losing all customers to competitors. When a firm has market power it faces a downward-sloping demand curve.

In perfectly competitive markets, market participants have no market power. A firm with market power has the ability to individually affect either the total quantity or the prevailing price in the market. If the demand curve is downward sloping (that is, the most common situation where price increases lead to a lower quantity demanded), then the decrease in supply as a result of the exercise of market power creates an economic deadweight loss in comparison with a situation of perfect competition. This is often viewed as socially undesirable, and as a result, many countries have anti-trust or other legislation with the aim of limiting the ability of firms to accrue market power. Such legislation often regulates mergers and sometimes introduces a judicial power to compel divestiture.

A firm usually has market power by virtue of it controlling a large portion of the market. In extreme cases - monopoly and monopsony - the firm controls the entire market. However, market size alone is not a good indicator of market power.

Highly concentrated markets may be contestable if there are no barriers to entry or exit, limiting the incumbent firm's ability to raise its price above competitive levels.

Market power gives firms the ability to engage in unilateral anti-competitive behaviour. Some of the behaviours that firms with market power are accused of engaging in include predatory pricing, product tying, and creation of overcapacity or other barriers to entry. If no individual participant in the market has significant market power, then anti-competitive behaviour can take place only through collusion, or the exercise of a group of participants' collective market power.

When several firms control a significant share of market sales, the resulting market structure is called an oligopoly or oligopsony. An oligopoly may engage in collusion, either tacit or overt, and thereby exercize market power. An explicit agreement in an oligopoly to affect market price or output is called a cartel. The behaviour of firms in perfect competition or monopoly can be treated as a simple optimization, but an oligopoly requires game theoretic analysis.

Monopoly power is an example of market failure which occurs when one or more of the participants has the ability to influence the price or other outcomes in some general or specialized market. The most commonly discussed form of market power is that of a monopoly, but other forms such as monopsony, and more moderate versions of these two extremes, exist. Market participants that have market power are sometimes referred to as "price makers", while those without are sometimes called "price takers".

A well known example of monopolistic market power is Microsoft's market share in PC operating systems. The United States v. Microsoft case concerned the allegation that Microsoft illegally exercised its market power by bundling its web browser with its operating system. Some have suggested that Wal Mart exercises monopsonistic market power; its size allows it to extract extremely low prices from its suppliers.

**Monopoly**

In economics, is defined as a persistent market situation where there is only one provider of a product or service. Monopolies are characterized by a lack of economic competition for the good or service that they provide and a lack of viable substitute goods.

Monopoly should be distinguished from monopsony, in which there is only one buyer of the product or service; it should also, strictly, be distinguished from the (similar) phenomenon of a cartel. In a monopoly a single firm is the sole provider of a product or service; in a cartel a centralized institution is set up to partially coordinate the actions of several independent providers.

## STRATEGIES IN MARKETING

Marketing strategy is a powerful process that gives an organization a competitive advantage in the marketplace. While just defining a marketing strategy will not automatically create a competitive advantage, it will allow the organization to concentrate its (always limited) resources on the greatest opportunities to increase sales and achieve a sustainable competitive advantage.

The word strategy comes from the Greek word strategos meaning general. Strategy is what generals use to win battles. Thus properly understood, marketing strategy is a high-level exercise involving the "generals" of the organization in determining how to build on the firm's strengths while (ethically) taking advantage of competitors' weaknesses. Marketing strategy is most effective when it is a vital component of corporate strategy, defining how the organization will engage customers, prospects and the competition in the market arena for consistent success.

A marketing strategy also serves as the foundation of a marketing plan. A marketing plan contains a set of specific actions required to successfully implement a specific marketing strategy. For example: "Use a low cost product to attract consumers. Once our organization, via our low cost product, has established a relationship with consumers, our organization will sell additional, higher-margin products and services that enhance the consumer's interaction with the low-cost product or service."

A strategy is different from a tactic. While it is possible to write a tactical marketing plan without a sound, well-considered strategy, it is not recommended. Without a sound marketing strategy, a marketing plan has no foundation. Marketing strategies serve as the fundamental underpinning of marketing plans designed to reach marketing objectives. It is important that these objectives have measurable results.

A good marketing strategy should integrate an organization's marketing goals, policies, and action sequences (tactics) into a cohesive whole. The objective of a marketing strategy is to provide a foundation from which a tactical plan is developed. This allows the organization to carry out its mission effectively and efficiently.

Marketing strategies are partially derived from broader corporate strategies, corporate missions, and corporate goals. They should flow from the firm's mission statement. They are also influenced by a range of microenvironmental factors.

Marketing strategies are dynamic and interactive. They are partially planned and partially unplanned.

## COMMERCIAL PLANNING

"In the modern world of business, it is useless to be a creative original thinker unless you can also sell what you create. Management cannot be expected to recognize a good idea unless it is presented to them by a good salesman." David M. Ogilvy

The success of a new product depends not only on the idea behind the product, but also on the marketing of the new product before, during and after the product launch. Commercializing a product is commonly known as Commercial Planning. No concrete methods are currently available for New Product Launching (NPL). However, several articles are published about NPL and the essential activities, to launch a new product. This article describes a set of activities and products, that are essential for launching a new product. New Product Launching is part of the New Product Development method.

## STRATEGIC MANAGEMENT

An organization's strategy must be appropriate for its resources, environmental circumstances, and core objectives. The process involves matching the company's [internal resources (eg IT) and capabilities (eg quality management)] to the external business environment the organization faces. Strategy formulation involves:

- Doing a situation analysis: both internal and external; both micro-environmental and macro-environmental.
- Concurrent with this assessment, objectives are set. This involves crafting vision statements (long term view of a possible future), mission statements (the role that the organization gives itself in society), overall corporate objectives (both financial and strategic), strategic business unit objectives (both financial and strategic), and tactical objectives.
- These objectives should, in the light of the situation analysis, suggest a strategic plan. The plan provides the details of how to achieve these objectives.

This three-step strategy formulation process is sometimes referred to as determining where you are now, determining where you want to go, and then determining how to get there. These three questions are the essence of strategic planning. SWOT Analysis: I/O Economics for the external factors and RBV for the internal factors.

Strategy implementation involves:

- Allocation of sufficient resources (financial, personnel, time, technology support)
- Establishing a chain of command or some alternative structure (such as cross functional teams)

- Assigning responsibility of specific tasks or processes to specific individuals or groups
- It also involves managing the process. This includes monitoring results, comparing to benchmarks and best practices, evaluating the efficacy and efficiency of the process, controlling for variances, and making adjustments to the process as necessary.
- When implementing specific programs, this involves acquiring the requisite resources, developing the process, training, process testing, documentation, and integration with (and/or conversion from) legacy processes.

Strategy formulation and implementation is an on-going, never-ending, integrated process requiring continuous reassessment and reformation. Strategic management is dynamic. It involves a complex pattern of actions and reactions. It is partially planned and partially unplanned. Strategy is both planned and emergent, dynamic, and interactive. Some people (such as Andy Grove at Intel) feel that there are critical points at which a strategy must take a new direction in order to be in step with a changing business environment. These critical points of change are called strategic inflection points.

Strategic management operates on several time scales. Short term strategies involve planning and managing for the present. Long term strategies involve preparing for and preempting the future. Marketing strategist Derek Abell (1993), has suggested that understanding this dual nature of strategic management is the least understood part of the process. He claims that balancing the temporal aspects of strategic planning requires the use of dual strategies simultaneously.

Strategic Management is actually a solid foundation or a framework within which all the functionning managerial operations are bundled together. This is the highest level corporate activity that sets the terms and goals for a company that it should follow for prosperity.

Strategic management techniques can be viewed as bottom-up, top-down, or collaborative processes. In the bottom-up approach, employees submit proposals to their managers who, in turn, funnel the best ideas further up the organization. This is often accomplished by a capital budgeting process. Proposals are assessed using financial criteria such as return on investment or cost-benefit analysis. The proposals that are approved form the substance of a new strategy, all of which is done without a grand strategic design or a strategic architect. The top-down approach is the most common by far. In it, the CEO, possibly with the assistance of a strategic planning team, decides on the overall direction the company should take. Some organizations are starting to experiment with collaborative strategic planning techniques that recognize the emergent nature of strategic decisions.

In most (large) corporations there are several levels of strategy. Strategic management is the highest in the sense that it is the broadest, applying to all parts of the firm. It gives direction to corporate values, corporate culture, corporate goals, and corporate missions. Under this broad corporate strategy there are often functional or business unit strategies.

Functional strategies include marketing strategies, new product development strategies, human resource strategies, financial strategies, legal strategies, and information technology management strategies. The emphasis is on short and medium term plans and is limited to the domain of each department's functional responsibility. Each functional department attempts to do its part in meeting overall corporate objectives, and hence to some extent their strategies are derived from broader corporate strategies.

Many companies feel that a functional organizational structure is not an efficient way to organize activities so they have reengineered according to processes or strategic business units (called SBUs). A strategic business unit is a semi-autonomous unit within an organization. It is usually responsible for its own budgeting, new product decisions, hiring decisions, and price setting. An SBU is treated as an internal profit centre by corporate headquarters. Each SBU is responsible for developing its business strategies, strategies that must be in tune with broader corporate strategies.

The "lowest" level of strategy is operational strategy. It is very narrow in focus and deals with day-to-day operational activities such as scheduling criteria. It must operate within a budget but is not at liberty to adjust or create that budget. Operational level strategy was encouraged by Peter Drucker in his theory of management by objectives (MBO). Operational level strategies are informed by business level strategies which, in turn, are informed by corporate level strategies. Business strategy, which refers to the aggregated operational strategies of single business firm or that of an SBU in a diversified corporation refers to the way in which a firm competes in its chosen arenas.

Corporate strategy, then, refers to the overarching strategy of the diversified firm. Such corporate strategy answers the questions of "in which businesses should we compete?" and "how does being in one business add to the competitive advantage of another portfolio firm, as well as the competitive advantage of the corporation as a whole?"

Since the turn of the millennium, there has been a tendency in some firms to revert to a simpler strategic structure. This is being driven by information technology. It is felt that knowledge management systems should be used to share information and create common goals. Strategic divisions are thought to hamper this process. Most recently, this notion of strategy has been captured under the rubric of dynamic strategy, popularized by the strategic management textbook authored by Carpenter and Sanders. This work builds on that of Brown and Eisenhart as well as Christensen and portrays firm strategy, both business and corporate, as necessarily embracing ongoing strategic change, and the seamless integration of strategy formulation and implementation. Such change and implementation are usually built into the strategy through the staging and pacing facets.

Management by Objectives (MBO) is a process of agreeing upon objectives within an organization so that management and employees buy in to the objectives and understand what they are. Management By Objectives term was first popularized by Peter Drucker in 1954 in his book 'The Practice of Management'.

It is all too easy for managers to fail to outline, and agree with their employees, what it is that everyone is trying to achieve. MBO substitutes for good intentions a process that requires rather precise written description of objectives (for the period ahead) and timelines for their monitoring and achievement. The process requires that the manager and the employee agree to what the employee will attempt to achieve in the period ahead, and (very important) that the employee accept and buy into the objectives (otherwise commitment will be lacking).

For example, whatever else a manager and employee may discuss and agree in their regular discussions, let us suppose that they feel that it will be sensible to introduce a key performance indicator to show the development of sales revenue in a part of the firm. Then the manager and the employee need to discuss what is being planned, what the time-schedule is and what the indicator might or might not be. Thereafter the two of them should liaise to ensure that the objective is being attended to and will be delivered on time.

Organizations have scarce resources and so it is incumbent on the managers to consider the level of resourcing but also to consider whether the objectives that are jointly agreed within the firm are the right ones and represent the best allocation of effort. Also, reliable Management information systems are needed to establish relevant objectives and monitor their "reach ratio" in an objective way.

MBO is often achieved using set targets. MBO introduced the SMART criteria: Objectives for MBO must be SMART (Specific, Measurable, Agreed, Realistic, and Time-Specific). However, it has been reported in recent years that this style of management receives criticism in that it triggers employees' unethical behaviour of distorting the system or financial figures to achieve the targets set by their short-term, narrow bottom-line, and completely self-centered thinking.

## MARKETING STRATEGY TOOLS AND MODELS

### ANSOFFS MATRIX

A common tool used within marketing was developed by Igor Ansoff in 1957. His model gives organisation five strategic business options.

1. Market Penetration: This involves increasing sales of an existing product and penetrating the market further by either promoting the product heavily or reducing prices to increase sales.
2. Product Development: The organisation develops new products to aim within their existing market, in the hope that they will gain more custom and market share. For Example Sony launching the Playstation 2 to replace their existing model.
3. Market Development: The organisation here adopts a strategy of selling existing products to new markets. This can be done either by a better understanding of segmentation, i.e who else can possibly purchase the product or selling the product to new markets overseas.
4. Diversification: Moving away from what you are selling (your core activities) to providing something new eg Moving over from selling foods to selling cars.
5. Consolidation: Where the organisation adopts a strategy of withdrawing from particular markets, scaling back on operations and concentrating on its existing products in existing markets.

### PRODUCT LIFE CYCLE

The product life cycle concept suggests that a product passes through four stages of evolution. Introduction, growth, maturity and decline. As a product evolves and passes through theses four stages profit is affected, and different strategies have to be employed to ensure that the product is a success within its market.

As a new product much time will be spent by the organisation to create awareness of it presence amongst its target market. Profits are negative or low because of this reason.

Growth: If consumer clearly feels that this product will benefit them in some ways and they accept it, the organisation will see a period of rapid sales growth.

Maturity: Rapid sales growth cannot last forever. Sales slow down as the product sales reach peak as it has been accepted by most buyers.

Decline: Sales and profits start to decline, the organisation may try to change their pricing strategy to stimulate growth, however the product will either have to be re-modified, or replaced within the market.

## VALUE CHAIN ANALYSIS

Michael Porter in 1985 introduced in his book ' The competitive advantage' the concept of the Value Chain. He suggested that activities within the organisation add value to the service and products that the organisation produces, and all these activities should be run at optimum level if the organisation is to gain any real competitive advantage. If they are run efficiently the value obtained should exceed the costs of running them i.e. customers should return to the organisation and transact freely and willingly. Michael Porter suggested that the organisation is split into 'primary activities' and 'support activities'.

### Primary Activities

Inbound logistics : Refers to goods being obtained from the organisations suppliers ready to be used for producing the end product.

Operations : The raw materials and goods obtained are manufactured into the final product. Value is added to the product at this stage as it moves through the production line.

Outbound logistics : Once the products have been manufactured they are ready to be distributed to distribution centres, wholesalers, retailers or customers.

Marketing and Sales: Marketing must make sure that the product is targeted towards the correct customer group. The marketing mix is used to establish an effective strategy, any competitive advantage is clearly communicated to the target group by the use of the promotional mix.

Services: After the product/service has been sold what support services does the organisation have to offer. This may come in the form of after sales training, guarantees and warranties.

With the above activities, any or a combination of them, maybe essential for the firm to develop the competitive advantage which Porter talks about in his book.

**Support Activities**

The support activities assist the primary activities in helping the organisation achieve its competitive advantage. They include:

Procurement: This department must source raw materials for the organisation and obtain the best price for doing so. For the price they must obtain the best possible quality

Technology development: The use of technology to obtain a competitive advantage within the organisation. This is very important in today's technological driven environment. Technology can be used in production to reduce cost thus add value, or in research and development to develop new products, or via the use of the internet so customers have access to online facilities.

Human resource management: The organisation will have to recruit, train and develop the correct people for the organisation if they are to succeed in their objectives. Staff will have to be motivated and paid the 'market rate' if they are to stay with the organisation and add value to it over their duration of employment. Within the service sector eg airlines it is the 'staff' who may offer the competitive advantage that is needed within the field.

Firm infrastructure: Every organisations needs to ensure that their finances, legal structure and management structure works efficiently and helps drive the organisation forward.

As you can see the value chain encompasses the whole organisation and looks at how primary and support activities can work together effectively and efficiently to help gain the organisation a superior competitive advantage.

## SWOT ANALYSIS

A tool used by organisations to help the firm establish its Strengths, Weaknesses, Opportunities and Threats (SWOT). A SWOT analysis is used as a framework to help the firm develop its overall corporate, marketing, or product strategies. Note:Strengths and Weaknesses are internal factors which are controllable by the organisation. Opportunities & threats are external factors which are uncontrollable by the organisation.

Strength examples could include:

- A strong brand name.
- Market share.
- Good reputation.
- Expertise and skill.
- Weaknesses could include:
- Low or no market share.
- No brand loyalty.
- Lack of experience.
- Opportunities could include:
- A growing market.
- Increased consumer spending.
- Selling internationally.
- Changes in society beneficial to your company.

Threats could include:

- Competitors
- Government policy eg taxation, laws
- Changes in society not beneficial to your company

A SWOT analysis is an excellent tool to use if the organisation wants to take a step back and assess the situation they are in. Issues raised from the analysis are then used to assist the organisation in developing their marketing mix strategy. A SWOT analysis must form the part of any prudent marketing strategy.

**Generic Strategies**

For an organisation to obtain a sustainable competitive advantage Michael Porter suggested that they should follow either one of three generic strategies.

**Strategy one: Cost Leadership**

This strategy involves the organisation aiming to be the lowest cost producer within their industry. The orgainisation aims to drive cost down through all the elements of the production of the product from sourcing, to labour costs. The cost leader usually aims at a broad market, so sufficient sales can cover costs. Low cost producers include Easyjet airline, Ryan air, Asda and Walmart. Some organisation may aim to drive costs down but will not pass on these cost savings to their customers aiming for increased profits clearly because their brand can command a premium rate.

**Strategy 2: Differentiation**

To be different, is what organisations strive for. Having a competitive advantage which allows the company and its products ranges to stand out is crucial for their success. With a differentiation strategy the organisation aims to focus its effort on particular segments and charge for the added differentiated value. If we look at Brompton folding cycles their compact design differentiates them from other folding bike companies. New concepts which allow for differentiation can be patented, however patents have a certain life span and organisation always face the danger that their idea that gives the competitive advantage will be copied in one form or another.

**Strategy 3: Niche strategies**

Here the organisation focuses its effort on one particular segment and becomes well known for providing products/ services within the segment. They form a competitive advantage for this niche market and either succeed by being a low cost producer or differentiator within that particular segment. Examples include Roll Royce and Bentley.

**Are you 'Stuck in the Middle'**

The danger some organisation face is that they try to do all three and become what is known as stuck in the middle. The have no clear business strategy, be all to all consumers, which adds to their running costs causing a fall in sales and market share. 'Stuck in the middle' companies are usually subject to a takeover or merger.

**Industry Analysis Model**

Porters fives forces model is an excellent model to use to analyse a particular environment of an industry. So for example, if we were entering the PC industry, we would use porters model to help us find out about:

1) Competitive Rivalry
2) Power of suppliers
3) Power of buyers
4) Threats of substitutes
5) Threat of new entrants.

The above five main factors are key factors that influence industry performance, hence it is common sense and practical to find out about these factors before you enter the industry.

**Competitive Rivalry**

A starting point to analysing the industry is to look at competitive rivalry. If entry to an industry is easy then competitive rivalry will likely to be high. If it is easy for customers to move to substitute products for example from coke to water then again rivalry will be high. Generally competitive rivalry will be high if:

- There is little differentiation between the products sold between customers.
- Competitors are approximately the same size of each other.
- If the competitors all have similar strategies.
- It is costly to leave the industry hence they fight to just stay in (exit barriers)

**Power of Suppliers**

Suppliers are also essential for the success of an organisation. Raw materials are needed to complete the finish product of the organisation. Suppliers do have power. This power comes from:

- If they are the only supplier or one of few suppliers who supply that particular raw material.
- If it costly for the organisation to move from one supplier to another (known also as switching cost)
- If there is no other substitute for their product.

**Power of Buyers**

Buyers or customers can exert influence and control over an industry in certain circumstances. This happens when:

- There is little differentiation over the product and substitutes can be found easily.
- Customers are sensitive to price.
- Switching to another product is not costly.

**Threat of Substitutes**

Are there alternative products that customers can purchase over your product that offer the same benefit for the same or less price? The threat of substitute is high when:

- Price of that substitute product falls.
- It is easy for consumers to switch from one substitute product to another.
- Buyers are willing to substitute.

**Threat of New Entrant**

The threat of a new organisation entering the industry is high when it is easy for an organisation to enter the industry i.e. entry barriers are low.

An organisation will look at how loyal customers are to existing products, how quickly they can achieve economy of scales, would they have access to suppliers, would government legislation prevent them or encourage them to enter the industry.

So to summaries porters five forces model is essential to carry to help you understand your industry in depth before you enter it.

**Diffusion of Innovation**

This extension of the product life cycle was developed by Everett M. Rogers in 1962 and simply looks who adopts products at the different stages of the life cycle.

Rogers identified five types of purchasers as the product moves through its life cycle stage. He suggested:

1. Innovator who make up 2.5% of all purchases of the product, purchase the product at the beginning of the life cycle. They are not afraid of trying new products that suit their lifestyle and will also pay a premium for that benefit.
2. Early Adopters make up 13.5% of purchases, they are usually opinion leaders and naturally adopt products after the innovators. This group of purchasers are crucial because adoption by them means the product becomes acceptable, spurring on later purchasers.
3. Early Majority make up 34% of purchases and have been spurred on by the early adopters. They wait to

see if the product will be adopted by society and will purchase only when this has happened. They early majority usually have some status in society.

4. Late Majority make up another 34% of sales and usually purchase the product at the late stages of majority within the life cycle.
5. Laggards make up 16% of total sales and usually purchase the product near the end of its life. They are the 'wait and see' group. They wait to see if the product will get cheaper. Usually when they purchase the product a new version is already on the market. Some may call Laggards, bargain hunters!

**Boston Consultancy Group (BCG Matrix)**

This product portfolio matrix classifies product lines into four categories. The BCG models suggests that organisations should have a healthy balance of products within their range. The Boston Consultancy Group classified these products as following:

**Question Mark/Problem Child**

These are products with low market share but operate in high market growth rates. The company puts a lot of resources in this product in the hope that it will eventually increase market share and generate cash returns in the future.

**Star**

Stars have high market shares that operate in growing markets. The product at this stage should be generating positive returns for the company.

**Cash Cow**

Cash Cow are products at the mature stage of the lifecycle, they generate high amounts of cash for the company, but growth rate is slowing. There are chances that the product may slip into decline, appropriate marketing mix strategies should be employed to try to prevent this from happening.

## Chapter 4

# Marketing Tactics

The marketing mix principles (also known as the 4 p's.) are used by business as tools to assist them in pursuing their objectives. The marketing mix principles are controllable variables, which have to be carefully managed and must meet the needs of the defined target group.

**Product Strategies**

When an organisation introduces a product into a market they must ask themselves a number of questions.

1. Who is the product aimed at?
2. What benefit will they expect?
3. How do they plan to position the product within the market?
4. What differential advantage will the product offer over their competitors?

We must remember that Marketing is fundamentally about providing the correct bundle of benefits to the end user, hence the saying 'Marketing is not about providing products or services it is essentially about providing changing benefits to the changing needs and demands of the customer'.

Philip Kotler in Principles of Marketing devised a very interesting concept of benefit building with a product. Kotler suggested that a product should be viewed in three levels.

Level 1: Core Product. What is the core benefit your product offers?. Customers who purchase a camera are buying more then just a camera they are purchasing memories.

Level 2 Actual Product: All cameras capture memories. The aim is to ensure that your potential customers purchase your one. The strategy at this level involves organisations branding, adding features and benefits to ensure that their product offers a differential advantage from their competitors.

Level 3: Augmented product: What additional non-tangible benefits can you offer? Competition at this level is based around after sales service, warranties, delivery and so on. John Lewis a retail departmental store offers free five year guarantee on purchases of their Television sets, this gives their 'customers the additional benefit of 'piece of mind' over the five years should their purchase develop a fault.

**Product Decisions**

When placing a product within a market many factors and decisions have to be taken into consideration. These include:

Product design – Will the design be the selling point for the organisation as we have seen with the iMAC, the new VW Beetle or the Dyson vacuum cleaner.

Product quality: Quality has to consistent with other elements of the marketing mix. A premium based pricing strategy has to reflect the quality a product offers.

Product features: What features will you add that may increase the benefit offered to your target market? Will the organisation use a discriminatory pricing policy for offering these additional benefits?

Branding: One of the most important decisions a marketing manager can make is about branding. The value of brands in today's environment is phenomenal. Brands have the power of instant sales, they convey a message of confidence, quality and reliability to their target market.

Brands have to be managed well, as some brands can be cash cows for organisations. In many organisations they are represented by brand managers, who have hugh resources to ensure their success within the market.

A brand is a tool which is used by an organisation to differentiate itself from competitors. Ask yourself what is the value of a pair of Nike trainers without the brand or the logo? How does your perception change?

Increasingly brand managers are becoming annoyed by 'copycat' strategies being employed by supermarket food retail stores particular within the UK. Coca-Cola threatened legal action against UK retailer Sainsbury after introducing their Classic Cola, which displayed similar designs and fonts on their cans.

Internet branding is now becoming an essential part of the branding strategy game. Generic names like Bank.com and Business.com have been sold for £m's. Recently within the UK banking industry we have seen the introduction of Internet banks such as cahoot.com and marbles.com the task by brand managers is to make sure that consumers understand that these brands are banks!

**Pricing Strategies**

Pricing is one of the most important elements of the marketing mix, as it is the only mix, which generates a turnover for the organisation. The remaining 3p's are the variable cost for the organisation. It costs to produce and design a product, it costs to distribute a product and costs to promote it. Price must support these elements of the mix. Pricing is difficult and must reflect supply and demand relationship. Pricing a product too high or too low could mean a loss of sales for the organisation.

Pricing should take into account the following factors:

- Fixed and variable costs
- Competition
- Company objectives
- Proposed positioning strategies
- Target group and willingness to pay
- Pricing Strategies

An organisation can adopt a number of pricing strategies. The pricing strategies are based much on what objectives the company has set itself to achieve.

Penetration pricing: Where the organisation sets a low price to increase sales and market share.

Skimming pricing: The organisation sets an initial high price and then slowly lowers the price to make the product available to a wider market. The objective is to skim profits of the market layer by layer.

Competition pricing: Setting a price in comparison with competitors.

Product Line Pricing: Pricing different products within the same product range at different price points. An example would be a video manufacturer offering different video recorders with different features at different prices. The greater the features and the benefit obtained the greater the consumer will pay. This form of price discrimination assists the company in maximising turnover and profits.

Bundle Pricing: The organisation bundles a group of products at a reduced price.

Psychological pricing: The seller here will consider the psychology of price and the positioning of price within the market place. The seller will therefore charge 99p instead £1 or $199 instead of $200

Premium pricing: The price set is high to reflect the exclusiveness of the product. An example of products using this strategy would be Harrods, first class airline services, porsche etc.

Optional pricing: The organisation sells optional extras along with the product to maximise its turPlace strategies

Refers to how an organisation will distribute the product or service they are offering to the end user. The organisation must distribute the product to the user at the right place at the right time. Efficient and effective distribution is important if the organisation is to meet its overall marketing objectives. If organisation underestimate demand and customers cannot purchase products because of it profitability will be affected.

What channel of distribution will they use?

Two types of channel of distribution methods are available. Indirect distribution involves distributing your product by the use of an intermediary. Direct distribution involves distributing direct from a manufacturer to the consumer e.g. For example Dell Computers. Clearly direct distribution gives a manufacturer complete control over their product.

A successful product or service means nothing unless the benefit of such a service can be communicated clearly to the target market.

An organisations promotional strategy can consist of:

Advertising: Is any non personal paid form of communication using any form of mass media.

Public relations: Involves developing positive relationships with the organisation media public. The art of good public relations is not only to obtain favorable publicity within the media, but it is also involves being able to handle successfully negative attention.

Sales promotion: Commonly used to obtain an increase in sales short term. Could involve using money off coupons or special offers.

Personal selling: Selling a product service one to one.

Direct Mail: Is the sending of publicity material to a named person within an organisation. There has been a massive growth in direct mail campaigns over the last 5 years. Spending on direct mail now amounts to £18 bn a year representing 11.8% of advertising expenditure (Source: Royal Mail 2000). Organisations can pay thousands of pounds for databases, which contain names and addresses of potential customers.

Direct mail allows an organisation to use their resources more effectively by allowing them to send publicity material to a named person within their target segment. By personalising advertising, response rates increase thus increasing the chance of improving sales.

An effective communication campaign should comprise of a well thought out message strategy. What message are you trying to put accross to your target audience?. How will you deliver that message? Will it be through the appropiate use of branding? logos or slogan design?. The message should reinforce the benefit of the product and should also help the company in developing the positioning strategy of the product.

Media strategy refers to how the organisation is going to deliver their message. What aspects of the promotional mix will the company use to deliver their message strategy. Where will they promote? Clearly the company must take into account the readership and general behaviour of their target audience before they select their media strategy. What newspapers do their target market read? What TV programmes do they watch? Effective targeting of their media campaign could save the company on valuable financial resources.

Communication by the manufacturer is not only directed towards consumers to create demand. A push strategy is where the manufacturer concentrates some of their marketing effort on promoting their product to retailers to convince them to stock the product. A combination of promotional mix strategies are used at this stage aimed at the retailer including personal selling, and direct mail. The product is pushed onto the retailer, hence the name. A pull strategy is based around the manufacturer promoting their product amongst the target market to create demand. Consumers pull the product through the distribution channel forcing the wholesaler and retailer to stock it, hence the name pull strategy. Organisations tend to use both push and pull strategies to create demand from retailers and consumers.

## COMMUNICATION MODEL - AIDA

AIDA is a communication model which can be used by firms to aid them in selling their product or services. AIDA is an Acronym for Attention, Interest, Desire, Action.. When a product is launched the first goal is to grab attention. Think, how can an organisation use it skills to do this? Use well-known personalities to sell products? Once you grab attention how can you hold Interest, through promoting features, clearly stating the benefit the product has to offer? The third stage is desire, how can you make the product desirable to the consumer? By demonstrating it? The final stage is the purchase action, if the company has been successful with its strategy then the target customer should purchase the product.

As products move through the four stages of the product lifecycle different promotional strategies should be employed at these stages to ensure the healthy success and life of the product.

**Stages and Promotion Strategies**

When a product is new the organisations objective will be to inform the target audience of its entry. Television, radio, magazine, coupons etc may be used to push the product through the introduction stage of the lifecycle. Push and Pull Strategies will be used at this crucial stage.

**Growth**

As the product becomes accepted by the target market the organisation at this stage of the lifecycle the organisation works on the strategy of further increasing brand awareness to encourage loyalty.

**Maturity**

At this stage with increased competition the organisation take persuasive tactics to encourage the consumers to purchase their product over their rivals. Any differential advantage will be clearly communicated to the target audience to inform of their benefit over their competitors.

**Decline**

As the product reaches the decline stage the organisation will use the strategy of reminding people of the product to slow the inevitable.

**Place Strategies**

Refers to how an organisation will distribute the product or service they are offering to the end user. The organisation must distribute the product to the user at the right place at the right time. Efficient and effective distribution is important if the organisation is to meet its overall marketing objectives. If organisation underestimate demand and customers cannot purchase products because of it profitability will be affected.

What channel of distribution will they use?

Two types of channel of distribution methods are available. Indirect distribution involves distributing your product by the use of an intermediary. Direct distribution involves distributing direct from a manufacturer to the consumer e.g. For example Dell Computers. Clearly direct distribution gives a manufacturer complete control over their product.

**Distribution Strategies**

Depending on the type of product being distributed there are three common distribution strategies available:

1. Intensive distribution: Used commonly to distribute low priced or impulse purchase products eg chocolates, soft drinks.
2. Exclusive distribution: Involves limiting distribution to a single outlet. The product is usually highly priced, and requires the intermediary to place much detail in its sell. An example of would be the sale of vehicles through exclusive dealers.
3. Selective Distribution: A small number of retail outlets are chosen to distribute the product. Selective distribution is common with products such as computers, televisions household appliances, where consumers are willing to shop around and where manufacturers want a large geographical spread.

If a manufacturer decides to adopt an exclusive or selective strategy they should select a intermediary which has experience of handling similar products, credible and is known by the target audience.

**Brand Names**

How do you name a product? Simply put it, there is no easy option. Depending on how established an organisation is, there are a number of ways to brand a product.

Individual name: A product could be branded with an individual name. A firm may decide it wants a brand, which has no association with any of its other brands. Volkswagen in the UK, for example own the brand SEAT and Skoda

Family brand: Where a product is part of a family, e.g. Kellogg's, with Corn flakes, Rice Krispies, and Frosties. The brand is stretched to other products because customers trust it, and the firm is trying to maximize the equity it holds in the brand.

Combined brand name: A popular strategy involves the organisation combing the already established family name with a new individual brand name. The idea is to use the reputation of the established family or company name to launch a new associated product. For example Nestle may use their name to launch a new cereal or cereal bar.

## CONSUMER BUYING BEHAVIOUR

What influences consumers to purchase products or services? The consumer buying process is a complex matter as many internal and external factors have an impact on the buying decisions of the consumer.

When purchasing a product there several processes, which consumers go through. These will be discussed below.

1. Problem/Need Recognition: How do you decide you want to buy a particular product or service? It could be that your DVD player stops working and you now have to look for a new one, all those DVD films you purchased you can no longer play! So you have a problem or a new need. For high value items like a DVD player or a car or other low frequency purchased products this is the process we would

take. However, for impulse low frequency purchases e.g. confectionery the process is different.

2. Information search: So we have a problem, our DVD player no longer works and we need to buy a new one. What's the solution? Yes go out and purchase a new one, but which brand? Shall we buy the same brand as the one that blew up? Or stay clear of that? Consumer often go on some form of information search to help them through their purchase decision. Sources of information could be family, friends, neighbours who may have the product you have in mind, alternatively you may ask the sales people, or dealers, or read specialist magazines like What DVD? to help with their purchase decision. You may even actually examine the product before you decide to purchase it.
3. Evaluation of different purchase options: So what DVD player do we purchase? Shall it be Sony, Toshiba or Bush? Consumers allocate attribute factors to certain products, almost like a point scoring system which they work out in their mind over which brand to purchase. This means that consumers know what features from the rivals will benefit them and they attach different degrees of importance to each attribute. For example sound maybe better on the Sony product and picture on the Toshiba, but picture clarity is more important to you then sound. Consumers usually have some sort of brand preference with companies as they may have had a good history with a particular brand or their friends may have had a reliable history with one, but if the decision falls between the Sony DVD or Toshiba then which one shall it be? It could be that the a review the consumer reads on the particular Toshiba product may have tipped the balance and that they will purchase that brand.

4. Purchase decision: Through the evaluation process discussed above consumers will reach their final purchase decision and they reach the final process of going through the purchase action e.g. The process of going to the shop to buy the product, which for some consumers can be as just as rewarding as actually purchasing the product. Purchase of the product can either be through the store, the web, or over the phone.

**Post Purchase Behaviour**

Ever have doubts about the product after you purchased it? This simply is post purchase behaviour and research shows that it is a common trait amongst purchasers of products. Manufacturers of products clearly want recent consumers to feel proud of their purchase, it is therefore just as important for manufacturers to advertise for the sake of their recent purchaser so consumers feel comfortable that they own a product from a strong and reputable organisation. This limits post purchase behaviour. i.e. You feel reassured that you own the latest advertised product.

**Factors Influencing the Behaviour of Buyers**

Consumer behaviour is affected by many uncontrollable factors. Just think, what influences you before you buy a product or service? Your friends, your upbringing, your culture, the media, a role model or influences from certain groups?

Culture is one factor that influences behaviour. Simply culture is defined as our attitudes and beliefs. But how are these attitudes and beliefs developed? As an individual growing up, a child is influenced by their parents, brothers, sister and other family member who may teach them what is wrong or right. They learn about their religion and culture, which helps them develop these opinions, attitudes and beliefs (AIO).

These factors will influence their purchase behaviour however other factors like groups of friends, or people they look up to may influence their choices of purchasing a particular product or service. Reference groups are particular groups of people some people may look up towards to that have an impact on consumer behaviour. So they can be simply a band like the Spice Girls or your immediate family members. Opinion leaders are those people that you look up to because your respect their views and judgements and these views may influence consumer decisions. So it maybe a friend who works with the IT trade who may influence your decision on what computer to buy. The economical environment also has an impact on consumer behaviour; do consumers have a secure job and a regular income to spend on goods? Marketing and advertising obviously influence consumers in trying to evoke them to purchase a particular product or service.

People's social status will also impact their behaviour. What is their role within society? Are they Actors? Doctors? Office worker? and mothers and fathers also? Clearly being parents affects your buying habits depending on the age of the children, the type of job may mean you need to purchase formal clothes, the income which is earned has an impact. The lifestyle of someone who earns £250000 would clearly be different from someone who earns £25000. Also characters have an influence on buying decision. Whether the person is extrovert (out going and spends on entertainment) or introvert (keeps to themselves and purchases via online or mail order) again has an impact on the types of purchases made.

**Maslow's Hierarchy of Needs**

Abraham Maslow hierarchy of needs theory sets out to explain what motivated individuals in life to achieve. He set out his answer in a form of a hierarchy. He suggests individuals aim to meet basic psychological needs of hunger and thirst. When this has been met they then move up to the next stage of the hierarchy, safety needs, where the priority lay with job security and the knowing that an income will be available to them regularly. Social needs come in the next level of the hierarchy, the need to belong or be loved is a natural human desire and people do strive for this belonging. Esteem need is the need for status and recognition within society, status sometimes drives people, the need to have a good job title and be recognised or the need to wear branded clothes as a symbol of status.

Self-actualisation the realisation that an individual has reached their potential in life. The point of self-actualisation is down to the individual, when do you know you have reached your point of self-fulfilment?

But how does this concept help an organisation trying to market a product or service?

Well as we have established earlier within this website, marketing is about meeting needs and providing benefits, Maslows concept suggests that needs change as we go along our path of striving for self-actualisation. Supermarket firms develop value brands to meet the psychological needs of hunger and thirst. Harrods develops products and services for those who want have met their esteem needs. So Maslows concept is useful for marketers as it can help them understand and develop consumer needs and wants.

**Types of Buying Behaviour**

There are four typical types of buying behaviour based on the type of products that intends to be purchased. Complex buying behaviour is where the individual purchases a high value brand and seeks a lot of information before the purchase is made. Habitual buying behaviour is where the individual buys a product out of habit e.g. a daily newspaper, sugar or salt. Variety seeking buying behaviour is where the individual likes to shop around and experiment with different products. So an individual may shop around for different breakfast cereals because he/she wants variety in the mornings! Dissonance reducing buying behaviour is when buyer are highly involved with the purchase of the product, because the purchase is expensive or infrequent. There is little difference between existing brands an example would be buying a diamond ring, there is perceived little difference between existing diamond brand manufacturers.

Before an organisation can target a specific segment accurately it must ask itself a number of questions. It is important to evaluate the effectiveness of a targeting strategy and the viability of the segment, if this is not done then money will be wasted.

The market which is segmented must meet the following criteria:

Measurability of segment: Can you measure the size and growth of the segment. Is the segment growing? In the UK the market is growing at an extremely fast pace. The fast growth rate is attracting many players within the market.

Accessibility of segment: Is it easy for you to target and reach your segment? Can they be reached with basic communication tools such as radio and TV advertising? If you cannot target your segment effectively with marketing communication then it is not viable.

Suitability of segment: Is there enough spending power within the segment for the company to sustain itself.

Actionability of segment: Does the organisation have enough resources to reach their segments?. It is no point in targeting segments you do not have the resources to cater for. If you were a car manufacturer the organisation would not concentrate on the affluent and price sensitive market if they did not have the resources to do so.

## TARGETING

After the process of segmentation the next step is for the organisation to decide how it is going to target these particular groups. There are three targeting options an organisation can adopt.

Sometimes referred to as mass marketing the firm may decide to aim its resources at the entire market with one particular product. Coca Colas original marketing strategy was based on this form. One product aimed at the mass market in the hope that a sufficient amount of buyers would be attracted, although there are now changes in their product line to cater for growing dietary and caffeine free needs of consumers.

Differentiated marketing strategy - Where the firm decides to target several segments and develops distinct products/ services with separate marketing mix strategies aimed at the varying groups. An example of this would be airline companies offering first, business (segment 1) or economy class tickets (segment 2), with separate marketing programmes to attract the different groups.

Concentrated Marketing: Where the organisation concentrates its marketing effort on one particular segment. The firm will develop a product that caters for the needs of that particular group. For example Rolls Royce cars aim its vehicles at the premium segment, same as Harrods within the UK.

Kotler suggested that a product should be viewed in three levels.

Level 1: Core Product. What is the core benefit your product offers?. Customers who purchase a camera are buying more then just a camera they are purchasing memories.

Level 2 Actual Product: All cameras capture memories. The aim is to ensure that your potential customers purchase your one. The strategy at this level involves organisations branding, adding features and benefits to ensure that their product offers a differential advantage from their competitors.

Level 3: Augmented product: What additional non-tangible benefits can you offer? Competition at this level is based around after sales service, warranties, delivery and so on. John Lewis a retail departmental store offers free five year guarantee on purchases of their Television sets, this gives their 'customers the additional benefit of 'piece of mind' over the five years should their purchase develop a fault.

## SERVICE MARKETING

### Characteristics of a Service

What exactly are the characteristics of a service? How are services different from a product? In fact many organisations do have service elements to the product they sell, for example

McDonald's sell physical products i.e. burgers but consumers are also concerned about the quality and speed of service, are staff cheerful and welcoming and do they serve with a smile on their face?

There are five characteristics to a service which will be discussed below.

1. Lack of ownership: You cannot own and store a service like you can a product. Services are used or hired for a period of time. For example when buying a ticket to the USA the service lasts maybe 9 hours each way, but consumers want and expect excellent service for that time. Because you can measure the duration of the service consumers become more demanding of it.
2. Intangibility: You cannot hold or touch a service unlike a product. In saying that although services are intangible the experience consumers obtain from the service has an impact on how they will perceive it. What do consumers perceive from customer service? the location, and the inner presentation of where they are purchasing the service?.
3. Inseparability: Services cannot be separated from the service providers. A product when produced can be taken away from the producer. However a service is produced at or near the point of purchase. Take visiting a restaurant, you order your meal, the waiting and delivery of the meal, the service provided by the waiter/ress is all apart of the service production process and is inseparable, the staff in a restaurant are as apart of the process as well as the quality of food provided.
4. Perishibility: Services last a specific time and cannot be stored like a product for later use. If travelling by train, coach or air the service will only last the duration of the journey. The service is developed and used almost simultaneously. Again because of this time constraint consumers demand more.

5. Heterogeneity: It is very difficult to make each service experience identical. If travelling by plane the service quality may differ from the first time you travelled by that airline to the second, because the airhostess is more or less experienced.

A concert performed by a group on two nights may differ in slight ways because it is very difficult to standardise every dance move. Generally systems and procedures are put into place to make sure the service provided is consistent all the time, training in service organisations is essential for this, however in saying this there will always be subtle differences.

**Service Marketing Mix**

Having discussed the characteristics of a service, let us now look at the marketing mix of a service.

The service marketing mix comprises off the 7'p's. These include:

- Product
- Price
- Place
- Promotion
- People
- Process
- Physical evidence.

An essential ingredient to any service provision is the use of appropriate staff and people. Recruiting the right staff and training them appropriately in the delivery of their service is essential if the organisation wants to obtain a form of competitive advantage. Consumers make judgements and deliver perceptions of the service based on the employees they interact with. Staff should have the appropriate interpersonal skills, aptititude, and service knowledge to provide the service that consumers are paying for. Many British organisations aim to apply for the Investors In People accreditation, which tells consumers that staff are taken care off by the company and they are trained to certain standards.

***Process***

Refers to the systems used to assist the organisation in delivering the service. Imagine you walk into Burger King and you order a Whopper Meal and you get it delivered within 2 minutes. What was the process that allowed you to obtain an efficient service delivery? Banks that send out Credit Cards automatically when their customers old one has expired again require an efficient process to identify expiry dates and renewal. An efficient service that replaces old credit cards will foster consumer loyalty and confidence in the company.

### *Physical Evidence*

Where is the service being delivered? Physical Evidence is the element of the service mix which allows the consumer again to make judgements on the organisation. If you walk into a restaurant your expectations are of a clean, friendly environment. On an aircraft if you travel first class you expect enough room to be able to lay down!

Physical evidence is an essential ingredient of the service mix, consumers will make perceptions based on their sight of the service provision which will have an impact on the organisations perceptual plan of the service.

The Service marketing mix involves analysing the 7'p of marketing involving, Product, Price, Place, Promotion, Physical Evidence, Process and People.

To certain extent managing services are more complicated then managing products, products can be standardised, to standardise a service is far more difficult as there are more input factors i.e. people, physical evidence, process to manage then with a product.

## Consumer Goods Classification

Consumer goods are products which are purchased for personal consumption. Consumer goods are classified into three areas. These are:

### *Convenience Goods*

Convenience products are inexpensive frequent purchases, there is little effort needed to purchase them. Examples may include fast food and confectionery products. Convenience products are split into staples, such as milk, eggs and emergency products which are purchased when the need arises e.g. Umbrellas.

### *Shopping Goods*

Shopping goods are usually high risk products where consumers like to shop around to find the best features and price for that product.. Examples include buying fridges, freezers or washing machines.

### *Specialty Goods*

There are products that are purchased infrequently. The consumers will conduct extensive research to make sure that their purchase decision is right, because specialty goods are expensive and infrequent purchases. The organization will support the product with an extensive warranty package. Examples include watches and diamonds. There are usually little or no substitutes for these products.

### *Pricing Strategies*

Pricing is one of the most important elements of the marketing mix, as it is the only mix, which generates a turnover for the organisation. The remaining 3p's are the variable cost for the organisation. It costs to produce and design a product, it costs to distribute a product and costs to promote it. Price must support these elements of the mix. Pricing is difficult and must reflect supply and demand relationship. Pricing a product too high or too low could mean a loss of sales for the organisation. Pricing should take into account the following factors:

- Fixed and variable costs
- Competition
- Company objectives
- Proposed positioning strategies
- Target group and willingness to pay

### *Pricing Strategies*

An organisation can adopt a number of pricing strategies. The pricing strategies are based much on what objectives the company has set itself to achieve. Penetration pricing: Where the organisation sets a low price to increase sales and market share.

Skimming pricing: The organisation sets an initial high price and then slowly lowers the price to make the product available to a wider market. The objective is to skim profits of the market layer by layer.

Competition pricing: Setting a price in comparison with competitors.

Product Line Pricing: Pricing different products within the same product range at different price points. An example would be a video manufacturer offering different video recorders with different features at different prices. The greater the features and the benefit obtained the greater the consumer will pay. This form of price discrimination assists the company in maximising turnover and profits.

Bundle Pricing: The organisation bundles a group of products at a reduced price.

Psychological pricing: The seller here will consider the psychology of price and the positioning of price within the market place. The seller will therefore charge 99p instead £1 or $199 instead of $200

Premium pricing: The price set is high to reflect the exclusiveness of the product. An example of products using this strategy would be Harrods, first class airline services, porsche etc.

Optional pricing: The organisation sells optional extras along with the product to maximise its turnover. This strategy is used commonly within the car industry.

In Principles of Marketing, by Philip Kotler and Gary Armstrong a brand is defined as 'a name, term, sign symbol or a combination of these, that identifies the maker or seller of the product'

A brand name helps an organisation differentiate itself from its competitors. In todays competitive world no product can go without a brand. Customers often build up a relationship with a brand that they trust and will often go back to time and time again. For example, some people may only purchase a Sony TV although there are acceptable alternatives on the market, because of a past positive history with this brand.

Brand equity refers to the value of the brand. Brand equity does not develop instantaneously. A brand needs to be carefully nurtured and marketed so consumers feel real value and trust towards that brand. Nike, Adidas, Harrods, have high brand equity. These brand command high awareness and consumer loyalty. But how much are these brands worth? It is difficult to put a value on these brands. But how much is a pair of Nike trainers worth without the logo on it?

When a company manages its brands it has a number of strategies it can use to further increase its brand value. These are:

Line extension: This is where an organisation adds to its current product line by introducing, versions with new features, an example could be a Crisp manufacturer extending its line by adding more exotic flavours.

Brand extension: If your current brand name is successful, you may use the brand name to extend into new or existing areas. For example Virgin extending its brand from records, to airlines, to mobiles.

Multi Branding: The company decides to further introduce more brands into an already existing category. Kellogg's for example have a number of brands in the cereal market and the cereal bar market. Multi-branding can allow an organisation to maximise profits, but a company needs to be weary over their own brands competing with each other over market share.

New Brands: An organisation may decide to launch a new brand into a market. A new brand may be used to compete with existing rivals and may be marketed as something 'new and fresh'.

## PERCEPTUAL MAPPING/POSITIONING MAP

In helping you develop a market positioning strategy for your product or service, perceptual maps or positioning maps as they are sometimes referred to, are often used to help the organisation identify a positioning strategy.

When plotting a peceptual map two dimensions are commonly used. If we plot the UK chocolate market we can identify those brands which are high price and high quality. Belgium chocolates are plotted as high quality and high price, and twix is plotted one low quality low price brand. Once completed the perceptual map could help identify where an organisation could launch a new brand pherhapsat the medium price and quality range. In our basic map, you can see there is not much competition within that particular area.

We must remember that perceptual maps are plotted on the basis of someones perception and what maybe a quality product to one person, may not be percieved as quality to another.

## Chapter 5

# Finance Planning in Hotel Management

Accounting (methodology) is the measurement, disclosure or provision of assurance about financial information that helps managers, investors, tax authorities and other decision makers make resource allocation decisions. The names come from the use of financial accounts. Financial accounting is one branch of accounting and historically has involved processes by which financial information about a business is recorded, classified, summarized, interpreted, and communicated. Accounting is also widely referred to as the "language of business".

Auditing, a related but separate discipline, has two sub-disciplines: Internal and External auditing. External auditing is the process whereby an independent auditor examines an organization's financial statements and accounting records in order to express an opinion — that conveys reasonable but not absolute assurance — as to the truth and fairness of the statements and the accountant's adherence to Generally Accepted Accounting Principles (GAAP), in all material respects.

Internal auditing is an examination in which management, and not the external public, is the main beneficiary. It is carried out usually by auditors employed by the company, but sometimes by external service providers. The internal auditor's role is broader, and basically depends on what kind of assurance management wants. It usually certifies the efficiency and effectiveness of processes, departments, projects or internal controls. The Institute of Internal Auditors is generally accepted as the custodian of Internal Auditing best practice.

At the heart of accounting is the measurement of financial transactions which are transfers of legal property rights made under contractual relationships. Non-financial transactions are specifically excluded due to conservatism and materiality principles.

Practitioners of accountancy are known as accountants. There are many professional bodies for accountants throughout the world. Many allow their members to use titles indicating their membership. Examples are Chartered Certified Accountant (ACCA or FCCA), Chartered Accountant (FCA, CA or ACA) and Certified Public Accountant (CPA).

Accountancy attempts to create accurate financial reports that are useful to managers, regulators, and other stakeholders such as shareholders, creditors, or owners. The day-to-day record-keeping involved in this process is known as bookkeeping.

At the heart of modern financial accounting is the double-entry bookkeeping system. This system involves making at least two entries for every transaction: a debit in one account, and a corresponding credit in another account. The sum of all debits should always equal the sum of all credits. This provides an easy way to check for errors. This system was first used in medieval Europe, although claims have been made that the system dates back to Ancient Greece.

According to critics of standard accounting practices, it has changed little since. Accounting reform measures of some kind have been taken in each generation to attempt to keep bookkeeping relevant to capital assets or production capacity. However, these have not changed the basic principles, which are supposed to be independent of economics as such. In recent times, the divergence of accounting from economic principles has resulted in controversial reforms to make financial reports more indicative of economic reality.

Accountancy's infancy dates back to the earliest days of human agriculture and civilization (the Sumerians in Mesopotamia), when the need to maintain accurate records of the quantities and relative values of agricultural products first arose. Simple accounting is mentioned in the Christian Bible in the book of Matthew, in the Parable of the Talents (Matt. 25:19). Twelfth century writer Ibn Taymiyyah mentioned in his book Hisba (verification, calculation), detailed accounting systems used by the Muslims as early as in the mid-seventh century. The accounting practices were influenced by the Roman and the Persian civilizations that Muslims interacted with. The most detailed example of a complex governmental accounting system is the Divan of Umar, the second Caliph of Islam in which all revenues and disbursements were recorded. The Divan of Umar has been described in detail by various Islamic historians and was used by Muslim rulers with mofidications and enhancements until the fall of the Ottoman Empire.

## MODERN ACCOUNTANCY

The first book on accounting was written by a Croatian merchant Benedetto Cotrugli, who is also known as Benedikt Kotruljeviæ, from the city of Dubrovnik. During his life in Italy he met many merchants and decided to write, Della Mercatvra et del Mercante Perfetto (On Trade and the Perfect Merchant) in which he elaborated on the principles of modern, double-entry book-keeping. He finished his lifework in 1458. However, his work was not published until 1573, as a result of which his contributions to the field have been overlooked by the general public.

For this reason, Luca Pacioli, also known as Friar Luca dal Borgo, is credited for the "birth" of accounting. His Summa de arithmetica, geometrica, proportioni et proportionalita (Venice 1494), a synthesis of the mathematical knowledge of his time, includes the first published description of the method of keeping accounts that Venetian merchants used at that time, known as the double-entry accounting system. Although Pacioli codified rather than invented this system, he is widely regarded as the "Father of Accounting". The system he published included most of the accounting cycle as we know it today. He described the use of journals and ledgers, and warned that a person should not go to sleep at night until the debits equalled the credits! His ledger had accounts for assets (including receivables and inventories), liabilities, capital, income, and expenses — the account categories that are reported on an organization's balance sheet and income statement, respectively. He demonstrated year-end closing entries and proposed that a trial balance be used to prove a balanced ledger. His treatise also touches on a wide range of related topics from accounting ethics to cost accounting.

The first known book in the English language on accounting was published in London by John Gouge (or Gough) in 1543. It is described as A Profitable Treatyce called the Instrument or Boke to learn to knowe the good order of the kepyng of the famouse reconynge, called in Latin, Dare and Habere, and, in English, Debitor and Creditor.

A short book of instructions was also published in 1588 by John Mellis of Southwark, in which he says, "I am but the renuer and reviver of an ancient old copie printed here in London the 14 of August 1543: collected, published, made, and set forth by one Hugh Oldcastle, Scholemaster, who, as appeareth by his treatise, then taught Arithmetics, and this booke in Saint Ollaves parish in Marko Lane." John Mellis refers to the fact that the principle of accounts he explains (which is a simple system of double entry) is "after the forme of Venice".

A book described as The Merchants Mirrour, or directions for the perfect ordering and keeping of his accounts formed by way of Debitor and Creditor, after the (so termed) Italian manner, by Richard Dafforne, accountant, published in 1635, contains many references to early books on the science of accountancy. In a chapter in this book, headed "Opinion of Book-keeping's Antiquity," the author states, on the authority of another writer, that the form of book-keeping referred to had then been in use in Italy about two hundred years, "but that the same, or one in many parts very like this, was used in the time of Julius Caesar, and in Rome long before."

An early Dutch writer appears to have suggested that double-entry book-keeping was even in existence among the Greeks, pointing to scientific accountancy having been invented in remote times.

There were several editions of Richard Dafforne's book - the second edition in 1636, the third in 1656, and another in 1684. The book is a very complete treatise on scientific accountancy, beautifully prepared and containing elaborate explanations. The numerous editions tend to prove that the science was highly appreciated in the 17th century. From this time on, there has been a continuous supply of literature on the subject, many of the authors styling themselves accountants and teachers of the art, and thus proving that the professional accountant was then known and employed.

The requirements for entry in the profession of accounting vary from country to country. Accountants may be licensed by a variety of organisations, such as the British qualified accountancy bodies including Association of Chartered Certified Accountants (ACCA) and Institute of Chartered Accountants, and are recognized by titles such as Chartered Certified Accountant (ACCA or FCCA) and Chartered Accountant (UK, Australia, New Zealand, Canada, India, Pakistan, South Africa), Certified Public Accountant (Ireland, Japan, US, Singapore, Hong Kong, the Philippines), Certified Management Accountant (Canada, U.S.), Certified General Accountant (Canada), or Certified Practising Accountant (Australia). Some Commonwealth countries (Australia and Canada) often recognise both the certified and chartered accounting bodies. The majority of "public" accountants in New Zealand and Canada are Chartered Accountants; however, Certified General Accountants are also authorized by legislation to practise public accounting and auditing in all Canadian provinces, except Ontario and Quebec, as of 2005. There is, however, no legal requirement for an accountant to be a paid-up member of one of the many Institutes and other bodies which are effectively a form of professional trade union. Unlike the Law Society, which can legally stop a solicitor from practising, accountancy institutes do not have such authority. However, auditors are regulated.

Before the Enron and other accounting scandals, there were five large firms and were called the Big Five. Since Arthur Andersen's assurance practice split (after the firm was found guilty in the Enron scandal), with a plurality joining KPMG in the US and Deloitte & Touche outside of the US, Arthur Andersen left from the group. Previous to this there were also groupings referred to as the "Big Six" (Arthur Andersen, plus Coopers & Lybrand before its merger with Price Waterhouse) and the "Big Eight" (Ernst and Young prior to their merger were Ernst & Whinney and Arthur Young and Deloitte & Touche was formed by the merger of Deloitte, Haskins and Sells with the firm Touche Ross).

Enron turned out to be only the first of a series of accounting scandals that enveloped the accounting industry in 2002.

This is likely to have far-reaching consequences for the U.S. accounting industry. Application of International Accounting Standards originating in International Accounting Standards Board headquartered in London and bearing more resemblance to UK than current US practices is often advocated by those who note the relative stability of the UK accounting system (which reformed itself after scandals in the late 1980s and early 1990s). Accounting reform of a far more comprehensive sort is advocated by those who see issues with capitalism or economics, and seek ecological or social accountability.

According to Accountancy Age's 2005 league table, fee income amongst the Top 50 accounting firms in the UK rose from £6.3bn to £7.0bn. This followed two successive years in which fee income had declined, largely a result of the sale by some of the larger firms of their consultancy arms. As detailed in the next section, fee income in most business areas - audit, tax, corporate finance and consultancy - rose in the 2005 survey, with insolvency and wealth management being the only segments where revenue fell.

PricewaterhouseCoopers remains the largest firm with fee income totalling £1,780m followed by Deloitte (£1,350m), KPMG (£1,066m) and Ernst & Young (£945m). The combined revenue of the Big Four accounted for £5.0bn, 72% of the fee income of the Top 50, down from 78-79% in the years up to the 2002 survey and the third year in succession a decline in their share has occurred (Chart 1). Ernst & Young's fee income is the smallest of the largest four firms, but still over three times that of the next largest firm, Grant Thornton. The amount of fee income tapers off amongst the mid-tier firms so that in total there were only 25 firms that each generated more than £15m of revenue in the 2005 survey.

For more details regarding British qualified accountancy professionals, please refer to the page of British qualified accountants.

## MANAGEMENT ACCOUNTING

Management accounting is concerned with the provisions and use of accounting information to managers within organizations, to provide them with the basis in making informed business decisions that would allow them to be better equipped in their management and control functions. Unlike financial accountancy information (which, for the most part, is public information), management accounting information is used within an organization (typically for decision-making) and is usually confidential and access to which is only available to a select few.

According to CIMA, The Chartered Institute of Management Accountants, Management Accounting is "the process of identification, measurement, accumulation, analysis, preparation, interpretation and communication of information used by management to plan, evaluate and control within an entity and to assure appropriate use of and accountability for its resources. Management accounting also comprises the preparation of financial reports for non management groups such as shareholders, creditors, regulatory agencies and tax authorities" (CIMA Official Terminology)

**Aims**

1. Formulating strategies;
2. Planning and constructing business activities;
3. Making decisions;
4. Well use of resources;
5. Supporting financial reports preparation; and
6. Safeguarding assets.

In the late 1980s, accounting practitioners and educators were heavily criticized on the grounds that management accounting practices (and, even more so, the curriculum taught to accounting students) had changed little over the preceding 60 years, despite radical changes in the business environment. Professional accounting institutes, perhaps fearing that management accountants would increasingly be seen as superfluous in business organizations, subsequently devoted considerable resources to the development of a more innovative skills set for management accountants.

The distinction between 'traditional' and 'innovative' management accounting practices can be illustrated by reference to cost control techniques. Traditionally, management accountants' principal technique was variance analysis, which is a systematic approach to the comparison of the actual and budgeted costs of the raw materials and labour used during a production period.

While some form of variance analysis is still used by most manufacturing firms, it nowadays tends to be used in conjunction with innovative techniques such as life cycle cost analysis and activity-based costing, which are designed with specific aspects of the modern business environment in mind. Lifecycle costing recognizes that managers' ability to influence the cost of manufacturing a product is at its greatest when the product is still at the design stage of its product lifecycle (i.e., before the design has been finalised and production commenced), since small changes to the product design may lead to significant savings in the cost of manufacturing the product. Activity-based costing (ABC) recognizes that, in modern factories, most manufacturing costs are determined by the amount of 'activities' (e.g., the number of production runs per month, and the amount of production equipment idle time) and that the key to effective cost control is therefore optimizing the efficiency of these activities. Activity-based accounting is also known as Cause and Effect accounting.

Both lifecycle costing and activity-based costing recognize that, in the typical modern factory, the avoidance of disruptive events (such as machine breakdowns and quality control failures) is of far greater importance than (for example) reducing the costs of raw materials. Activity-based costing also deemphasizes direct labour as a cost driver and concentrates instead on acitivities that drive costs, such as the provision of a service or the production of a product component.

The most significant recent direction in managerial accounting is throughput accounting, which recognizes the interdependencies of modern production processes and provide managers with a tool that will allow them to measure the contribution per unit of constrained resource for any given product, customer or supplier. (For a detailed description of Throughput Accounting.)

A seldom expressed alternative view of management accounting is that it is neither a neutral or benign influence in organizations, rather a mechanism for management control through surveillance. This view locates management accounting specifically in the context of management control theory.

There are several related professional qualifications in the field of accountancy including:

- Management Accountancy Qualifications
  - CIMA — CMA
  - Institute of Cost and Works Accountants of India
  - AAFM

- Other Professional Accountancy Qualifications
  - Chartered Certified Accountant, (ACCA)
  - Chartered Accountant, (CA)
  - Certified Public Accountant, (CPA)

Accounting Management (Business) is the practical application of management techniques to control and report on the financial health of the organization. This involves the analysis, planning, implementation, and control of programs designed to provide financial data reporting for managerial decision making. This includes the maintenance of bank accounts, developing financial statements, cash flow and financial performance analysis. Accounting management is a mandatory knowledge module of any MBA programme.

Accounting is often referred to as billing management. The goal is to gather usage statistics for users.

Using the statistics the users can be billed and usage quota can be enforced.

Examples:

- Disk usage
- Link utilisation
- CPU time

For non-billed networks, 'Administration' replaces 'Accounting'. The goals of Administration is to administer the set of authorized users, by establishing users, passwords and permissions; and to administer the operations of the equipment such as by performing software backup and synchronization.

**Activity-based Costing**

Activity-based costing (ABC) is a method of allocating costs to products and services. It is generally used as a tool for planning and control. This is a necessary tool for doing value chain analysis.

The concepts of ABC were developed in the manufacturing sector of the U.S. during the 1970s and 80s. During this time, the Consortium for Advanced

Manufacturing-International, now known simply as CAM-I, provided a formative role for studying and formalizing the principles that have become more formally known as Activity-Based Costing. Robin Cooper and Robert Kaplan, proponent of the Balanced Scorecard, brought notice to these concepts in a number of articles published in Harvard Business Review beginning in 1988. Cooper and Kaplan described ABC as an approach to solve the problems of traditional cost management systems. These traditional costing systems are often unable to determine accurately the actual costs of production and of the costs of related services. Consequently managers were making decisions based on inaccurate data especially where there are multiple products.

Instead of using broad arbitrary percentages to allocate costs, ABC seeks to identify cause and effect relationships to objectively assign costs. Once costs of the activities have been identified, the cost of each activity is attributed to each product to the extent that the product uses the activity. In this way ABC often identifies areas of high overhead costs per unit and so directs attention to finding ways to reduce the costs or to charge more for costly products.

Activity-based costing was first clearly defined in 1987 by Robert S. Kaplan and W. Bruns as a chapter in their book Accounting and Management. They initially focused on manufacturing industry where increasing technology and productivity improvements have reduced the relative proportion of the direct costs of labour and materials, but have increased relative proportion of indirect costs. For example increased automation has reduced labour, which is a direct cost, but has increased depreciation, which is an indirect cost.

Traditionally cost accountants had arbitrarily added a broad percentage onto the direct costs to allow for the indirect costs. However as the percentages of overhead costs had risen, this technique became increasingly inaccurate because the indirect costs were not caused equally by all the products. For example one product might take more time in one expensive machine than another product, but since the amount of direct labour and materials might be the same, the additional cost for the use of the machine would not be recognised when the same broad 'on-cost' percentage is added to all products. Consequently, when multiple products share common costs, there is a danger of one product subsidising another.

Like manufacturing industries, financial institutions also have diverse products which can cause cross-product subsidies. Since personnel expenses represent the largest single component of non-interest expense in financial institutions, these costs must also be attributed more accurately to products and customers. Activity based costing, even though developed for manufacturing, can therefore be a useful tool for doing this. This extended use of ABC to financial institutions was presented in 1990 in an article appearing in the Journal of Bank Cost and Management Accounting (Volume 3, Number 2) by Richard Sapp, David Crawford and Steven Rebishcke.

Direct labour and materials are relatively easy to trace directly to products, but it is more difficult to directly allocate indirect costs to products. Where products use common resources differently, some sort of weighting is needed in the cost allocation process. The measure of the use of a shared activity by each of the products is known as the cost driver. For example, the cost of the activity of bank tellers can be ascribed to each product by measuring how long each product's transactions takes at the counter and then by measuring the number of each type of transaction.

Even in activity-based costing, some overhead costs are difficult to assign to products and customers, for example the chief executive's salary. These costs are termed 'business sustaining' and are not assigned to products and customers because there is no meaningful method. This lump of unallocated overhead costs must nevertheless be met by contributions from each of the products, but it is not as large as the overhead costs before ABC is employed.

Although some may argue that costs untraceable to activities should be "arbitrarily allocated" to products, it is important to realize that the only purpose of ABC is to provide information to management. Therefore, there is no reason to assign any cost in an arbitrary manner. Management accountants can be creative in finding other ways to represent these costs on internal reporting statements.

## BUDGETING

Budget generally refers to a list of all planned expenses and revenues. A budget is an important concept in microeconomics, which uses a budget line to illustrate the trade-offs between two or more goods.

A personal budget is among the most important concepts of personal finance. In a personal or family budget all sources of income (inflows) are identified and expenses (outflows) are planned with the intent of matching outflows to inflows (Making ends meet). There are a wide variety of personal budgeting methods and tools that can be employed to help individuals and families with the budgeting process. Also the level of planned finance available to a person, corporation or government, as set by a certain person.

The budget of a government is a summary or plan of the intended revenues and expenditures of that government. In the United States, the federal budget is prepared by the Office of Management and Budget, and submitted to Congress for consideration. Invariably, Congress makes many and substantial changes. Nearly all American states are required to have balanced budgets, but the federal government is allowed to run deficits. In the UK the budget is prepared by the Chancellor of the Exchequer, the second most important member of the government, and must be passed by Parliament. The Parliament seldom makes changes to the budget.

The budget of a company is compiled annually. A finished budget usually requires considerable effort and can be seen as a financial plan for the new financial year. While traditionally the Finance department compiles the company's budget, modern software allows hundreds or even thousands of people in the various departments (operations, human resources, IT etc) to contribute their expected revenues and expenses to the final budget.

If the actual numbers delivered through the financial year turn out to be close to the budget, this will demonstrate that the company understands their business and has been successfully driving it in the direction they had planned. On the other hand, if the actuals diverge wildly from the budget, this sends out an 'out of control' signal and the share

Cost-plus pricing is a pricing method commonly used by firms. It is used primarily because it is easy to calculate and requires little information. There are several varieties, but the common thread in all of them is that you first calculate the cost of the product, then include an additional amount to represent profit. Cost-plus pricing is often used on government contracts, and has been criticized as promoting wasteful expenditures.

**Calculating Price Using the Cost-plus Method**

There are several ways of determining cost, and the profit can be added as either a percentage markup or an absolute amount. One example is:

P = (AVC + FC%) * (1 + MK%)

where:

- P = price
- AVC = average variable cost
- FC% = percentage allocation of fixed costs
- MK% = percentage markup

For example: If variable costs are 30 yen, the allocation to cover fixed costs is 10 yen, and you feel you need a 50% markup then you would charge a price of 60 yen:

$$P = (30 + 10) \cdot (1 + 0.50)$$
$$P = 40 \cdot 1.5$$
$$P = 60$$

An alternative way of doing a similar calculation is:

P = (AVC + FC%) / (1 " MK%)

To make things simpler, some firms, particularly retailers, ignore fixed costs and just use the purchase price paid to their suppliers as the cost term. They indirectly incorporate the fixed cost allocation into the markup percentage. To simplify things even further, sometimes a fixed amount is applied rather than a percentage. This fixed amount is usually determined by head-office to make it easy for franchisees and store managers. This is sometimes referred to as turnkey pricing.

Another variant of cost plus pricing is activity based pricing. This involves being more careful in determining costs. Instead of using arbitrary expense categories when allocating overhead, every activity is linked to the resources it uses.

Cost will need to be recalculated and the percentage markup will likely need to be adjusted as the product goes through its life cycle. This is sometimes referred to as product life cycle pricing, although it is seldom done deliberately or in a planned and organized manner. Price skimming and penetration pricing are also types of product life cycle pricing but they are demand based pricing methods rather cost based.

**Advantages of Cost-plus Pricing**

1. Easy to calculate
2. Minimal information requirements
3. Easy to administer
4. Tends to stabilize markets - insulated from demand variations and competitive factors
5. Insures seller against unpredictable, or unexpected later costs
6. Ethical advantages

**Disadvantages**

1. Tends to ignore the role of consumers
2. Tends to ignore the role of competitors
3. Use of historical accounting costs rather than replacement value
4. Use of "normal" or "standard" output level to allocate fixed costs
5. Inclusion of sunk costs rather than just using incremental costs

6. Ignores opportunity costs
7. Contractors may not focus on performance because the cost is always covered by the client

In microeconomics, Production is simply the conversion of inputs into outputs. It is an economic process that uses resources to create a commodity that is suitable for exchange. This can include manufacturing, storing, shipping, and packaging. Some economists define production broadly as all economic activity other than consumption. They see every commercial activity other than the final purchase as some form of production.

Production is a process, and as such it occurs through time and space. Because it is a flow concept, production is measured as a "rate of output per period of time". There are three aspects to production processes:

1. The quantity of the commodity produced,
2. The form of the good produced,
3. The temporal and spatial distribution of the commodity produced.

A production process can be defined as any activity that increases the similarity between the pattern of demand for goods, and the quantity, form, and distribution of these goods available to the market place.

A production process is efficient if a given quantity of outputs cannot be produced with any less inputs. It is said to be inefficient when there exists another feasible process that, for any given output, uses less inputs. Some economists (in particular Leibenstein) use the term X-efficiency to indicate that production processes tend to be inherently inefficient due to satisficing behaviour. The "rate of efficiency" is simply the amount of (or value of) outputs divided by the amount of (or value of) inputs. If a production process uses 50 units of input (or $5000 worth of inputs) to produce one unit of output it is more efficient than a process that uses 55 units of input (or $5500 worth of inputs) to produce the same level of output. It is said to be 10% more efficient ({55-50}/50=1/10=10%).

The inputs or resources used in the production process are called factors by economists. The myriad of possible inputs are usually grouped into four or five categories. These factors are:

- Raw materials (natural capital)
- Labour services (human capital)
- Capital goods
- Land

Sometimes a fifth category is added, entrepreneurial and management skills, a subcategory of labour services. Capital goods are those goods that have previously undergone a production process. They are previously produced means of production. Some textbooks use "technology" as a factor of production.

In the "long run" all of these factors of production can be adjusted by management. The "short run" however, is defined as a period in which at least one of the factors of production is fixed. A fixed factor of production is one whose quantity cannot readily be changed. Examples include major pieces of equipment, suitable factory space, and key managerial personnel. A variable factor of production is one whose usage rate can be changed easily. Examples include electrical power consumption, transportation services, and most raw material inputs. In the short run, a firm's "scale of operations" determines the maximum number of outputs that can be produced. In the long run, there are no scale limitations.

The total product (or total physical product) of a variable factor of production identifies what outputs are possible using various levels of the variable input. This can be displayed in either a chart that lists the output level corresponding to various levels of input, or a graph that summarizes the data into a "total product curve". The diagram shows a typical total product curve. In this example, output increases as more inputs are employed up until point A. The maximum output possible with this production process is Qm. If there are other inputs used in the process, they are assumed to be fixed.

The average physical product is the total product divided by the number of units of variable input employed. It is the output of each unit of input. If there are 10 employees working on a production process that manufactures 50 units per day, then the average product of variable labour input is 5 units per day.

The average product typically varies as more of the input is employed, so this relationship can also be expresses as a chart or as a graph. A typical average physical product curve is shown (APP). It can be obtained by drawing a vector from the origin to various points on the total product curve and plotting the slopes of these vectors.

The marginal physical product of a variable input is the change in total output due to a one unit change in the variable input (called the discrete marginal product) or alternatively the rate of change in total output due to an infinitesimally small change in the variable input (called the continuous marginal product). The discrete marginal product of capital is the additional output resulting from the use of an additional unit of capital (assuming all other factors are fixed). The continuous marginal product of a variable input can be calculated as the derivative of quantity produced with respect to variable input employed. The marginal physical product curve is shown (MPP). It can be obtained from the slope of the total product curve.

Because the marginal product drives changes in the average product, we know that when the average physical product is falling, the marginal physical product must be less than the average. Likewise, when the average physical product is rising, it must be due to a marginal physical product greater than the average. For this reason, the marginal physical product curve must intersect the maximum point on the average physical product curve.

MPP keeps increasing till it reaches its maximum. Up until this point every additional unit has been adding more value to the total product than the previous one. From this point onwards, every additional unit adds less to the total product compared to the previous one. But the average product is still increasing till MPP touches APP. At this point, an additional unit is adding the same value as the average product. From this point onwards, MPP starts to reduce and so does APP because every additional unit is adding less to APP than the average product. But the total product is still increasing because every additional unit is still contributing positively. Therefore, during this period, both, the average as well as marginal products, are decreasing, but the total product is still increasing. Finally we reach a point when MPP crosses the x-axis. At this point every additional unit starts to diminish the product of previous units, possibly by getting into their way. Therefore the total product starts to decrease at this point. This is point A on the total product curve.

Diminishing returns can be divided into three categories: 1. Diminishing Total returns, which implies reduction in total product with every additional unit of input. This occurs after point A in the graph. 2. Diminishing Average returns, which refers to the portion of the APP curve after its intersection with MPP curve. 3. Diminishing Marginal returns, refers to the point where the MPP curve starts to slope down and travels all the way down to the x-axis and beyond. Putting it in a chronological order, at first the marginal returns start to diminish, then the average returns, followed finally by the total returns.

These curves illustrate the principle of diminishing marginal returns to a variable input (not to be confused with diseconomies of scale which is a long term phenomenon in which all factors are allowed to change). This states that as you add more and more of a variable input, you will reach a point beyond which the resulting increase in output starts to diminish. This point is illustrated as the maximum point on the marginal physical product curve. It assumes that other factor inputs (if they are used in the process) are held constant. An example is the employment of labour in the use of trucks to transport goods. Assuming the number of available trucks (capital) is fixed, then the amount of the variable input labour could be varied and the resultant efficiency determined. At least one labourer (the driver) is necessary. Additional workers per vehicle could be productive in loading, unloading, navigation, or around the clock continuous driving. But at some point the returns to investment in labour will start to diminish and efficiency will decrease. The most efficient distribution of labour per piece of equipment will likely be one driver plus an additional worker for other tasks (2 workers per truck would be more efficient than 5 per truck).

Resource allocations and distributive efficiencies in the mix of capital and labour investment will vary per industry and according to available technology. Trains are able to transport much more in the way of goods with fewer "drivers" but at the cost of greater investment in infrastructure. With the advent of mass production of motorized vehicles, the economic niche occupied by trains (compared with transport trucks) has become more specialized and limited to long haul delivery.

There is an argument that if the theory is holding everything constant, the production method should not be changed, i.e., division of labour should not be practiced. However, the rise in marginal product means that the workers use other means of production method, such as in loading, unloading, navigation, or around the clock continuous driving. For this reason, some economists think that the "keeping other things constant" should not be used in this theory.

The total, average, and marginal physical product curves mentioned above are just one way of showing production relationships. They express the quantity of output relative to the amount of variable input employed while holding fixed inputs constant. Because they depict a short run relationship, they are sometimes called short run production functions. If all inputs are allowed to be varied, then the diagram would express outputs relative to total inputs, and the function would be a long run production function. If the mix of inputs is held constant, then output would be expressed relative to inputs of a fixed composition, and the function would indicate long run economies of scale.

Rather than comparing inputs to outputs, it is also possible to assess the mix of inputs employed in production. An isoquant relates the quantities of one input to the quantities of another input. It indicates all possible combinations of inputs that are capable of producing a given level of output.

Rather than looking at the inputs used in production, it is possible to look at the mix of outputs that are possible for any given production process. This is done with a production possibilities frontier. It indicates what combinations of outputs are possible given the available factor endowment and the prevailing production technology.

You can use a lot of labour with a minimal amount of capital, or you could invest heavily in capital equipment that requires a minimal amount of labour to operate, or any combination in between. For most goods, there are more than just two inputs. For example in agriculture, the amount of land, water, and fertilizer can all be varied to produce different amounts of a crop. An isoquant, in the two input case, is a curve that shows all the ways of combining two inputs so as to produce a given level of output. In the three input case it will be a surface. Iso is Latin for equal and quant is short for quantity. Movement along an isoquant depicts a constant rate of output, but a changing input ratio. A unique isoquant can be constructed for every level of output, and a family of isoquants can be created to represent various output levels. Isoquants further from the origin represent greater amounts of output. Isoquants are usually considered to be everywhere dense, meaning an infinite number of them could be plotted in any two input space.

A typical isoquant is illustrated in the diagram to the right. At point A in the diagram Ka units of capital are combined with La units of labour to produce 100 units of output. It is downward sloping, convex to the origin, and non-intersecting (additional isoquants, not shown, would be drawn parallel to this one). A complete isoquant is actually a closed curve, but only the "down sloping to the right" portion makes economic sense. The upward sloping parts of isoquants, for example, indicate that that level of output could be produced by less of both inputs so this section is of little interest to decision makers. The economic section of the isoquants is defined by a pair of lines called ridge lines.

The "downward to the right" slope of the economic region of an isoquant is due to the possibility of substituting one input for another in the production process while keeping the level of output constant.

Isoquants are typically convex to the origin reflecting the fact that the two factors are substitutable for each other at varying rates. This rate of substitutability is called the "marginal rate of technical substitution" (MRTS) or occasionally the "marginal rate of substitution in production". It measures the reduction in one input per unit increase in the other input that is just sufficient to maintain a constant level of production. For example, the marginal rate of substitution of labour for capital gives the amount of capital that can be replaced by one unit of labour while keeping output unchanged.

To move from point A to point B in the diagram, the amount of capital is reduced from Ka to Kb while the amount of labour is increased only from La to Lb. To move from point C to point D, the amount of capital is reduced from Kc to Kd while the amount of labour is increased from La to Lb. The marginal rate of technical substitution of labour for capital is equivalent to the absolute slope of the isoquant at that point (change in capital divided by change in labour). It is equal to 0 where the isoquant becomes horizontal, and equal to infinity where it becomes vertical.

The opposite is true when going in the other direction. In this case we are looking at the marginal rate of technical substitution capital for labour (which is the reciprocal of the marginal rate of technical substitution labour for capital).

It can also be shown that the marginal rate of substitution labour for capital, is equal to the marginal physical product of labour divided by the marginal physical product of capital.

In the unusual case of two inputs that are perfect substitutes for each other in production, the isoquant would be linear (linear, a straight line, with a function y = a - bx). If, on the other hand, there is only one production process available, factor proportions would be fixed, and these zero-substitutability isoquants would be shown as horizontal or vertical lines.

## FIXED ASSETS MANAGEMENT

Fixed assets management is an accounting process that seeks to track fixed assets for the purposes of financial accounting, preventive maintenance, and theft deterrence.

Many organizations face a significant challenge to track the location, quantity, condition, maintenance and depreciation status of their fixed assets. A popular approach to tracking fixed assets utilizes serial numbered Asset Tags, often with bar codes for easy and accurate reading. Periodically, the owner of the assets can take inventory with a mobile barcode reader and then produce a report.

Off-the-shelf software packages for fixed asset management are marketed to businesses small and large. Some Enterprise Resource Planning systems are available with fixed assets modules.

## FREE CASH FLOW

Free cash flow measures a firm's net increase in

- Cash from operations (this includes the reduction for interest),
- Less the dividends paid to preferred shareholders, and
- Less expenditures necessary to maintain assets.

Increases in non-cash current assets may, or may not be deducted, depending on whether they are considered to be maintaining the status quo, or to be investments for growth.

### Problems with CapX

1. The expenditures for maintenance of assets is only part of the capx reported on the Statement of Cash

Flows. It must be separated from the expenditures for growth purposes. This split is not a requirement under GAAP, and is not audited. Management is free to disclose maintenance capx or not. Therefore this input to the calculation of free cash flow is easy to manipulate. Since it is a very large number, maintenance capx's questionable validity is the basis for some people's dismissal of 'free cash flow'.

2. A second problem with the maintenance capx measurement is its intrinsic 'lumpyness'. By their nature, expenditures for capital assets that will last decades are infrequent, but costly when they occur. 'Free cash flow', in turn, will be very different from year to year. No particular year will be a 'norm' that can be expected to be repeated.

**Uses of the Metric**

1. Free cash flow measures the ease with which businesses can grow and pay dividends to shareholders. Even profitable businesses may have negative cash flows. Their requirement for increased financing will result in increased financing costs reducing future income. It is easier to grow with organic cash flows than with additional financing.
2. According to the discounted cash flow valuation model, the intrinsic value of a company is the present value of all future free cash flows, plus the cash proceeds from its eventual sale. The presumption is that the cash flows are used to pay dividends to the shareholders. Bear in mind the lumpyness discussed above.
3. Some investors prefer using free cash flow instead of net income to measure a company's financial performance, because free cash flow is more difficult to manipulate than net income. The problems with this presumption are itemized at cash flow and return of capital.

4. The payout ratio is a metric used to evaluate the sustainability of distributions from REITs, Oil & Gas Royalty Trusts, and Income Trust. The distributions are divided by the free cash flow. Distributions may include any of income, flowed-through capital gains or return of capital.

This metric is used only by shareholders. Debt holders are not concerned with maintaining the operating capital assets, or with growing the business. Nor are they concerned with taxes paid since their payments come first. The appropriate metric for debt holders is EBITDA.

# Chapter 6

# Managerial Skill Development

## PROFESSIONAL DEVELOPMENT

Professional development often refers to skills required for maintaining a specific career path or to general skills offered through continuing education, including the more general skills area of personal development. It can be seen as training to keep current with changing technology and practices in a profession or in the concept of lifelong learning. Developing and implementing a programme of professional development is often a function of the human resources department of a large corporation or institution.

In a very broad sense professional development may include formal types of vocational education, typically post-secondary or polytechnical training leading to qualification or a credential required to get or retain employment. Informal or individualized programs of professinal development may also include the concept of personal of coaching.

Professional development on the job may develop or enhance process skills, sometimes referred to as leadership skills, as well as task skills. Some examples for process skills are 'effectiveness skills', 'team functioning skills', and 'systems thinking skills'. Some examples of task skills are computer software applications, customer service skills and safety training.

Examples of skills relevant to a current occupation are leadership training for managers and training for specific techniques or equipment for educators, technicians, metal workers, medical practitioners and engineers. For some occupations there is a provision for accreditation tied to "continuing professional education" and proving competence regulated by a professional body.

In the USA, many states have professional development requirements for school teachers (preK-grade 12). For example, in New Jersey, state regulations mandate that all active teachers and educational services personnel in New Jersey complete 100 hours of professional development every five years, consistent with the New Jersey Professional Development Standards. In the state of Florida, instructional personnel must earn 120 inservice hours or 2 college courses every 5 years in each area of certification.

Professional development standards are becoming a legislated mandate in a number of states in the USA. In the state of Florida, each district is reviewed every three years to ensure that professional development meets standards in the areas of planning, delivery, follow-up and evaluation Apprenticeship.

Apprenticeship which is still popular in some countries, is a system of training a new generation of skilled crafts practitioners. Apprentices (or in early modern usage "prentices") build their careers from apprenticeships. Most of their training is done on the job while working for an employer who helps the apprentices learn their trade. Often some informal, theoretical education is also involved.

The system of apprenticeship first developed in the later Middle Ages and came to be supervised by craft guilds and town governments. A master craftsman was entitled to employ young people as an inexpensive form of labour in exchange for providing formal training in the craft. Most apprentices were males, but female apprentices can be found in a number of crafts associated with embroidery, silk-weaving etc. Apprentices were young (usually about fourteen to twenty-one years of age), unmarried and would live in the master craftsman's household. Most apprentices aspired to becoming master craftsmen themselves on completion of their contract (usually a term of seven years), but some would spend time as a journeyman and a significant proportion would never acquire their own workshop.

Subsequently governmental regulation and the licensing of polytechnics and vocational education formalised and bureaucratised the details of apprenticeship.

The modern concept of an internship is similar to an apprenticeship.Universities still use apprenticeship schemes in their production of scholars: bachelors are promoted to masters and then produce a thesis under the oversight and the of a supervisor before the corporate body of the university recognises the reaching of the standard of a doctorate.

Also similar to apprenticeships are the professional development arrangements for new graduates in the professions of accountancy and the law a British example was training contracts known as 'articles of clerkship'.

Apprenticeships have a long tradition in the United Kingdom's education system. In early modern England 'parish' apprenticeships under the Poor Law came to be used as a way of providing for poor children of both sexes alongside the regular system of apprenticeships, which tended to provide for boys from slightly more affluent backgrounds.

In modern times, the system became less and less important, especially as employment in heavy industry and artisan trades declined. Traditional apprenticeships reached their lowest point in the 1970s: by that time, training programmes were rare and people who were apprentices learnt mainly by example. In 1986, National Vocational Qualifications (NVQs) were introduced, in an attempt to revitalise vocational training. Still, by 1990, apprenticeship took up only two-thirds of one percent of total employment.

In 1994, the government introduced Modern Apprenticeships (in England - but not Scotland or Wales - the name was changed to Apprenticeships in 2004), again to try to improve the image of work-based learning and to encourage young people and employers to participate. (Modern) Apprenticeships are based on frameworks devised initially by National Training Organisations and now by their successors, Sector Skills Councils, state-sponsored but supposedly 'employer-led' bodies responsible for defining training requirements in their sector (such as Business Administration or Accounting). Frameworks consist of National Vocational Qualifications, a technical certificate and Key Skills including literacy and numeracy. Those who complete all elements of the framework receive a certificate, but the Apprenticeship is not a discrete qualification.

There are now more than 160 Apprenticeship frameworks (2005). Unlike traditional apprenticeships, the current scheme extends beyond 'craft' and skilled trades to areas of the service sector with no apprenticeship tradition. Employers who participate in the scheme have an employment contract with their apprentices, but off-the-job training and assessment is wholly funded by the state through various agencies - formerly the Training and Enterprise Councils, now the Learning and Skills Council in England or its equivalents in Scotland and Wales. These agencies contract with 'learning providers' who organise and/or deliver training and assessment services to employers. Providers are usually private training companies but might also be Further Education colleges, voluntary sector organisations, Chambers of Commerce or employer 'Group Training Associations'; only about 5 % of apprenticeships are directly contracted with single employers participating in the scheme. There is no minimum time requirement for apprenticeships, although the average time spent completing a framework is roughly 21 months.

In 2000 the Government established the Modern Apprenticeships Advisory Committee (MAAC) to recommend 'how best to ensure that the quality of Modern Apprenticeships fully matches the standards set by leading nations worldwide'. Its 2001 report noted that 'England currently does not have a strong apprenticeships system'; critical weaknesses identified included: declining participation by young people; low completion rates, with only about a third of all apprentices completing their frameworks; and weaknesses in training, assessment and data collection. Many young people and employers were still unaware of exactly what an apprenticeship involved.

Changes recommended by the Committee at first seemed to have little effect: between 2000 and 2003, the number of people starting apprenticeships fell from 76,800 to 47,300. In 2001, just over one fifth of young people under age 22 took up an apprenticeship: of these, only 33% actually completed it, making approximately 7% of young British people under 22 who completed an apprenticeship in 2001. Between 2001/02 and 2004/05, however, the percentage of young people completing apprenticeships rose from 24% to 39% and in 2005 it was announced that the target of getting 28% of 16-21 year olds to start an apprenticeship had been met. Recognising that demand for apprenticeship places exceeds supply from employers, and that many young people, parents and employers still associate apprenticeship with craft trades and manual occupations, the Government developed a major marketing campaign in 2004.

Refinement of the Apprenticeship system continues - in 2005 the Learning and Skills Council, Department for Education and Skills, and Qualifications and Curriculum Authority, together with their equivalents in Wales and the Sector Skills Councils, launched the Apprenticeship Blueprint for England and Wales, which revises and redefines the essential and flexible elements of an apprenticeship framework.

Apprenticeships are part of Germany's successful dual education system, and as such form an integral part of many people's working life. Young people can learn one of 356 (2005) apprenticeship occupations (Ausbildungsberufe), such as Doctor's Assistant, Banker, Dispensing Optician or Oven Builder. The dual system means that apprentices spend most of their time in companies and the rest in formal education. Usually, they work for three to four days a week in the company and then spend one or two days at a vocational school (Berufsschule). These Berufsschulen have been part of the education system since the 19th century.

In 1969, a law (the Berufsausbildungsgesetz) was passed which regulated and unified the vocational training system and codified the shared responsibility of the state, the unions, associations and chambers of trade and industry. The dual system was successful in both parts of divided Germany: in the GDR, three quarters of the working population had completed apprenticeships.

Although the rigid training system of the GDR, linked to the huge collective combines, did not survive reunification, the system remains popular in modern Germany: in 2001, two thirds of young people aged under 22 began an apprenticeship, and 78% of them completed it, meaning that approximately 51% of all young people under 22 have completed an apprenticeship. One in three companies offered apprenticeships in 2003; in 2004 the government signed a pledge with industrial unions that all companies except very small ones must take on apprentices.

The precise skills and theory taught on apprenticeships are strictly regulated, meaning that everyone who has, for example, had an apprenticeship as an Industriekaufmann (someone who works in an industrial company as a personnel assistant or accountant, etc) has learned the same skills and had the same courses in procurement and stocking up, cost and activity accounting, staffing, accounting procedures, production, profit and loss accounting and various other subjects. The employer is responsible for the entire programme; apprentices are not allowed to be employed and have only an apprenticeship contract. The time taken is also regulated; each occupation learnt takes a different time, but the average is 35 months. People who have not taken this apprenticeship are not allowed to call themselves an Industriekaufmann; the same is true for all the 356 occupations.

In France, apprenticeships also developed between the ninth and thirteenth centuries, with guilds structured around apprentices, journeymen and master craftsmen, continuing in this way until 1791, when the guilds were suppressed.

In 1851 the first law on apprenticeships came into force. From 1919, young people had to take 150 hours of theory and general lessons in their subject a year. This minimum training time rose to 360 hours a year in 1961, then 400 in 1986.

The first training centres for apprentices appeared in 1961, and in 1971 apprenticeships were legally made part of professional training. In 1986 the age limit for beginning an apprenticeship was raised from 20 to 25. From 1987 the range of qualifications achieveable through an apprenticeship was widened to include the brevet professionnel, the bac professionnel, the brevet de technicien superieur, engineering diplomas and more.

On January 18, 2005, President Jacques Chirac announced the introduction of a law on a programme for social cohesion comprising the three pillars of employment, housing and equal opportunities. The French government pledged to further develop apprenticeship as a path to success at school and to employment, based on its success: in 2005, 80% of young French people who had completed an apprenticeship entered employment. In France, the term denotes manual labour only. The plan aimed to raise the number of apprentices from 365,000 in 2005 to 500,000 in 2009. To achieve this aim, the government is, for example, granting tax relief for companies when they take on apprentices.

The minister in charge of the campaign, Jean-Louis Borloo, also hoped to improve the image of apprenticeships with an information campaign, as they are often connected with academic failure at school and an ability to grasp only practical skills and not theory. After the civil unrest end of 2005, the government, led by prime minister Dominique de Villepin, announced a new law. Dubbed "law on equality of chances", it created the First Employment Contract as well as manual apprenticeship as soon as 14 years old. From this age, students are allowed to quit the compulsory school system in order to quickly learn a vocation. This measure has long been a revendication of conservative French political parties, and was met by tough opposition from trade unions and students.

Persons interested in learning to become electricians can join one of several apprenticeship programs offered jointly by the International Brotherhood of Electrical Workers and the National Electrical Contractors Association. No background in electrical work is required. A minimum age of 18 is required. There is no maximum age. Men and women are equally invited to participate. The organization in charge of the programme is called the National Joint Apprenticeship and Training Committee.

Apprentice electricians work 37 to 40 hours per week at the trade under the supervision of a journeyman electrician and receive pay and benefits. They spend an additional 6 hours per week in classroom training. At the conclusion of training (5 years for commercial and industrial construction, less for residential construction), apprentices become journeymen (and women). All of this is offered at no charge except for the cost of books which is approximately $200 per year. Persons completing this programme are considered highly skilled by employers and command high pay and benefits.

In the United States, education officials and nonprofit organizations who seek to emulate the apprenticeship system in other nations have created the School to work education reforms. They seek to link academic education to careers. Some programs include job shadowing, watching a real worker for a short period of time, or actually spending significant time at a job at no or reduced pay that would otherwise be spent in academic classes working at a local business. Some legislators raised the issue of child labour laws for unpaid labour or jobs with hazards.

The standards based education reform movement was based on research by the NCEE, headed by Marc Tucker, in Japan, Denmark, Singapore and Germany. The study "America's Choice, High Skills or Low Wages" found that each country has central ministry which requires a standard curriculum that all students must take with no exceptions, and proposed creating internationally-benchmarked standards. All education programs would lead to a skill certificate that "certifies that an individual has mastered occupational skills at levels that are a least as challenging as skill standards endorsed by the National Skills Standards Board". The National Skill Standards Board was set as part of Goals 2000 to match the competencies cited by the Department of Labor's Scans report. Marc Tucker, in "A Human Resources Development Plan for the United States" stated "These new professional and technical certificates and degrees typically are won within three years of acquiring the general education certificate captures all of the essentials of the apprenticeship idea redefines college can access the system through the requirement that their employers spend an amount equal to 1 and 1/2 percent of their salary and wage bill on training leading to national skill certification."

In contrast to the scenario of the NCEE study "America's Choice, High Skills or Low Wages", European students in nations such as Germany are actually tracked by test scores between college-bound, skilled apprenticship, and unskilled labour tracks, rather than held to one uniform passing standard. After elementary school, half of German students are tracked to the Hauptschule for manual trades. At fifteen, students enter a trade school and become apprentices in their chosen professions, graduating with trade certifications at age 18. About one in four are assigned to the Realschule for white-collar jobs in finance or administration, switching to job training at age sixteen. Originally only one quarter of German students attended the Gymnasium which is the college-preparatory high school, which awards the degree of Abitur necessary for a university. Effectively, compared to US comprehensive high schools, apprenticeships essentially end full time academic studies by age sixteen.

In the United States, School to work programs work within the framework of comprehensive high schools which were introduced in the 20th century to educate the entire range of student ability and interest tracks in one learning community, rather than prepare a small number for college. Traditionally this tracked students within a wide choice of courses based on ability with vocational such as auto repair and carpentry tending to be at the lower end of academic ability and college-bound trigonometry and pre-calculus at the upper end.

American education reform seeks to end such tracking, which is seen as a barrier to opportunity. By contrast, the world-class system studied by the NCEE actually relies heavily tracking based on test scores. Education officials in the US, based largely on school redesign proposals by NCEE and other organizations have chosen to use criterion-referenced tests that define one high standard that must be achieved by all students to receive a uniform diploma. In contrast to the German sorting system, US education officials from local to the federal level have made it a goal to eliminate the achievement gap between populations, and the need for remedial classes in college once the belief that all students will pass the standard becomes reality.

Many states are now requiring passing a High school graduation examination to insure that all graduates across all ethnic, gender and income groups will possess the same skills that were previously only required by the college-bound. In states such as Washington which have started the standards based reform process, many have questioned whether this insures success for all, or just creates massive failure, as only half of 10th graders have demonstrated they have passed the standards defined 10 years ago for their diploma. The traditional education system rejected by education officials was based on a rank-order rather than a standards-based definition of success and grade level expected of all students, and gave diplomas to students even if they did not demonstrate meeting high world class academic standards, or aspired to careers which did not require college degrees.

Traditional expectations rejected by the standards movement are that different students will achieve at different levels, and should study different diverse curricula between. The standards based education reform model adopted by most states and school districts since the 1990s is based on the belief that all students will succeed if held to a high standard of what students must know and be able to do, and that all students should have the opportunity to learn the same mathematics and writing skills as the most successful. An important principle of School to work is that all students will participate in school to work programs, and will graduate with skills necessary to job the workforce, rather than using tests to sort students between tracks.

## CAREER MANAGEMENT

Career management is defined by Ball (1997) as:

1. Making career choices and decisions – the traditional focus of careers interventions. The changed nature of work means that individuals may now have to revisit this process more frequently than in the past.
2. Managing the organisational career – concerns the career management tasks of individuals within the workplace, such as decision-making, life-stage transitions, dealing with stress etc.
3. Managing 'boundaryless' careers – refers to skills needed by workers whose employment is beyond the boundaries of a single organisation, a workstyle common among, for example, artists and designers.
4. Taking control of one's personal development – as employers take less responsibility, employees need to take control of their own development in order to maintain and enhance their employability.

Now that the job-for-life covenant between employer and employee has been superseded by an insecure and uncertain job market, career management has become a necessary survival skill rather than being an activity pursued by Ivy League alumni or people born with a silver spoon in the mouth. Job security is now based on knowledge, skills and added-value rather than length of service or loyalty to an employer. Career management is nothing more than a small investment of time, money and energy to protect the major source of revenue—one's job.

## ORGANIZATION DEVELOPMENT

Organization development, according to Richard Beckhard, is defined as:

1. A planned effort...
2. Organization-wide...
3. Managed from the top...
4. To increase organization effectiveness and health...
5. Through planned interventions in the organization's 'processes', using behavioural science knowledge.

According to Warren Bennis, organization development (OD) is a complex strategy intended to change the beliefs, attitudes, values, and structure of organizations so that they can better adapt to new technologies, markets, and challenges.

Warner Burke emphasizes that OD is not just "anything done to better an organization"; it is a particular kind of change process designed to bring about a particular kind of end result. OD involves organizational reflection, system improvement, planning, and self-analysis.

The term "Organization Development" is often used interchangeably with Organizational effectiveness, especially when used as the name of a department or a part of the Human Resources function within an organization.

At the core of OD is the concept of an organization, defined as two or more people working together toward one or more shared goals. Development in this context is the notion that an organization may become more effective over time at achieving its goals.

"OD is a long range effort to improve organization's problem solving and renewal processess, particularly through more effective and collaborative management of organization culture-with specific emphasis on the culture of formal workteams-with the assistance of a change agent or catalyst and the use of the theory and technology of applied behavioral science including action research"

Kurt Lewin is widely recognized as the founding father of OD, although he died before the concept became current in the mid-1950s. From Lewin came the ideas of group dynamics, and action research which underpin the basic OD process as well as providing its collaborative consultant/client ethos. Institutionally, Lewin founded the Research Center for Group Dynamics at MIT, which moved to Michigan after his death. RCGD colleagues were among those who founded the National Training Laboratories (NTL), from which the T-group and group-based OD emerged. In the UK, working as close as was possible with Lewin and his colleagues, the Tavistock Institute of Human Relations was important in developing systems theories. Important too was the joint TIHR journal Human Relations, although nowadays the Journal of Applied Behavioral Sciences is seen as the leading OD journal.

OD is taught in many institutions worldwide, with no one legitimately able to claim to be the center of OD training. Leading institutions include the The Johns Hopkins University, Tavistock Institute of Human Relations, American University, Benedictine University that offers the only PhD programme in OD, Bowling Green State University, Case Western Reserve University, Claremont Graduate University, Fielding Graduate University, Pepperdine, Phillips Graduate Institute, the University of Southern California, Alliant International University, Sheffield Hallam University in England, the University of Monterrey in Monterrey, Mexico and Assumption University of Thailand.

## ORGANIZATIONAL EFFECTIVENESS

Organizational effectiveness is the concept of how effective an organization is in achieving the outcomes the organization intends to produce. The idea of organizational effectiveness is especially important for non-profit organizations as most people who donate money to non-profit organizations and charities are interested in knowing whether the organization is effective in accomplishing its goals.

An organization's effectiveness is also dependent on an its communicative competence and ethics. The relationship between these three are simultaneous. Ethics is a foundation found within organizational effectivenss. An organization must exemplify respect, honesty, integrity and equity to allow communicative competence with the participating members. Along with ethics and communicative competence, members in that particular group can finally achieve their intended goals.

Foundations and other sources of grants and other types of funds are interested in organzational effectiveness of those people who seek funds from the foundations. Foundations always have more requests for funds or funding proposals and treat funding as an investment using the same care as a venture capitalist would in picking a company in which to invest.

Organizational effectiveness is an abstract concept and is basically impossible to measure. Instead of measuring organizational effectiveness, the organization determines proxy measures which will be used to represent effectiveness. Proxy measures used may include such things as number of people served, types and sizes of population segements served, and the demand within those segments for the services the organization supplies.

For instance, a non-profit organization which supplies meals to house bound people may collect statistics such as the number of meals cooked and served, the number of volunteers delivering meals, the turnover and retention rates of volunteers, the demographics of the people served, the turnover and retention of consumers, the number of requests for meals turned down due to lack of capacity (amount of food, capacity of meal preparation facilities, and number of delivery volunteers), and amount of wastage. Since the organization has as its goal the preparation of meals and the delivery of those meals to house bound people, it measures its organizational effectiveness by trying to determine what actual activities the people in the organization do in order to generate the outcomes the organization wants to create.

Activities such as fundraising or volunteer training are important because they provide the support needed for the organization to deliver its services but they are not the outcomes per se. These other activities are overhead activities which assist the organization in achieving its desired outcomes.

The term Organizational Effectiveness is often used interchangeably with Organization Development, especially when used as the name of a department or a part of the Human Resources function within an organization.

## ORGANIZATIONAL COMMITMENT

In the study of organizational behaviour, organizational commitment is the employee's psychological attachment to the organization. It can be contrasted with other work-related attitudes, such as Job Satisfaction (an employee's feelings about their job) and Organizational Identification (the degree to which an employee experiences a 'sense of oneness' with their organization).

Organizational scientists have developed many definitions of organizational commitment, and numerous scales to measure them. Exemplary of this work is Meyer & Allen's model of commitment, which was developed to integrate numerous definitions of commitment that had proliferated in the research literature. According to Meyer and Allen's (1991) three-component model of commitment, prior research indicated that there are three "mind sets" which can characterize an employee's commitment to the organization:

- Affective Commitment: AC is defined as the employee's emotional attachment to the organization. As a result, he or she strongly identifies with the goals of the organization and desires to remain a part of the organization. This employee commits to the organization because he/she "wants to". In developing this concept, Meyer and Allen drew largely on Mowday, Porter, and Steers's (1982) concept of commitment.
- Continuance Commitment: The individual commits to the organization because he/she perceives high costs

of losing organizational membership (cf. Becker's 1960 "side bet theory"), including economic losses (such as pension accruals) and social costs (friendship ties with co-workers) that would have to be given up. The employee remains a member of the organization because he/she "has to".

- Normative Commitment: The individual commits to and remains with an organization because of feelings of obligation. For instance, the organization may have invested resources in training an employee who then feels an obligation to put forth effort on the job and stay with the organization to 'repay the debt.' It may also reflect an internalized norm, developed before the person joins the organization through family or other socialization processes, that one should be loyal to one's organization. The employee stays with the organization because he/she "ought to".

Note that according to Meyer and Allen, these components of commitment are not mutually exclusive: an employee can simultaneously be committed to the organization in an affective, normative, *and* continuance sense, at varying levels of intensity. This idea led Meyer and Herscovitch to argue that at any point in time, an employee has a "commitment profile" that reflects high or low levels of all three of these mind-sets, and that different profiles have different effects on workplace behaviour such as job performance, absenteeism, and the chance that they will quit.

Meyer and Allen developed the Affective Commitment Scale (ACS), the Normative Commitment Scale (NCS) and the Continuance Commitment Scale (CCS) to measure these components of commitment. Many researchers have used them to determine what impact an employee's level of commitment has on outcomes such as quitting behaviour, job performance, and absenteeism. However, some researchers have questioned how well these scales actually assess an employee's commitment.

In addition to methodological investigations of the validity and reliability of these scales, recent research has focused on determining the cross-cultural validity of Meyer and Allen's measures (do employees in other countries/ cultures experience commitment the same way as employees in the USA?), and on expanding the three-component model to other foci (such as commitment to one's occupation, department, organization change initiatives, and work team.

# Chapter 7

# Managing Change

## CHANGE MANAGEMENT

Change management can take many forms and include many change environments. The most common usage to the term refers to organizational change management.

Organizational change management is the process of developing a planned approach to change in an organization. Typically the objective is to maximize the collective benefits for all people involved in the change and minimize the risk of failure of implementing the change. The discipline of change management deals primarily with the human aspect of change, and is therefore related to pure and industrial psychology.

Many technical disciplines (for example Information technology) have developed similar approaches to formally control the process of making changes to environments.

Change management can be either 'reactive', in which case management is responding to changes in the macroenvironment (that is, the source of the change is external), or proactive, in which case management is initiating the change in order to achieve a desired goal (that is, the source of the change is internal). Change management can be conducted on a continuous basis, on a regular schedule (such as an annual review), or when deemed necessary on a programme-by-programme basis.

Change management can be approached from a number of angles and applied to numerous organizational processes.

Its most common uses are in information technology management, strategic management, and process management. To be effective, change management should be multi-disciplinary, touching all aspects of the organization. However, at its core, implementing new procedures, technologies, and overcoming resistance to change are fundamentally human resource management issues.

Attitudes towards change result from a complex interplay of emotions and [cognitive] processes. Because of this complexity everyone reacts to change differently. On the positive side, change is seen as akin to opportunity, rejuvenation, progress, innovation, and growth. But just as legitimately, change can also be seen as akin to instability, upheaval, unpredictability, threat, and disorientation. Whether employees perceive change with fear, anxiety and demoralization, or with excitement and confidence, or somewhere in between, depends partially on the individual's psychological makeup, partially on management's actions, and partially on the specific nature of the change.

An early model of change developed by Kurt Lewin (1951) described change as a three-stage process. The first stage he called "unfreezing". It involved overcoming inertia and dismantling the existing "mind set". Defense mechanisms have to be bypassed. In the second stage the change occurs. This is typically a period of confusion. We are aware that the old ways are being challenged but we do not have a clear picture to replace them with yet. The third and final stage he called "refreezing". The new mind set is crystallizing and one's comfort level is returning to previous levels.

The ADKAR model developed by Jeff Hiatt for individual change management presents five building blocks that an individual must obtain to realize change successfully. These include awareness, desire, knowledge, ability and reinforcement. It is management's job to create an environment in which people can go through these stages as quickly as possible, including:

- Building awareness of why the change is needed
- Creating desire to support and participate in the change
- Developing knowledge of how to change
- Fostering ability to implement new skills and behaviors
- Providing reinforcements to sustain the change

Organizations are ruled by laws of complexity (The systemic/complexity principle) Emerging evidence from systems thinking and complexity science indicates that large systems show a different behaviour from their single parts. System theory talks about organizations as "non-trivial machines" (like the human body, etc.), whose behaviour cannot be predicted or calculated by a computer. These new sciences are applied to organizational development and change, for example in Appreciative Inquiry, Open Space Technology, Systemic Constellations, etc.

Most of our day-to-day assumptions are still based on classical Newtonian mechanics, which usually are applied to working with organizations. For example, most people would assume that if A is true, B is false. There is a growing number of thinkers who relate change in organizations to Quantum Mechanics, which teaches us that if A is true, B is equally true - just another side of the coin -, and that A could not exist without B. Observers (or consultants, or leaders) are always part of a field, which they influence but by which they are influenced themselves instantly. Some examples for the application of Quantum Mechanics to Change Management: - Process Oriented Psychology by Arnold Mindell, talks about the field in which each human relationship exists. Its application field, Worldwork, intends to transform systems by shifting roles that people unconsciously hold in a system. - Dialogue (by David Bohm) is a new form of communication in large groups which is based on the suspension of assumptions, thus letting the common knowledge of 'container' emerge. - Appreciative Inquiry, one of the most frequently applied approaches to organizational change, is partly based on the assumption that change in a system is instantanously ('Change at the Speed of Imagination')

**Key Concepts**

Below are several well known concepts in which the Change Management practice is rooted. There is some overlapping in these concepts and its practice, the tools derived from these ideas are often used interchangeably.

- Process Oriented Psychology
- Theme Centred Interaction
- Transactional Analysis
- Systems Thinking / Family Therapy
- Neurolinguistic Programming
- Communication Theory
- Whole Systems Change
- Total Quality Management
- ADKAR (a model used in Change management that connects organizational change management to individual change management).
- Change Management Excellence: Putting NLP to Work

The Formula for Change was developed by Richard Beckhard and David Gleicher and is sometimes referred to as Gleicher's Formula. The Formula illustrates that the combination of organisational dissatisfaction, vision for the future and the possibility of immediate, tactical action must be stronger than the resistance within the organisation in order for meaningful change to occur.

Management's first responsibility is to detect trends in the macroenvironment so as to be able to identify changes and initiate programs. It is also important to estimate what impact a change will likely have on employee behaviour patterns, work processes, technological requirements, and motivation. Management must assess what employee reactions will be and craft a change programme that will provide support as workers go through the process of accepting change. The programme must then be implemented, disseminated throughout the organization, monitored for effectiveness, and adjusted where necessary.

In general terms, a change programme should:

- Describe the change process to all people involved and explain the reasons why the changes are occurring. The information should be complete, unbiased, reliable, transparent, and timely.
- Be designed to effectively implement the change while being aligned with organizational objectives, macroenvironmental trends, and employee perceptions and feelings.
- Provide support to employees as they deal with the change, and wherever possible involve the employees directly in the change process itself.
- Be consistently monitored and reviewed for effectiveness. A successful change management project is typically also a flexible project.

Proper management of change to industrial facilities and processes is recognized as critical to safety, since complex processes can be very sensitive to even small changes. In the US, OSHA has regulations that govern how changes are to be made and documented. The main requirement is that a thorough review of a proposed change be performed by a multi-disciplinary team to ensure that as many possible viewpoints are used as possible to minimize the chances of missing a hazard. Change management in this context is referred to as Management of Change. Management of change is just one component of Process Safety Management. There were several large industrial accidents in the 60s and 70s that could be seen as the impetus for this regulation. As other examples, poor change management most likely played a part in the plane crash that killed John Denver, and was questioned in modifications to the fishing vessel in the book The Perfect Storm that may have made the ship less stable.

## QUALITY

Quality can refer to:

1. A specific characteristic of an object (the qualities of ice - i.e. its properties)
2. The achievement or excellence of an object (good quality ice - i.e. not of inferior grade)
3. The essence of an object (the quality of ice - i.e. "iceness")
4. The meaning of excellence itself

The first meaning is technical, the second practical, the third artistic and the fourth metaphysical. All four meanings, and therefore the meaning of quality, are synonymous with good.

Philosophy and common sense tend to see quality as related either to subjective feelings or to objective facts. The subject-object in question might be a concrete and functional (e.g. Arisotelian) value to be learnt and applied (a and b), or a psychic (e.g. platonic) ideal to be apprehended and represented (c). A third view tends to see quality not as a secondary value that something has, rather a primary truth which comprises apparent subjects and objects (d).

So the quality of something depends on the criteria being applied to it. Something might be good because it is useful, because it is beautiful, or simply because it exists. Determining or finding quality therefore involves an understanding of use, beauty and existence - what is useful, what is beautiful and what exists.

Many different techniques and concepts have evolved to improve product or service quality, including SPC, Zero Defects, Six Sigma, quality circles, TQM, Theory of Constraints (TOC),Quality Management Systems (ISO 9000 and others) and continuous improvement.

The meaning for the term quality has developed over time. Various interpretations are given below:

1. "degree to which a set of inherent characteristic fulfils requirements" as ISO 9000.
2. "Conformance to requirements" (Philip B. Crosby in the 1980s). The difficulty with this is that the requirements may not fully represent what the customer wants; Crosby treats this as a separate problem.
3. "Fitness for use". Fitness is defined by the customer.
4. A two-dimensional model of quality. The quality has two dimensions: "must-be quality" and "attractive quality". The former is near to the "fitness for use" and the latter is what the customer would love, but has not yet thought about. Supporters characterise this model more succinctly as: "Products and services that meet or exceed customers' expectations". One writer believes that this is today the most used interpretation for the term quality.
5. "Value to some person"

   "Costs go down and productivity goes up, as improvement of quality is accomplished by better management of design, engineering, testing and by improvement of processes. Better quality at lower price has a chance to capture a market. Cutting costs without improvement of quality is futile."
6. Energy quality, associated with both the energy engineering of industrial systems and the qualitative differences in the trophic levels of an ecosystem.
7. One key distinction to make is there are two common applications of the term Quality as form of activity or function within a business. One is Quality Assurance which is the "prevention of defects", such as the deployment of a Quality Management System and preventative activities like FMEA. The other is Quality Control which is the "detection of defects", most commonly associated with testing which takes place withn a Quality Management System typically referred to as Verification and Validation.

The quality of a product or service refers to the perception of the degree to which the product or service meets the customer's expectations. Quality has no specific meaning unless related to a specific function and/or object. Quality is a perceptual, conditional and somewhat subjective attribute. The dimensions of quality refer to the attributes that quality achieves in Operations Management

In the manufacturing industry it is commonly stated that "Quality drives productivity". Improved productivity is a source of greater revenues, employment opportunities and technological advances. Most discussions of quality refer to a finished part, wherever it is in the process. Inspection, which is what quality insurance usually means, is historical, since the work is done. The best way to think about quality is in process control. If the process is under control, inspection is not necessary.

## EMPLOYMENT PLANNIMG

Employment is a contract between two parties, one being the employer and the other being the employee. An employee may be defined as: "A person in the service of another under any contract of hire, express or implied, oral or written, where the employer has the power or right to control and direct the employee in the material details of how the work is to be performed."

In a commercial setting, the employer conceives of a productive activity, generally with the intention of creating profits, and the employee contributes labour to the enterprise, usually in return for payment of wages. Employment also exists in the public, non-profit and household sectors.

In the United States, the "standard" employment contract is considered to be at-will meaning that the employer and employee are both free to terminate the employment at any time and for any cause, or for no cause at all. However, if a termination of employment by the employer is deemed unjust by the employee, there can be legal recourse to challenge such a termination. In unionised work environments in particular, employees who are receiving discipline, up to and including termination of employment can ask for assistance by their shop steward to advocate on behalf of the employee. If an informal negotiation between the shop steward and the company does not resolve the issue, the shop steward may file a grievance, which can result in a resolution within the company, or mediation or arbitration, which are typically funded equally both by the union and the company. In non-union work environments, in the United States, unjust termination complaints can be brought to the United States Department of Labour. In the Canadian province of Ontario, formal complaints can be brought to the Ministry of Labour.

To the extent that employment or the economic equivalent is not universal, unemployment exists. Employment is almost universal in capitalist societies. Opponents of capitalism such as Marxists oppose the capitalist employment system, considering it to be unfair that the people who contribute the majority of work to an organization do not receive a proportionate share of the profit. However, the surrealist and the situationist movements were among the few groups to actually oppose work, and during the partially surrealist-influenced events of May 1968 the walls of the Sorbonne were covered with anti-work graffiti.

Labourers often talk of "getting a job", or "having a job". This conceptual metaphor of a "job" as a possession has led to its use in slogans such as "money for jobs, not bombs". Similar conceptions are that of "land" as a possession (real estate) or intellectual rights as a possession (intellectual property). The Online Etymology Dictionary explains that the origin of "job" is from the obsolete phrase "jobbe of work" in the sense of "piece of work", and most dictionaries list the Middle English "gobbe" meaning "lump" (gob) as the origin of "jobbe". Attempts to link the word to the biblical character Job seem to be folk etymology.

An employer is a person or institution that hires employees or workers. Employers offer wages or a salary to the workers in exchange for the worker's labour power, depending upon whether the employee is paid by the hour or a set rate per pay period. A salaried employee is typically not paid more for more hours worked than the minimum, whereas wages are paid for all hours worked, including overtime.

Employers include everything from individuals hiring a babysitter to governments and businesses which may hire many thousands of employees. In most western societies governments are the largest single employers, but most of the work force is employed in small and medium businesses in the private sector.

Note that although employees may contribute to the evolution of an enterprise, the employer maintains autonomous control over the productive base of land and capital, and is the entity named in contracts. The employer typically also maintains ownership of intellectual property created by an employee within the scope of employment and as a function thereof. These are known as "works for hire".

Within large organisations, the management of employees is often handled by Human Resources departments at "arm's length". Hiring, discipline and terminations are typically rendered by the HR department, whereas supervisors and managers of individual departments provide instructions concerning daily activities, goals, etc. On the national scale, employers can be organised within employers' organisations. Employees can be organised in trade unions or in trade associations, such as the Construction Specifications Institute, which represents specification writers.

An employee contributes labour and expertise to an endeavour. Employees perform the discrete activity of economic production. Of the three factors of production, employees usually provide the labour.

Specifically, an employee is any person hired by an employer to do a specific "job".eg cleners In most modern economies the term employee refers to a specific defined relationship between an individual and a corporation, which differs from those of customer, or client. Most individuals attain the status of employee after a thorough process of interviews with several departments within a company. If the individual is determined to be a satisfactory fit for the position, he is given an official offer of employment within that company for a defined starting salary and position. This individual then has all the rights and privileges of an employee, which may include medical benefits and vacation days. The relationship between a corporation and its employees is usually handled through the human resources department, which handles the incorporation of new hires, and the disbursement of any benefits which the employee may be entitled, or any grievances that employee may have. An offer of employment, however, does not guarantee employment for any length of time and each party may terminate the relationship at any time. This is referred to as at will employment. While the terms accountant, lawyer and photographer might refer to professions, they are not employee titles, which may include Controller, Vice President of Legal Affairs, and Head of Media Development.

There are differing classifications of workers within a company. Some are full-time and permanent and receive a guaranteed salary, while others are hired for short term contracts or work as temps or consultants. These latter differ from permanent employees in that the company where they work is not their employer, but they may work through a temp-agency or consulting firm. In this respect, it is important to distinguish independent contractors from employees, since the two are treated differently both in law and in most taxation systems.

Some companies feel that a happier work force is a better one and thus offer extra benefits to improve team spirit and performance. However, other employers try to increase profits by giving low wages and few benefits. To resist this, employees can organize into labor unions (American English), or trade unions (British English), who represent most of the available work force and must therefore be listened to by the management. This can lead to considerable ill-will and sometimes even violence between the two sides, but it can also lead to a peaceful and prosperous society, especially in countries in which the government plays an active mediator role in collective bargaining. This has helped produce prosperous economies in many countries due to the employees' increased spending power. Collective bargaining has in addition proved to be a powerful conflict resolution tool that has also enabled social dialog.

Associate is a term used by some companies instead of employee. Big box retailers like Wal-Mart and Home Depot, for example, use this term for non-management employees. Other firms use terms such as teammate or team member instead of employee.

Many companies further classify employees as exempt or non-exempt. This designation is used to separate employees that are eligible for overtime from those that are not. An exempt employee is one that is typically salaried and is not eligible to earn overtime. Non-exempt employees are typically paid hourly and are eligible for overtime pay.

When an individual entirely owns the business for which he or she labours, this is known as self-employment. If a self-employed individual has only one client for whom he or she performs work, he or she may be considered an employee of that client for tax purposes. Self-employment often leads to incorporation. Incorporation offers certain protections of one's personal assets. Laws of incorporation vary from state to state with California having the most incorporated businesses of any state in the U.S.

Workers who are not paid wages, such as volunteers, are generally not considered as being employed. One exception to this is an internship, an employment situation in which the worker receives training or experience (and possibly college credit) as the chief form of compensation.

Someone who works under obligation for the purpose of fulfilling a debt without pay is known as a slave and slaveowners are also not considered employers. Some historians suggest that slavery is older than employment, but both arrangements have existed for all recorded history.

## CUSTOMER SERVICE

Customer service is the provision of labour and other resources, for the purpose of increasing the value that buyers receive from their purchases and from the processes leading up to the purchase. With the rising dominance of the service sector in the global economy, customer service has grown in importance, as its impact on individuals, households, firms, and societies has become widespread.

The modern concept of customer service has its roots in the craftsman economy of the 1800s, when individuals and small groups of manufacturers competed to produce arts and crafts to meet public demand. In the 1970s, international competition increased, and producers responded by improving the quality of their products and services.

The overall quality of customer service - in society and in specific industries - will continue to be determined by the relative balance of power between suppliers and consumers; it will improve as competition becomes more intense, and decline as competition decreases.

### Strategic Advantage

A company can outperform rivals only if it can establish a difference that it can preserve. Customer service can be such a difference. It is very difficult to control, and therefore difficult to imitate. It is difficult to control because of its variability. The level of service may vary greatly between two providers in the same organization. It may also vary from one moment to another, even as delivered by the same provider. The difficulty is compounded in multi-unit operations: in addition to variability within units, there is also variability among units.

That is both the challenge and the opportunity. The consistent delivery of superior service requires the careful design and execution of a whole system of activities that includes people, capital, technology, and processes. The few companies that can manage this system do stand out, and are sought out. This is the foundation of their sustainable competitive advantage.

For an organization's members to deliver superior service consistently, they must be acculturated, i.e. instilled with the values, traits, patterns, and behaviors associated with a service culture. The mechanisms of this acculturation include recruitment, training, empowerment, and accountability, within the framework of an organization's ideology of service.

An organization's ideology comprises its purpose (Why are we here?) and values (What do we stand for?). Organizations renowned for providing excellent customer service have typically defined their purpose in terms of service – to serve their customers, and to serve their members. Their values typically include integrity, trustworthiness, reliability, personal responsibility, industriousness, continuous improvement, respect, and consistency.

Training is focused on enabling personnel to deliver service in a manner that is beneficial to both the organization's customers, and to itself.

Technology has made available a wide range of very powerful customer service tools. They range from support websites and the ability to have live chats with technical staff to databases tracking individual customers' preferences, pattern of buying, payment methods etc., and tailoring products and service responses based on this advanced data. Specialist software that is designed for the tracking of service levels and for helping recognize areas for improvement are often integrated into other enterprise operational software tools such as ERP software.

Whereas outstanding service organizations allow their people to make mistakes and learn from their failures, there is little or no tolerance for violations of its core service values. People who do not fit into the culture are removed.

Delivering customer service begins with understanding what customers want. And this understanding begins with the understanding that they do not always know what they want, or why they want it. Traditional market research assumes that they do. Newer methods recognize that as much as 95% of our decision making is subconscious.

Common research methods (e.g., surveys and focus groups) reveal what customers think their motivations are, rather than what their motivations truly are. When respondents do not comprehend their true motivations, they tend to state how they think they ought to be motivated. Recent progress in neuroscience and in observational technologies have yielded more reliable, less biased results. Companies have Interaction Designers that use User Centred Design methods, among others, to understand what customers need. They often use Personas to represent the research outcomes i.e., to describe the customer they are designing for.

In a competitive environment, however, satisfaction may not be enough. To stay in business, firms must provide at least as much satisfaction as their competitors. Moreover, firms that aim to gain profitable growth must increase the number of their customers while reducing the cost of customer acquisition. This is particularly true of companies that compete in mature industries. The objective then is not merely to satisfy customers, but to convert them into promoters (customers who recommend a company to others). Promoters serve to increase a firm's clientele, without increasing its cost of acquisition – i.e. with no additional marketing or promotional expense.

But customers do not make recommendations lightly. When they make a recommendation, they put their own reputations on the line. Firms must earn that recommendation through the consistent delivery of outstanding customer service.

Customer experience management (CEM) is "the process of strategically managing a customer's entire experience with a product or a company".

Marketing research has shown that about 70 to 80% of all products are perceived as commodities, that is, seen as being more-or-less the same as competing products. This makes marketing the product difficult. Marketers have taken various approaches to this problem including: branding, product differentiation, market segmentation, and relationship marketing.

Relationship marketing, (also called loyalty marketing) focuses on establishing and building a long term relationship between a company and a customer. There are several approaches that have been espoused including customer experience management, customer relationship management, loyalty programs, and database marketing.

The development of customer experience management originally started with a critique of three existing marketing concepts. It concluded that the following three concepts do not go far enough:

- Marketing concept—Since the 1970s there has been a gradual shift from a product-, technology-, and sales-focused orientation towards a customer- and market-oriented approach by determining the wants and needs of customers and satisfying them more efficiently or effectively as compared to competitors. However, the approach is still mostly functional, with similarities and differences between competitors being defined mostly by product features and customer benefits. In addition, the customer is perceived as being rational, which is in most cases not the case, as e.g. Kahneman and Tversky's Prospect theory has proven. Also, it is asserted that market research is mostly analytical leaving little room for qualitative assessments of customer relationships towards products, services, or brands. It is claimed (by Shultz) that traditional marketing, in practice, takes an inside-out approach (starting with internal variables like production capabilities and available capital then moving to external variables like customer needs), rather than taking an outside-in approach as marketing theory requires.
- Customer relationship management is claimed to be deficient because it primarily consists of database and software programs used in call centers and thus, focuses too much on quantitative data. By doing this, it is led by transactions rather than a desire to build lasting relationships with customers.

- Customer satisfaction is an outcome-oriented attitude deriving from customers who compare the performance or value of the product with their expectations of it. It is claimed that the customer satisfaction approach depends too heavily on outcome oriented measures like satisfaction and too superficially on direct experiential measures. A customer is said to be satisfied when a product's performance is above the customer's expectations. Thus, traditional customer satisfaction techniques are deficient if they don't help firms to understand and manage customers' experiences, experiences that lead to the following equation: good experience = satisfaction.

CEM recognizes, as does all of marketing since the early 1970s, that customers are a company's most valuable asset. What makes CEM different from traditional marketing is that it claims that marketing theory has seldom been implemented adequately.

CEM is a methodology that tries to overcome the gap between theory and practice by reformulating basic marketing principles. The result is that CEM stresses four aspects of marketing management :

- CEM focuses on all sorts of customer-related issues
- CEM combines the analytical and the creative
- CEM considers both, strategy and implementation
- CEM operates internally and externally

Although all marketing management and strategic management does all of these, CEM supporters claim that they have a methodology that will yield better results. Being convinced that the marketing concept is too product-centered, Customer relationship management too focused on quantitative data, and customer satisfaction too functional, CEM looks for another perspective on the relationship of a consumer with a product or service. And what's key? The experience linked to it is the key. This enables companies to

strategically manage a customer's experience with a brand and by doing so, achieve a truly customer focused management concept.

To accomplish this, a framework is required based on clearly defined company objectives. Schmitt's book "Customer Experience Management" offers the following five step framework that should help managers understand and manage the "customer experience":

Step 1: Analyzing the Experiential world of the customer

- Analyze sociocultural context of the customer (needs/ wants/lifestyle)
- Analyze business concept (requirements/solutions)

Step 2: Building the Experiential platform

- Connection between strategy and implementation
- Specifies the value that the customer can expect from the product (EVP = experiential value promise)

Whereas steps 1 (Analysis) and 2 (Strategy) form the basis for CEM, steps 3, 4, and 5 are focusing on Implementation.

Step 3: Designing the Brand experience

- Experiential features, product aesthetics, "look and feel", e.g. logos

Step 4: Structuring the Customer interface

- All sorts of dynamic exchanges and contract points with customers
- Intangible elements (i.e. value, attitude, behaviour)

Step 5: Engaging in Continuous Experiential innovation

- Anything that improves end customers' personal lives and business customers' working lives

And finally, to bring all pieces together, a holistic approach is required that provides a linkage between the different steps and connects them with the organization.

Organizing for CEM includes three tasks:

- Financial planning of CEM in terms of customers - CEM's ultimate goal is a fair and mutually beneficial long-term business relationship between a company and its customers. Customers will reward the company financially by doing business with it. The value of the customer to the firm, referred to as customer equity, will increase, and the company will grow and be profitable.

- Allocation of organizational resources - Improving the customer experience, and thus increasing customer equity, requires internal resources. The company needs to ask what financial, structural, and personnel resources it needs to engage in CEM to deliver an ongoing desirable experience to customers. Resources must be allocated to the brand experience, the customer interface, and innovation.
- Enhancement of the employee experience - The concept of experience applies also to the internal customers, the company's employees. What all employees, across all levels, get from an experience-oriented organization is a more rewarding employee experience that includes a new form of professional and personal development. Employees of such an organization live a more experiential and thus more satisfying and productive life. They are also more motivated and capable of delivering a great experience to customers.

## CUSTOMER RELATIONSHIP MANAGEMENT

Customer relationship management (CRM) covers methods and technologies used by companies to manage their relationships with clients. Information stored on existing customers (and potential customers) is analyzed and used to this end. Automated CRM processes are often used to generate automatic personalized marketing based on the customer information stored in the system.

Customer relationship management is a corporate level strategy, focusing on creating and maintaining relationships with customers. Several commercial CRM software packages

are available which vary in their approach to CRM. However, CRM is not a technology itself, but rather a holistic approach to an organisation's philosophy, placing the emphasis firmly on the customer.

CRM governs an organization's philosophy at all levels, including policies and processes, front-of-house customer service, employee training, marketing, systems and information management. CRM systems are integrated end-to-end across marketing, sales, and customer service.

A CRM system should:

- Identify factors important to clients.
- Promote a customer-oriented philosophy
- Adopt customer-based measures
- Develop end-to-end processes to serve customers
- Provide successful customer support
- Handle customer complaints
- Track all aspects of sales
- Create a holistic view of customers' sales & services information

There are three fundamental components in CRM:

- Operational - automation of basic business processes (marketing, sales, service)
- Analytical - analysis of customer data and behaviour using business intelligence
- Collaborative - communicating with clients

Operational CRM provides automated support to "front office" business processes (sales, marketing and service). Each interaction with a customer is generally added to a customer's history, and staff can retrieve information on customers from the database as necessary.

According to Gartner Group, operational CRM typically involves three general areas:

**Sales Force Automation (SFA) or Sales Force Management Systems**

These automate some of a company's critical sales and sales force management tasks, such as forecasting, sales administration, tracking customer preferences and demographics, performance management, lead management, account management, contact management and quote management.

**Customer Service and Support (CSS)**

CSS automates certain service requests, complaints, product returns and enquiries.

**Enterprise Marketing Automation (EMA)**

EMA provides information about the business environment, including information on competitors, industry trends, and macroenvironmental variables. EMA applications are used to improve marketing efficiency.

Integrated CRM software is often known as a "front office solution", as it deals directly with customers.

Many call centers use CRM software to store customer information. When a call is received, the system displays the associated customer information (determined from the number of the caller). During and following the call, the call center agent dealing with the customer can add further information.

Some customer services can be fully automated, such as allowing customers to access their bank account details online or via a WAP phone.

Analytical CRM analyses data (gathered as part of operational CRM, or from other sources) in an attempt to identify means to enhance a company's relationship with its clients. The results of an analysis can be used to design targeted marketing campaigns, for example:

- Acquisition: Cross-selling, up-selling
- Retention: Retaining existing customers (antonym: customer attrition)

- Information: Providing timely and regular information to customers

Other examples of the applications of analyses include:

- Contact optimization
- Evaluating and improving customer satisfaction
- Optimizing sales coverage
- Fraud detection
- Financial forecasts
- Price optimization
- Product development
- Programme evaluation
- Risk assessment and management
- Strategic Marketing
- Operational marketing

Data collection and analysis is viewed as a continuing and iterative process. Ideally, business decisions are refined over time, based on feedback from earlier analyses and decisions. Most analytical CRM projects use a data warehouse to manage data.

Collaborative CRM focuses on the interaction with customers (personal interaction, letter, fax, phone, Internet, e-mail etc.)

Collaborative CRM includes:

- Providing efficient communication with customers across a variety of communications channels
- Providing online services to reduce customer service costs
- Providing access to customer information while interacting with customers

Driven by authors from the Harvard Business School (Kracklauer/Mills/Seifert), Collaborative CRM also seems to be the new paradigma to succeed the leading Efficient Consumer Response and Category Management concept in the industry/ trade relationship.

In its broadest sense, CRM covers all interaction and business with customers. A good CRM programme allows a business to acquire customers, provide customer services and retain valued customers.

Customer services can be improved by:

- Providing online access to product information and technical assistance around the clock
- Identifying what customers value and devising appropriate service strategies for each customer
- Providing mechanisms for managing and scheduling follow-up sales calls
- Tracking all contacts with a customer
- Identifying potential problems before they occur
- Providing a user-friendly mechanism for registering customer complaints
- Providing a mechanism for handling problems and complaints
- Providing a mechanism for correcting service deficiencies
- Storing customer interests in order to target customers selectively
- Providing mechanisms for managing and scheduling maintenance, repair, and on-going support

The following factors need to be considered:

- Scalability: The system should be highly scalable, as the volume of data stored in the system grows over time
- Communication channels: CRM can interface with a variety of different channels (phone, WAP, Internet etc.)
- Workflow - A company's business processes need to be represented by the system with the ability to track the individual stages and transfer information between steps

- Assignment - The ability to assign requests, such as service requests, to a person or group.
- Database - the means of storing customer data and histories (in a data warehouse)
- Customer privacy Considerations, such as data encryption and legislation.

CRM applications often track customer interests and requirements, as well as their buying habits. This information can be used to target customers selectively. Furthermore, the products a customer has purchased can be tracked throughout the product's life cycle, allowing customers to receive information concerning a product or to target customers with information on alternative products once a product begins to be phased out.

Repeat purchases rely on customer satisfaction, which in turn comes from a deeper understanding of each customer and their individual needs. CRM is an alternative to the "one size fits all" approach. In industrial markets, the technology can be used to coordinate the conflicting and changing purchase criteria of the sector

The data gathered as part of CRM raises concerns over customer privacy and enables persuasive sales techniques. However, CRM does not necessarily involve gathering new data, but also includes making better use of customer information gathered as a result of routine customer interaction.

The privacy debate generally focuses on the customer information stored in the centralized database itself, and fears over a company's handling of this information. For example, there is virtually no way a consumer can determine if the company shares private (personally identifiable) data with third parties. Furthermore, companies may not always accurately declare to the consumer the types of information collected by CRM systems and the specific purposes for which the information is used.

CRM is also important to non-profit organizations, which sometimes use the terms "constituent relationship management", "contact relationship management" or "community relationship management" to describe their information systems for managing donors, volunteers and other supporters. salesforce.com, a popular CRM service that is on demand, offers its products for free to nonprofit organizations. hdhdhd

Price and quality of service have become negligible differentiators for companies in the communications, media and entertainment industries (e.g., wireline, wireless, broadband cable, and satellite service providers). The customer experience is emerging as the primary way service providers can stand apart from competitors. This new differentiation requires a new way of doing business: integrated customer management.

Integrated customer management, or ICM for short, was conceived as a business strategy that helps service providers create and, more importantly, deliver an intentional customer experience. Why intentional? Because the customer experience is too valuable to be an unintended, often haphazard by-product of internal business processes. ICM enables service providers to deliver an on-purpose experience that is consistently simple, uniquely personal and immediately valuable for customers at every point of service. The desired end result is stronger, more profitable customer relationships.

ICM can be achieved through three operational fundamentals:

Alignment: All people, processes and systems must be aligned to meet both business goals and customers desires. For example, bundling products is a good example of an initiative that crosses lines of business and/or departments. The product development, marketing and sales departments for local and long distance, wireless and data services must work in conjunction to enable the company to assemble and sell bundled services. Beyond this, customer service, accounting and other functions must also align support resources to shield

customers from the complexity of all behind-the-scene operations that make these and all offers possible. Alignment allows customers to perceive and interact with their service providers as one company, not as disparate lines of business.

Agility: In industries where the pace of change has greatly accelerated, service providers must be able to quickly and efficiently react to changing market conditions and customer demands. Entering new businesses or bringing new products to market quickly and cost-effectively is critical and is often a key differentiator between large organizations and their newer, more nimble niche players (e.g., a former utility, wireline service company versus VoIP provider; a traditional financial institution versus a credit card company). Agile organizations can change direction when it makes sense for them to do so—or when their customers demand it—without being hampered by organizational stovepipes, or by inflexible business processes or IT infrastructure.

Customer-centricity: In the past, ostensibly due to the original utility status of many communication service providers, the customer experience was not a primary concern. Providers sought only to make their products and services available, not necessarily easy to access or use. Therefore, the customer experience was primarily a by-product of internally focused processes designed to achieve the desired result (market or activate a service, generate a bill, enable customer service) efficiently and cost-effectively. Today, consumers have more authority and less patience with a slow, frustrating or otherwise unfulfilling customer experience. Whether they're interacting with a customer service representative, responding to an advertised offer, downloading content or paying their bill, customers demand that their experience be simple and, optimally, create value for them. Therefore, service providers must put the customer at the center of their business. Customer-centricity means making the business easier for customers to do business with. It also involves understanding customers' needs and desires and mapping processes and resources to meet them.

The phrase, "integrated customer management," was coined by Amdocs in 2004. Even though Amdocs pioneered it, ICM has become an accepted concept in the communication industry. For example, reporting on the 3GSM World Congress in Barcelona February 14, 2005, Financial Times printed the headline: "Vendors unveil systems for the real world; Integrated customer management and boosting revenues are the main issues for operators."

## SERVICES MARKETING

A Services marketing is marketing based on relationship and value. It may be used to market a service or a product.

"Managing the evidence" refers to the act of informing customers that the service encounter has been performed successfully. It is best done in subtle ways like providing examples or descriptions of good and poor service that can be used as a basis of comparison. The underlying rationale is that a customer might not appreciate the full worth of the service if they do not have a good benchmark for comparisons.

However, it is worth remembering that many of the concepts, as well as many of the specific techniques, will work equally well whether they are directed at products or services. In particular, developing a marketing strategy is much the same for products and services, in that it involves selecting target markets and formulating a marketing mix. Thus, Theodore Levitt suggested that "instead of talking of 'goods' and of 'services', it is better to talk of 'tangibles' and 'intangibles'". Levitt also went on to suggest that marketing a physical product is often more concerned with intangible aspects (frequently the `product service' elements of the total package) than with its physical properties. Charles Revson made a famous comment regarding the business of Revlon Inc.: `In the factory we make cosmetics. In the store we sell hope.' Arguably, service industry marketing merely approaches the problems from the opposite end of the same spectrum.

## Chapter 8

# Risk Management

The owner of a fast food franchise in East Los Angeles panicked when his drive-through cashier was robbed at gunpoint. While the criminals escaped with all the day's receipts, an even greater loss was the owner's peace of mind. Since his wife and daughter both worked at the restaurant, he stood to lose a lot more than money if the robbers returned. What could the owner have done to make his business and his family safe?

In this case, a simple bulletproof one-way drive-through window would have made the robbery impossible. More importantly, such a deterrent might make criminals think twice about their chosen target.

American businesses lose billions of dollars each year as a result of crime. Small operations are especially likely to be victims, losing at least 20 times more money than do large corporations. In fact, shoplifting, robbery and burglary put such a disproportionate strain on small firms that many disintegrate as a result. Business owners can even be held liable for crimes against people that are committed on their property, meaning their livelihood can be threatened by random acts of violence as well.

Employees of a sportswear manufacturing facility in Los Angeles were devastated when a man came in during working hours and murdered two of their coworkers before killing himself. The company's owner was shocked to learn that he could be held financially responsible for the trauma his staff experienced because access to the work area was not controlled effectively.

However, if the sportswear manufacturer had been able to prove to a judge that he had taken precautions — even minimal ones — to safeguard his building and his employees, he would have been absolved of liability.

No matter what kind of venture you own, you have assets and employees that require protection. Many entrepreneurs fail to realize the amount of damage crime can cause. They are also unaware that the most important security measures are inexpensive and simple to implement. As a business owner, you need to step back occasionally and conduct a security review, keeping in mind the three Ds of crime prevention: deter, delay and detect.

Deterring criminals is the key to making sure your business is not an easy target. Simple and inexpensive measures such as replacing old locks, hiding expensive equipment from passers-by, and putting bars on windows can cause would-be criminals to seek more vulnerable prey. Anything that tells potential thieves you have paid attention to the security of your building can be an effective deterrent.

Delaying a crime, or preventing quick access to valuable merchandise or equipment, is the second crucial step in protecting your business. The owner of a California office supply store learned the importance of delaying criminals after experiencing repeated burglaries, each of which resulted in losses of almost $10,000 in merchandise. Although the store had a locked accordion gate behind glass entrance doors, the gate was secured with a cheap lock. A sturdier, slightly more expensive lock could have occupied the burglars long enough for the police to reach the scene after the alarm was activated.

The last of the three Ds, detection, is accomplished by more complex technology like alarms or surveillance equipment. However, these products — such as window glass bugs or motion detectors — can actually give a false sense of security. For experienced criminals know that alarm

companies and police communications centers must go through a number of steps before reaching the location of a break-in. This gives them ample opportunity to escape with valuable equipment or merchandise. For this reason, law enforcement officials maintain that alarms and surveillance should only be used as back-up security devices.

Although detection is generally not effective at preventing a crime, it can decrease the amount of time a burglar has inside the building and is therefore an important component of building security. However, don't spend disproportionate amounts of money on high-tech equipment. Focus instead on inexpensive, low-tech tools for deterring or delaying criminals.

After you install new security precautions, the job is not finished until you have also made adjustments to your daily operations and employee training. "Not enough people are looking at the big picture," asserts Michael Harding, a Southern California law enforcement officer. "Your physical security will not be effective without operational security and good employee training. The three are tied together."

In the case of the Los Angeles fast-food franchise that was robbed at gunpoint, Harding found simple solutions to the many security problems existing there. The restaurant's back door and a storage room door were left unlocked during business hours, for example, and employees tended to leave them wide open for the sake of fast movement between areas of the building. "All I had to do was tell them to close and lock their doors," says Harding. "It sounds obvious, but it could really save a lot of worry."

With careful thought, you can probably identify most of your own security weaknesses. First, determine exactly what requires protection in your office, store or factory. Use common sense. For instance, don't spend a lot of money on alarms and access control for a storage area that only houses basic supplies such as boxes or business forms. For areas such as this, good locks should be sufficient.

In addition, step back and look realistically at your neighborhood and personnel. Don't go overboard by surrounding your building with Dobermans, or conversely, take unnecessary risks with valuable resources by depending only on trust for security.

Also evaluate how well your existing security arrangements address likely threats to your business. Be sure to go over every detail from the types of locks you install and your system of key distribution to employee identification and after-hours use of the facility. Even simple things like lighting can be extremely important.

If you are uncertain about the vulnerable points in your building and how to protect them, consider calling in a security professional to conduct a comprehensive evaluation of your premises and daily operations.

The best analysis will only be possible after the consultant observes typical personnel activity and thoroughly examines the various access points at all sides of the building and on the roof. Ask for a complete report of the evaluations and recommendations after the professional has explained them to you in a face-to-face consultation.

Keep in mind as you look for a consultant that the person you hire may have a product to sell other than knowledge about security. Although the professional often provides excellent advice, use common sense about any product recommendations the consultant makes.

Officer Harding recommends consultants who are currently in law enforcement because they have the greatest expertise in crime prevention and nothing to sell but the most up-to-date information. Just as fashion and food trends change with the times, so do crimes. "We get to interview the bad guys when we arrest them for a break-in," Harding says, "so we know all their latest secrets."

Aside from carefully controlling traffic through your premises, access control keypads and card readers provide many benefits that will save you money and worry in the long run.

To keep track of who goes in and out of the various doors in their four buildings, Insignia Commercial Group in Austin, Texas has used access control keypads for years. Michael Osborne, chief engineer, says he utilizes the system for much more than security purposes, however. "We've got the access system tied into energy control too," he says. "That way, only designated people can turn on the air conditioning and lights after hours by using their codes."

The system, designed by Hirsch Electronics in Irvine, California, has appeared in films like "Jurassic Park." "The keypads have a high-tech look that many business owners really like. Employees feel safer, and visitors know they're dealing with the latest in security," reports Rob Zivney of Hirsch Electronics. Osborne agrees that appearance is one of the added benefits of electronic access control.

Just as with other building security measures, access control systems require thorough user training to work well. Osborne says all the companies located in Insignia's buildings have a tenant manual that describes exactly how to operate the system. As he explains, "The manual reminds people not to let anyone in behind them as they enter, for example, and never to punch in a code while someone is watching."

When looking around the inside of your building, do you see valuable equipment or merchandise that a thief could collect in five minutes or less? Then maybe your alarm system just isn't enough. Consider the steps and time involved between the alarm being triggered and the arrival of a police officer at your site.

1. The alarm goes off when someone breaks in or trespasses.
2. The security company must identify the location of the alarm.
3. The security company calls the location to make sure the alarm was not set off accidentally by someone authorized with a special code.
4. The security company contacts the local sheriff or other police communication center.

5. The police enter the location into a computer and look for an on-duty officer in the area.
6. The police communication center sends an officer to the location.
7. The officer arrives on the scene of the break-in, often five minutes or more after the alarm originally sounded.

Whether a business operates out of a factory, garage, store or office suite, good key control can protect the people, property and information inside.

The little words "Do Not Duplicate" on all of your office keys sound like good insurance against unauthorized entry. Unfortunately, they mean almost nothing in most cases, says Alan Stelzer of Antrim's Security Co. in Pasadena, California. Stelzer strongly recommends keys that can only be duplicated by the manufacturers or their agents when you present a registration card and positive identification. All of the copies should then be listed by their consecutive serial numbers and the employees who use them.

One of the best features of the latest locks is that they can be installed into existing door hardware. A locksmith inserts or removes a columnar unit rather than installing expensive new materials. "This system, including a master key which only you use to unlock all of the doors, is a must for security, especially since it requires little time and investment," says Stelzer.

In today's high-tech world, a decidedly low-tech solution can still be effective. For many types of businesses like automobile dealerships, construction sites or warehouses, guard dogs can be an excellent crime deterrent.

Unlike security systems or alarms, guard dogs can cover large outdoor areas, and they continue to work during a power outage. Unlike a human guard, a well-trained dog stays alert throughout the night, and a dog's heightened senses of smell and hearing can detect intruders long before humans can. Dogs are also the least expensive guards, costing about $500 a month for full service.

At the minimum, a good guard dog service should provide nightly delivery and pick-up, in which case you and your employees do not have to come into actual contact with the animal. Your guard dog service must also must carry liability insurance, which protects you from responsibility for injuries the dog might inflict on passers-by or trespassers.

If you are thinking about using a guard dog to protect your premises, consider several issues. First, a good guard dog is an effective deterrent, but should only be used for that purpose. "If people want to steal, they're going to steal," claims J.R. Ewing of Century Dogs in Los Angeles, California.

The second thing to remember is that a determined criminal can find ways around almost any defense, including guard dogs. For example, mace, sedatives or other weapons can effectively disable even the most vigilant of animals. However, the presence of a guard dog does make your business far less appealing to would-be thieves who might decide to move on to more poorly protected premises.

To thoroughly safeguard your business, combine guard dog service — if appropriate — with other measures like good fences, locks and an alarm system.

The following is a simplified list of building features a security consultant would examine. Assess whether your security provisions are good, satisfactory, unsatisfactory or nonexistent.

Fixing a few simple problems can go a long way in preventing crime.

**1. Perimeter**

Lighting: Do you have lights at all entrances? Are they protected from vandals and thieves?

Fences / Walls: Is it possible to get over or under them? What are they made of? Are they in good condition?

Gates: Are any left unsecured? Are they in good condition?

Storage Yard: Do you have materials next to the fence or entrance? Are the materials hidden from passers-by?

Parking Lots: Is employee parking separate from parking for the general public? How close to the building is it? Is there enough lighting?

Address Numbers: Are they legible and visible from the street?

Pedestrian / Vehicle Access: How well is it monitored? Is it in front of the building?

**2. Doors**

Can they be pried open? Are they solid in construction? Do they have reliable dead bolts? What kind of strike plates do they have? Are your closing procedures listed and uniform?

**3. Windows**

Are they secured with screw locks, pins or sturdy cranks? Are louvers glued shut or otherwise secured? Are there drapes or blinds that prevent would-be thieves from seeing inside your property?

**4. Roof**

Are all skylights, vents and hatchways secured or covered? Do trees, drain pipes or walls allow easy access to the roof?

**5. Interior**

Lighting: Do you have lights on after hours? Is there an emergency back-up system?

Valuables: Are they out of view of any passers-by?

Storage / Offices / Saferoom: Are they secured with high-quality locks? Are there phones in each room to allow emergency calls?

**6. Special Areas**

Loading Docks: Are they well-marked and secure?

Employee Training: Have your employees been trained in crime awareness and prevention?

Key Control: Do you have a foolproof system to keep track of key distribution? Do you know many copies have been made? Trash Areas: Are your trash bins enclosed and locked?

**7. Security Systems**

Alarm System: Is it monitored? Does it include a panic device? Do you have prominent signs announcing its presence?

Closed-Circuit TV: How is it monitored? Is there a time delay?

Guards: What kind of training do they have? Are they bonded? How thorough a background check have you conducted on them?

Guard Dogs: How many do you have? During what hours are they present? Have you posted warnings prominently? Are you aware of your liability in case of attack?

If you are unable to answer many of these questions, a professional security consultation is in order. Remember that by investing a few hundred dollars now, you may be saving thousands of dollars in the long term.

Excerpted with permission from "Small Business Success" magazine, Volume X, produced by Pacific Bell Directory in partnership with the U.S. Small Business Administration and the Partners for Small Business Excellence.

## RISK MANAGEMENT FUNDAMENTALS

Risk management is attempting to identify and then manage threats that could severely impact or bring down the organization. Generally, this involves reviewing operations of the organization, identifying potential threats to the organization and the likelihood of their occurrence, and then taking appropriate actions to address the most likely threats.

Traditionally, risk management was thought of as mostly a matter of getting the right insurance. Insurance coverage usually came in rather standard packages, so people tended to not take risk management seriously. However, this impression of risk management has changed dramatically.

With the recent increase in rules and regulations, employee-related lawsuits and reliance on key resources, risk management is becoming a management practice that is every bit as important as financial or facilities management.

There are several basic activities which a nonprofit organization can conduct to dramatically reduce its chances of experiencing a catastrophic event that ruins or severely impairs the organization.

Organizations should regularly undertake comprehensive, focused assessment of potential risks to the organization. This focused assessment should occur at least twice a year by a team of staff members representing all the major functions of the organization. The assessment should be carefully planned, documented and methodically carried out.

Comprehensive checklists help a great deal to quickly review a wide range of organizational aspects. Other aspects require more careful review.

Checklists in the following sections cover almost 140 considerations to ensure a well run and highly protected organization.

## GOOD MANAGEMENT

Efforts undertaken to manage an organization well also contributes to sound risk management. For example, a fully attentive board with a wide range of skills may be the most important guard against major threats to an organization.

Careful strategic planning and effective supervision helps ensure organizational resources are closely aligned to accomplishing the organization's mission, and that staff and volunteers are treated fairly and comply with rules and regulations.

Every organization must have up-to-date policies which guide the relationships between staff and management. There has been a noticeable increase in lawsuits regarding wrongful termination, harassment and discrimination, disagreements about promotions or salary actions, etc. Parties to lawsuits include the organization, management and/or board members. Therefore, personnel policies must be reviewed at least once a year by an outside advisor who is an expert about all of the employee-related laws and regulations.

Be sure that management is well versed about the policies. Typically, courts will interpret actions by organizational personnel as representative of the organization's preferred course of action and superseding related, documented policies.

You might first review this information and then invite an insurance agent (or better yet, an insurance broker) to visit your organization to provide you an overview of the types of insurance typically sold to nonprofits. Note that many insurance professionals might not understand the nature of nonprofits. Therefore, you might first ask a few people from fellow nonprofits for references.

As dreadful as it may sound, you must schedule two hours sometime during the year to close your door and study your insurance policies. Note any questions and pose them to your insurance professional. Ask him or her to provide you a written, clear description regarding any ambiguities and to do so on company letterhead with his or her signature.

Note that Directors and Officers Insurance (D & O, and covered in the above "Insurance Against Liabilities" section) is increasingly considered because of the increasing number of lawsuits. In addition, D & O insurance helps attract highly experienced board members. Be sure your D & O insurance covers "insured vs. insured" which covers employee-related lawsuits and also covers ongoing costs to address a lawsuit (rather than paying only when the outcome of a lawsuit has been decided).

## RESOURCE MANAGEMENT

### People

This aspect of risk management is often overlooked. Each key role in an organization should have some type of resource to back up performance of that role. For example, another person in the organization should have general understanding of another person's role in case that other person for some reason is not able to perform the role. The use of up-to-date job descriptions, todo lists and receiving regular status reports both help to ensure understanding of how others carry out their roles Have a staff member back up another member who is on vacation. During staff meetings, have a staff member give a presentation about their role and how they carry it out. Ensure that each critical role has at least one backup person who can step in to conduct the role. The backup assignment should be part of the person's job description to help the person take the assignment seriously.

**General Facilities:**

1. Always lock your doors. This seems obvious, but too many organizations fail to do so.
2. Ensure your fire protection systems are fully functional by scheduing to test fire alarms twice a year or demanding that your facility's owner test alarms twice a year. Note that certain electrical equipment can be severely damaged from water sprinklers. Arrange adequate covering or arrangement to minimize water seepage if overhead sprinklers open up.
3. Conduct inspections twice a year, including to:
   a) Inspect floors for ripped carpets
   b) Look for cables or wires laying on the floor (tape over them if you have to)
   c) Notice any electical outlets with black soot hear outlets (this indicates electrical shortages)
   d) Ask all staff if their office accommodations are sufficient, e.g., their chairs are entirely comfortable (tilted correctly for their backs and at the right heights), is lighting sufficient for desk and computer work, etc.
   e) Notice any heavy items on or near the floor which staff must continually stoop to lift, e.g., boxes of paper for the copier or printers; open

boxes before they're set on the floor or stack heavy items in a storage room on a shelf

f) Ensure all doors have fully functional door knobs (it's amazing how long people can tolerate something as small as a knob that continually jams so the door is difficult to open)

g) Ensure there is a well-stocked first-aid kit available to all staff

h) Post emergency numbers on the wall near the central phone

i) During the winter, ensure adequate ice removal, e.g., spread sand over ice or use salt to melt ice

j) Schedule ten minutes in a staff meeting once a year for the entire staff to reflect on the quality of the facilities

Organizations should regularly undertake comprehensive, focused assessment of potential risks to the organization. This focused assessment should occur at least twice a year by a team of staff members representing all the major functions of the organization. The assessment should be carefully planned, documented and methodically carried out.

Comprehensive checklists help a great deal to quickly review a wide range of organizational aspects. Other aspects require more careful review.

Checklists in the following sections cover almost 140 considerations to ensure a well run and highly protected organization.

**Good Management**

Efforts undertaken to manage an organization well also contributes to sound risk management. For example, a fully attentive board with a wide range of skills may be the most important guard against major threats to an organization.

Careful strategic planning and effective supervision helps ensure organizational resources are closely aligned to accomplishing the organization's mission, and that staff and volunteers are treated fairly and comply with rules and regulations.

Every organization must have up-to-date policies which guide the relationships between staff and management. There has been a noticeable increase in lawsuits regarding wrongful termination, harassment and discrimination, disagreements about promotions or salary actions, etc. Parties to lawsuits include the organization, management and/or board members. Therefore, personnel policies must be reviewed at least once a year by an outside advisor who is an expert about all of the employee-related laws and regulations.

Be sure that management is well versed about the policies. Typically, courts will interpret actions by organizational personnel as representative of the organization's preferred course of action and superseding related, documented policies.

You might first review this information and then invite an insurance agent (or better yet, an insurance broker) to visit your organization to provide you an overview of the types of insurance typically sold to nonprofits. Note that many insurance professionals might not understand the nature of nonprofits. Therefore, you might first ask a few people from fellow nonprofits for references.

As dreadful as it may sound, you must schedule two hours sometime during the year to close your door and study your insurance policies. Note any questions and pose them to your insurance professional. Ask him or her to provide you a written, clear description regarding any ambiguities and to do so on company letterhead with his or her signature.

Note that Directors and Officers Insurance (D & O, and covered in the above "Insurance Against Liabilities" section) is increasingly considered because of the increasing number of lawsuits. In addition, D & O insurance helps attract highly experienced board members. Be sure your D & O insurance covers "insured vs. insured" which covers employee-related lawsuits and also covers ongoing costs to address a lawsuit (rather than paying only when the outcome of a lawsuit has been decided).

## PREVENTING EMPLOYEE THEFT

Many people consider accounting a tedious job, but not John Lewis. Throughout his three-year tenure with Unified Trucking he had ostensibly been a model employee, missing only a few days of work and conquering the Herculean task of bookkeeping single-handedly. The companyOs continued growth and profitability were the only indications management had ever needed to determine that John performed his job well. His professionalism and dedication made supervision unnecessary. John insisted on handling any problems or discrepancies personally, and made it clear that the buck stopped with him.

In fact, many bucks did stop with him, followed him home and neatly deposited themselves into his bank account. In three short years John managed to use his authority and exclusive bookkeeping access to bilk the company of nearly $100,000. As often happens, Johnos illicit activities were only revealed by accident. If janitorial workers had not discovered a suspicious amount of discarded receipts, the theft would have continued undetected.

Specialists say the cost of employee theft and embezzlement adds up to billions of dollars annually. For most companies, employee theft is a much more serious concern than burglars or shoplifters. In the retail industry, where theft of all types is a recurring problem, businesses recover an average of $1,350 from each employee apprehended for stealing, compared to $196 recovered from shoplifters. With dramatic figures like these, taking steps to eliminate theft and graft within a firm are sure to yield returns.

Should you consider your business immune to employee theft, think again. Security experts estimate that as many as 30 percent of all employees do steal, and that another 60 percent will steal if given sufficient motive and opportunity. The current economic hard times only add to the temptation of personnel to take what does not belong to them.

Yet protecting yourself from pilfering may be easier than you think. A comprehensive programme to eliminate employee theft can be simple and inexpensive, while at the same time increasing productivity and providing avenues for improved management-worker relations.

Know the Frequently Used Schemes having an elementary understanding of the more common forms of employee theft will help you formulate a strategy for subverting them. Here are just a few:

- Forging Receipts: Salespersons can charge a customer one sum, ring up a receipt for less, and pocket the difference.
- Hiding Receipts: When bookkeeping is sloppy and little supervision exists, employees can keep cash and receipts without raising an eyebrow.
- Pocketing Loose Change: Small sums of money, such as fees or petty cash, may not be missed at all.
- Pilfering Merchandise: Goods your firm purchases may never even make it to the shelves.
- Fictitious Payroll: Occasionally personnel managers will authorize salary for fictitious workers, then keep it for themselves.
- Overbilling Expenses: Managers with expense accounts may submit receipts twice and be reimbursed twice, or inflate actual expenses incurred.
- Purchasing Fraud: Employees sometimes declare themselves suppliers of nonexistent goods, and subsequently reimburse themselves handsomely.

Watch for the tell-tale signs of internal theft. One subtle but noticeable indication of dishonest employees may be an unexplained rise in their living standards. Be careful, however, as newfound wealth or sudden success may occur for a number of reasons of which you might not be aware. Be absolutely certain about a staff memberOs misconduct before making accusations that can strain worker relations, or even elicit a lawsuit.

Pay close attention to management-level personnel who insist on handling routine clerical tasks themselves. And be on guard for clients complaining about overcharging or inconsistencies in shipping and billing practices. Following up on customer grievances often reveals clandestine theft.

Some employees have theft in mind from the start. You should be able to weed out these people by performing thorough background checks on all new hire prospects, particularly for sensitive positions involving the flow of money. Call previous employers to verify resume and application information. Invest sufficient time to make sure applicants do not have a history of stealing from previous employers, and that all credentials and references are valid. Do not be overly zealous, however. Some good workers have made mistakes they genuinely regret and have never repeated them.

Many businesses conduct honesty testing in their hiring procedures and evaluations of current staff members. Honesty tests are standardized, commercially available written examinations that provide psychological evaluations of a candidateOs ethical dispositions and attitudes toward work. These tests can purportedly identify problem employees who have either stolen in the past or who will be unproductive workers. Honesty testing has been hailed by some for helping to eliminate pilfering, reduce employee turnover and increase productivity. It has also been criticized and challenged by those who feel the tests are either inaccurate or a violation of rights to privacy and other civil rights.

While the majority of workers will not go out of their way to steal, the best defense is careful supervision that removes any easy opportunities. Even though delegation of tasks is unavoidable, try to have a management-level supervisor oversee inventory and bookkeeping. If this is not possible, consider dividing these tasks among several staff members so no single employee has too much authority. Shifting responsibilities from one person to another allows them to check each otherOs work for accuracy and suspicious activities. It also makes collusion between employees, or between an employee and an outside source, such as a distributor, considerably less likely.

Occasional inspections or audits of inventory and bookkeeping help in preventing fraud and theft. Have an outside auditor or top manager perform the inspection on a periodic but unscheduled basis, thereby keeping records current and reducing theft opportunities. Requiring accounting employees to take vacations can also help the monitoring of bookkeeping records. Those who cover during vacation absences serve as an additional check on accounting discrepancies.

Most successful embezzlement schemes would have failed if inventory and accounting records were organized and up to date. If records are always behind and the work is sloppy, theft will be much harder to detect. You should regularly reconcile invoices and payments, as well as shipping and receiving bills. At least one software package is available that automatically examines your records and checks them for suspicious activities. Even without the sophistication of specialized software, your current accounting system may be able to give you useful information, such as revealing accounts that consistently show discrepancies.

It is possible to install physical obstacles to theft, such as alarm systems and secured, restricted areas. However, be aware that such obvious measures can have a negative effect on morale. While overt tactics to deter theft help prevent losses, they also convey very clearly to employees that they are not trusted.

Workers will be less likely to steal if you create an environment in which they think there is a good chance of being caught. Training and "employee awareness" programs can inform workers about stealing problems and keep them on the lookout for theft of any kind. A good programme can be motivational and enjoyable – highlighted, for example, by group rewards for departments that show decreased rates of theft. When management and labour work together to solve the problem, an additional result can be improved relations and higher morale.

To make a security programme such as this effective, it is crucial employees know they can turn over incriminating information on anyone in the firm without fearing job loss or other repercussions. Stress that management and supervisors are not above suspicion and that employee complaints will be taken seriously. Some programs feature special phone numbers or other means for workers to leave anonymous tips. Others offer rewards for informants while still guaranteeing their anonymity. A more positive approach may be to institute a profit-sharing plan which fosters loyalty, encourages personnel to monitor one another, and brings each employeeOs interests closer in line with those of the company.

The most troubling cases of employee theft occur when workers are in desperate financial straits. Common problems, such as heavy medical expenses, can temporarily put people into situations where stealing seems necessary for survival. Let employees know in advance that they can come to management for assistance rather than resorting to theft. Although no company is a charitable organization, consider helping distressed staff members find financial counseling. Some businesses even go so far as to provide short-term loans for reliable personnel.

Intimately linked with financial problems and theft is employee substance abuse. If your firm does not already have a procedure for screening workers for drugs or alcohol, it may benefit from one. Even if the company doesnOt actually test, the mere threat has an effect and may weed out some people who might otherwise steal to support their drug or alcohol habit. A programme that assists with counseling for personnel who admit to problems could help ameliorate the stranglehold these substances put on employees lives, including their finances.

To reinforce these other measures, a company should distribute clear, written policies on ethical behaviour to be signed by each employee —including the owner. It should be emphasized that there is no such thing as an "acceptable amount" of employee crime, and that, in fact, none at all will be tolerated. There should also be no double standard at work: all infractions should be punished regardless of how important the person or how small the infraction.

When formulating policies for theft and graft, some difficult decisions are involved. For example, should every employee found stealing be dismissed, or worse yet prosecuted? Or should the punishment fit the nature of the crime and be sensitive to extenuating circumstances, such as financial troubles? Be aware that severe punishments can sometimes do more harm than good, straining relations with employees and causing those who do steal to be extra careful in covering their tracks.

Employees need to know that one uniform ethical standard applies to everyone in the firm. Executives and managers should be positive role models for workers. If management is found dipping into petty cash, fudging on expense accounts or taking home equipment, personnel will feel justified in doing the same. As is always ideally the case, leadership and direction begin at the highest level.

When an envelope containing an entire dayOs worth of transactions disappeared, Dianne Oliver — owner of an eight-employee Merle Norman cosmetic franchise in Concord, California — immediately decided to institute a more formal system of storing money. "It's now put into a locked cash drawer under the computer after each transaction, with the employee entering the stock number if a product was sold, the method of payment, and how much was paid. The computer indicates the amount of change to be given. Each night, We tabulate to see that everything matches up." Oliver, who finds this method also helps her "keep control of inventory," does frequent checks on popular items to ensure no stock is missing. "And employees can buy all beauty products at wholesale, which helps eliminate temptation." "High ticket" items are placed at the back of the 1,000-foot store, with only a few display products kept up front near the door. In addition to a wide range of beauty supplies, Oliver also sells watches and jewelry, which are kept in locked cases.

"The watch case is even chained to the countertop," she explains. "And whenever an employee permanently departs, every lock is changed."

## PROJECT MANAGEMENT

Project management is a carefully planned and organized effort to accomplish a specific (and usually) one-time effort, for example, construct a building or implement a new computer system. Project management includes developing a project plan, which includes defining project goals and objectives, specifying tasks or how goals will be achieved, what resources are need, and associating budgets and timelines for completion. It also includes implementing the project plan, along with careful controls to stay on the "critical path", that is, to ensure the plan is being managed according to plan. Project management usually follows major phases (with various titles for these phases), including feasibility study, project planning, implementation, evaluation and support/ maintenance. (Programme planning is usually of a broader scope than project planning, but not always.)

Almost any human activity that involves carrying out a non-repetitive task can be a project. So we are all project managers! We all practise project management (PM).

But there is a big difference between carrying out a very simple project involving one or two people and one involving a complex mix of people, organisations and tasks.

This has been true for millennia, but large-scale projects like the Pyramids often used rather simple control and resource techniques including brute force to 'motivate' the workforce!

The art of planning for the future has always been a human trait. In essence a project can be captured on paper with a few simple elements: a start date, an end date, the tasks that have to be carried out and when they should be finished, and some idea of the resources (people, machines etc) that will be needed during the course of the project.

When the plan starts to involve different things happening at different times, some of which are dependent on each other, plus resources required at different times and in different quantities and perhaps working at different rates, the paper plan could start to cover a vast area and be unreadable.

This was a problem facing the US Navy in the development of the Polaris missile system. There were so many aspects to the project that a new technique had to be invented to cope with it: the PERT technique. This and later developments led to mathematical techniques that can be used to find the critical path through a series of planned tasks that interconnect during the life of a project.

You could begin the story of modern project management from this time. But that would be unfair as project management is not only about planning but also about human attributes like leadership and motivation.

Nevertheless, the idea that complex plans could be analysed by a computer to allow someone to control a project is the basis of much of the development in technology that now allow projects of any size and complexity not only to be planned but also modelled to answer 'what if?' questions.

The original programs and computers tended to produce answers long after an event had taken place. Now, there are many project planning and scheduling programs that can provide real time information, as well as linking to risk analysis, time recording, costing, estimating and other aspects of project control.

But computer programs are not project management: they are tools for project managers to use. Project management is all that mix of components of control, leadership, teamwork, resource management etc, that goes into a successful project.

Project managers can be found in all industries. Their numbers have grown rapidly as industry and commerce has realised that much of what it does is project work. And as project-based organisations have started to emerge, project management is becoming established as both a professional career path and a way of controlling business.

So opportunities in project management now exist not only in being a project manager, but also as part of the support team in a project or programme office or as a team leader for part of a project. There are also qualifications that can be attained through the professional associations.

One reason for the rapid growth is the need to understand how to look after complex projects, often in high tech areas, which are critical to business success but also have to use scarce resources efficiently.

Most people still want their projects to be on time, meet quality objectives, and not cost more than the budget. These form the classic time, quality, cost triangle.

In fact if you have an unlimited budget and unlimited time, project management becomes rather easy. For most people, however, time and money are critical and that is what makes project management so important today.

## PLANNING A PROJECT

Before describing the role and creation of a specification, we need to introduce and explain a fairly technical term: a numbty is a person whose brain is totally numb. In this context, numb means "deprived of feeling or the power of unassisted activity"; in general, a numbty needs the stimulation of an electric cattle prod to even get to the right office in the morning. Communication with numbties is severely hampered by the fact that although they think they know what they mean (which they do not), they seldom actually say it, and they never write it down. And the main employment of numbties world-wide is in creating project specifications. You must know this - and protect your team accordingly.

A specification is the definition of your project: a statement of the problem, not the solution. Normally, the specification contains errors, ambiguities, misunderstandings and enough rope to hang you and your entire team. Thus before you embark upon the the next six months of activity working on the wrong project, you must assume that a numbty was the chief author of the specification you received and you must read, worry, revise and ensure that everyone concerned with the project (from originator, through the workers, to the end-customer) is working with the same understanding. The outcome of this deliberation should be a written definition of what is required, by when; and this must be agreed by all involved. There are no short-cuts to this; if you fail to spend the time initially, it will cost you far more later on.

The agreement upon a written specification has several benefits:

- The clarity will reveal misunderstandings
- The completeness will remove contradictory assumptions
- The rigour of the analysis will expose technical and practical details which numbties normally gloss over through ignorance or fear
- The agreement forces all concerned to actually read and think about the details

The work on the specification can seen as the first stage of Quality Assurance since you are looking for and countering problems in the very foundation of the project - from this perspective the creation of the specification clearly merits a large investment of time.

From a purely defensive point of view, the agreed specification also affords you protection against the numbties who have second thoughts, or new ideas, half way through the project. Once the project is underway, changes cost time (and money). The existence of a demonstrably-agreed specification enables you to resist or to charge for (possibly in terms of extra time) such changes. Further, people tend to forget what they originally thought; you may need proof that you have been working as instructed.

The places to look for errors in a specification are:

- The global context: numbties often focus too narrowly on the work of one team and fail to consider how it fits into the larger picture. Some of the work given to you may actually be undone or duplicated by others. Some of the proposed work may be incompatible with that of others; it might be just plain barmy in the larger context.

- The interfaces: between your team and both its customers and suppliers, there are interfaces. At these points something gets transferred. Exactly what, how and when should be discussed and agreed from the very beginning. Never assume a common understanding, because you will be wrong. All it takes for your habitual understandings to evaporate is the arrival of one new member, in either of the teams. Define and agree your interfaces and maintain a friendly contact throughout the project.
- Time-scales: numbties always underestimate the time involved for work. If there are no time-scales in the specification, you can assume that one will be imposed upon you (which will be impossible). You must add realistic dates. The detail should include a precise understanding of the extent of any intermediate stages of the task, particularly those which have to be delivered.
- External dependencies: your work may depend upon that of others. Make this very clear so that these people too will receive warning of your needs. Highlight the effect that problems with these would have upon your project so that everyone is quite clear about their importance. To be sure, contact these people yourself and ask if they are able to fulfil the assumptions in your specification.
- Resources: the numbty tends to ignore resources. The specification should identify the materials, equipment and manpower which are needed for the project. The agreement should include a commitment by your managers to allocate or to fund them. You should check that the actual numbers are practical and/or correct. If they are omitted, add them - there is bound to be differences in their assumed values.

This seems to make the specification sound like a long document. It should not be. Each of the above could be a simple sub-heading followed by either bullet points or a table - you are not writing a brochure, you are stating the definition of the project in clear, concise and unambiguous glory.

Of course, the specification may change. If circumstances, or simply your knowledge, change then the specification will be out of date. You should not regard it as cast in stone but rather as a display board where everyone involved can see the current, common understanding of the project. If you change the content everyone must know, but do not hesitate to change it as necessary.

Having decide what the specification intends, your next problem is to decide what you and your team actually need to do, and how to do it. As a manager, you have to provide some form of framework both to plan and to communicate what needs doing. Without a structure, the work is a series of unrelated tasks which provides little sense of achievement and no feeling of advancement. If the team has no grasp of how individual tasks fit together towards an understood goal, then the work will seem pointless and they will feel only frustration.

To take the planning forward, therefore, you need to turn the specification into a complete set of tasks with a linking structure. Fortunately, these two requirements are met at the same time since the derivation of such a structure is the simplest method of arriving at a list of tasks.

## WORK BREAKDOWN STRUCTURE

Once you have a clear understanding of the project, and have eliminated the vagaries of the numbties, you then describe it as a set of simpler separate activities. If any of these are still too complex for you to easily organise, you break them down also into another level of simpler descriptions, and so on until you can manage everything. Thus your one complex project is organised as a set of simple tasks which together achieve the desired result.

The reasoning behind this is that the human brain (even yours) can only take in and process so much information at one time. To get a real grasp of the project, you have to think about it in pieces rather than trying to process the complexity of its entire details all at once. Thus each level of the project can be understood as the amalgamation of a few simply described smaller units.

In planning any project, you follow the same simple steps: if an item is too complicated to manage, it becomes a list of simpler items. People call this producing a work breakdown structure to make it sound more formal and impressive. Without following this formal approach you are unlikely to remember all the niggling little details; with this procedure, the details are simply displayed on the final lists.

One common fault is to produce too much detail at the initial planning stage. You should be stop when you have a sufficient description of the activity to provide a clear instruction for the person who will actually do the work, and to have a reasonable estimate for the total time/effort involved. You need the former to allocate (or delegate) the task; you need the latter to finish the planning.

## TASK ALLOCATION

The next stage is a little complicated. You now have to allocate the tasks to different people in the team and, at the same time, order these tasks so that they are performed in a sensible sequence.

Task allocation is not simply a case of handing out the various tasks on your final lists to the people you have available; it is far more subtle (and powerful) than that. As a manager you have to look far beyond the single project; indeed any individual project can be seen as merely a single step in your team's development. The allocation of tasks should thus be seen as a means of increasing the skills and experience of your team - when the project is done, the team should have gained.

In simple terms, consider what each member of your team is capable of and allocate sufficient complexity of tasks to match that (and to slightly stretch). The tasks you allocate are not the ones on your finals lists, they are adapted to better suit the needs of your team's development; tasks are moulded to fit people, which is far more effective than the other way around. For example, if Arthur is to learn something new, the task may be simplified with responsibility given to another to guide and check the work; if Brenda is to develop, sufficient tasks are combined so that her responsibility increases beyond what she has held before; if Colin lacks confidence, the tasks are broken into smaller units which can be completed (and commended) frequently.

Sometimes tasks can be grouped and allocated together. For instance, some tasks which are seemingly independent may benefit from being done together since they use common ideas, information, talents. One person doing them both removes the start-up time for one of them; two people (one on each) will be able to help each other.

The ordering of the tasks is really quite simple, although you may find that sketching a sequence diagram helps you to think it through (and to communicate the result). Pert charts are the accepted outcome, but sketches will suffice. Getting the details exactly right, however, can be a long and painful process, and often it can be futile. The degree to which you can predict the future is limited, so too should be the detail of your planning. You must have the broad outlines by which to monitor progress, and sufficient detail to assign each task when it needs to be started, but beyond that - stop and do something useful instead.

At the initial planning stage the main objective is to get a realistic estimate of the time involved in the project. You must establish this not only to assist higher management with their planning, but also to protect your team from being expected to do the impossible. The most important technique for achieving this is known as: guesstimation.

Guesstimating schedules is notoriously difficult but it is helped by two approaches:

- Make your guesstimates of the simple tasks at the bottom of the work break down structure and look for the longest path through the sequence diagram
- Use the experience from previous projects to improve your guesstimating skills

The corollary to this is that you should keep records in an easily accessible form of all projects as you do them. Part of your final project review should be to update your personal data base of how long various activities take. Managing this planning phase is vital to your success as a manager.

Some people find guesstimating a difficult concept in that if you have no experience of an activity, how can you make a worthwhile estimate? Let us consider such a problem: how long would it take you to walk all the way to the top of the Eiffel Tower or the Statue of Liberty? Presuming you have never actually tried this (most people take the elevator part of the way), you really have very little to go on. Indeed if you have actually seen one (and only one) of these buildings, think about the other. Your job depends upon this, so think carefully. One idea is to start with the number of steps - guess that if you can. Notice, you do not have to be right, merely reasonable. Next, consider the sort of pace you could maintain while climbing a flight of steps for a long time. Now imagine yourself at the base of a flight of steps you do know, and estimate a) how many steps there are, and b) how long it takes you to climb them (at that steady pace). To complete, apply a little mathematics.

Now examine how confident you are with this estimate. If you won a free flight to Paris or New York and tried it, you would probably (need your head examined) be mildly surprised if you climbed to the top in less than half the estimated time and if it took you more than double you would be mildly annoyed. If it took you less than a tenth the time, or ten times as long, you would extremely surprised/annoyed.

In fact, you do not currently believe that that would happen (no really, do you?). The point is that from very little experience of the given problem, you can actually come up with a working estimate - and one which is far better than no estimate at all when it comes to deriving a schedule. Guesstimating does take a little practice, but it is a very useful skill to develop.

There are two practical problems in guesstimation. First, you are simply too optimistic. It is human nature at the beginning of a new project to ignore the difficulties and assume best case scenarii - in producing your estimates (and using those of others) you must inject a little realism. In practice, you should also build-in a little slack to allow yourself some tolerance against mistakes. This is known as defensive scheduling. Also, if you eventually deliver ahead of the agreed schedule, you will be loved.

Second, you will be under pressure from senior management to deliver quickly, especially if the project is being sold competitively. Resist the temptation to rely upon speed as the only selling point. You might, for instance, suggest the criteria of: fewer errors, history of adherence to initial schedules, previous customer satisfaction, "this is how long it takes, so how can you trust the other quotes".

**ESTABLISHING CONTROLS**

When the planning phase is over (and agreed), the "doing" phase begins. Once it is in motion, a project acquires a direction and momentum which is totally independent of anything you predicted. If you come to terms with that from the start, you can then enjoy the roller-coaster which follows. To gain some hope, however, you need to establish at the start (within the plan) the means to monitor and to influence the project's progress.

There are two key elements to the control of a project

- Milestones (clear, unambiguous targets of what, by when)
- Established means of communication

For you, the milestones are a mechanism to monitor progress; for your team, they are short-term goals which are far more tangible than the foggy, distant completion of the entire project. The milestones maintain the momentum and encourage effort; they allow the team to judge their own progress and to celebrate achievement throughout the project rather than just at its end.

The simplest way to construct milestones is to take the timing information from the work breakdown structure and sequence diagram. When you have guesstimated how long each sub-task will take and have strung them together, you can identify by when each of these tasks will actually be completed. This is simple and effective; however, it lacks creativity.

A second method is to construct more significant milestones. These can be found by identify stages in the development of a project which are recognisable as steps towards the final product. Sometimes these are simply the higher levels of your structure; for instance, the completion of a market-evaluation phase. Sometimes, they cut across many parallel activities; for instance, a prototype of the eventual product or a mock-up of the new brochure format.

If you are running parallel activities, this type of milestone is particularly useful since it provides a means of pulling together the people on disparate activities, and so:

- They all have a shared goal (the common milestone)
- Their responsibility to (and dependence upon) each other is emphasised
- Each can provide a new (but informed) viewpoint on the others' work
- The problems to do with combining the different activities are highlighted and discussed early in the implementation phase
- You have something tangible which senior management (and numbties) can recognise as progress

- You have something tangible which your team can celebrate and which constitutes a short-term goal in a possibly long-term project
- It provides an excellent opportunity for quality checking and for review

Of course, there are milestones and there are mill-stones. You will have to be sensitive to any belief that working for some specific milestone is hindering rather than helping the work forward. If this arises then either you have chosen the wrong milestone, or you have failed to communicate how it fits into the broader structure.

Communication is your everything. To monitor progress, to receive early warning of danger, to promote cooperation, to motivate through team involvement, all of these rely upon communication. Regular reports are invaluable - if you clearly define what information is needed and if teach your team how to provided it in a rapidly accessible form. Often these reports merely say "progressing according to schedule". These you send back, for while the message is desired the evidence is missing: you need to insist that your team monitor their own progress with concrete, tangible, measurements and if this is done, the figures should be included in the report. However, the real value of this practice comes when progress is not according to schedule - then your communication system is worth all the effort you invested in its planning.

At the planning stage, you can deal with far more than the mere project at hand. You can also shape the overall pattern of your team's working using the division and type of activities you assign.

Ask your team. They too must be involved in the planning of projects, especially in the lower levels of the work breakdown structure. Not only will they provide information and ideas, but also they will feel ownership in the final plan.

This does not mean that your projects should be planned by committee - rather that you, as manager, plan the project based upon all the available experience and creative ideas. As an initial approach, you could attempt the first level(s) of the work breakdown structure to help you communicate the project to the team and then ask for comments. Then, using these, the final levels could be refined by the people to whom the tasks will be allocated. However, since the specification is so vital, all the team should vet the penultimate draft.

There are two pitfalls to avoid in project reviews:

- They can be too frequent
- They can be too drastic

The constant trickle of new information can lead to a vicious cycle of planning and revising which shakes the team's confidence in any particular version of the plan and which destroys the very stability which the structure was designed to provide. You must decide the balance. Pick a point on the horizon and walk confidently towards it. Decide objectively, and explain beforehand, when the review phases will occur and make this a scheduled milestone in itself.

Even though the situation may have changed since the last review, it is important to recognise the work which has been accomplished during the interim. Firstly, you do not want to abandon it since the team will be demotivated feeling that they have achieved nothing. Secondly, this work itself is part of the new situation: it has been done, it should provide a foundation for the next step or at least the basis of a lesson well learnt. Always try to build upon the existing achievements of your team.

No plan is complete without explicit provision for testing and quality. As a wise manager, you will know that this should be part of each individual phase of the project. This means that no activity is completed until it has passed the (objectively) defined criteria which establishes its quality, and these are best defined (objectively) at the beginning as part of the planning.

When devising the schedule therefore you must include allocated time for this part of each activity. Thus your question is not only: "how long will it take", but also: "how long will the testing take". By asking both questions together you raise the issue of "how do we know we have done it right" at the very beginning and so the testing is more likely to be done in parallel with the implementation. You establish this philosophy for your team by include testing as a justified (required) cost.

Another reason for stating the testing criteria at the beginning is that you can avoid futile quests for perfection. If you have motivated your team well, they will each take pride in their work and want to do the best job possible. Often this means polishing their work until is shines; often this wastes time. If it clear at the onset exactly what is needed, then they are more likely to stop when that has been achieved. You need to avoid generalities and to stipulate boundaries; not easy, but essential.

The same is also true when choosing the tools or building-blocks of your project. While it might be nice to have use of the most modern versions, or to develop an exact match to your needs; often there is an old/existing version which will serve almost as well (sufficient for the purpose), and the difference is not worth the time you would need to invest in obtaining or developing the new one. Use what is available whenever possible unless the difference in the new version is worth the time, money and the initial, teething pains.

A related idea is that you should discourage too much effort on aspects of the project which are idiosyncratic to that one job. In the specification phase, you might try to eliminate these through negotiation with the customer; in the implementation phase you might leave these parts until last. The reason for this advice is that a general piece of work can be tailored to many specific instances; thus, if the work is in a general form, you will be able to rapidly re-use it for other projects. On the other hand, if you produce something which is cut to fit exactly one specific case, you may have to repeat the work entirely even though the next project is fairly similar. At the planning phase, a manager should bare in mind the future and the long-term development of the team as well as the requirements of the current project.

As a manager, you have to regulate the pressure and work load which is imposed upon your team; you must protect them from the unreasonable demands of the rest of the company. Once you have arrived at what you consider to be a realistic schedule, fight for it. Never let the outside world deflect you from what you know to be practical. If they impose a deadline upon you which is impossible, clearly state this and give your reasons. You will need to give some room for compromise, however, since a flat NO will be seen as obstructive. Since you want to help the company, you should look for alternative positions.

You could offer a prototype service or product at an earlier date. This might, in some cases, be sufficient for the customer to start the next stage of his/her own project on the understanding that your project would be completed at a later date and the final version would then replace the prototype.

The complexity of the product, or the total number of units, might be reduced. This might, in some cases, be sufficient for the customer's immediate needs. Future enhancements or more units would then be the subject of a subsequent negotiation which, you feel, would be likely to succeed since you will have already demonstrate your ability to deliver on time.

You can show on an alternative schedule that the project could be delivered by the deadline if certain (specified) resources are given to you or if other projects are rescheduled. Thus, you provide a clear picture of the situation and a possible solution; it is up to your manager then how he/she proceeds.

The most common error in planning is to assume that there will be no errors in the implementation: in effect, the schedule is derived on the basis of "if nothing goes wrong, this will take...". Of course, recognising that errors will occur is the reason for implementing a monitoring strategy on the project. Thus when the inevitable does happen, you can react and adapt the plan to compensate. However, by carefully considering errors in advance you can make changes to the original plan to enhance its tolerance. Quite simply, your planning should include time where you stand back from the design and ask: "what can go wrong?"; indeed, this is an excellent way of asking your team for their analysis of your plan.

You can try to predict where the errors will occur. By examining the activities' list you can usually pinpoint some activities which are risky (for instance, those involving new equipment) and those which are quite secure (for instance, those your team has done often before). The risky areas might then be given a less stringent time-scale - actually planning-in time for the mistakes. Another possibility is to apply a different strategy, or more resources, to such activities to minimise the disruption. For instance, you could include training or consultancy for new equipment, or you might parallel the work with the foundation of a fall-back position.

At the end of any project, you should allocate time to reviewing the lessons and information on both the work itself and the management of that work: an open meeting, with open discussion, with the whole team and all customers and suppliers. If you think that this might be thought a waste of time by your own manager, think of the effect it will have on future communications with your customers and suppliers.

**PLANNING FOR THE FUTURE**

With all these considerations in merely the "planning" stage of a project, it is perhaps surprising that projects get done at all. In fact projects do get done, but seldom in the predicted manner and often as much by brute force as by careful planning. The point, however, is that this method is non-optimal. Customers feel let down by late delivery, staff are demotivated by constant pressure for impossible goals, corners get cut which harm your reputation, and each project has to overcome the same problems as the last.

With planning, projects can run on time and interact effectively with both customers and suppliers. Everyone involved understands what is wanted and emerging problems are seen (and dealt with) long before they cause damage. If you want your projects to run this way - then you must invest time in planning.

Significant organizational change occurs, for example, when an organization changes its overall strategy for success, adds or removes a major section or practice, and/or wants to change the very nature by which it operates. It also occurs when an organization evolves through various life cycles, just like people must successfully evolve through life cycles. For organizations to develop, they often must undergo significant change at various points in their development. That's why the topic of organizational change and development has become widespread in communications about business, organizations, leadership and management.

Leaders and managers continually make efforts to accomplish successful and significant change — it's inherent in their jobs. Some are very good at this effort (probably more than we realize), while others continually struggle and fail. That's often the difference between people who thrive in their roles and those that get shuttled around from job to job, ultimately settling into a role where they're frustrated and ineffective. There are many schools with educational programs about organizations, business, leadership and management. Unfortunately, there still are not enough schools with programs about how to analyze organizations, identify critically important priorities to address (such as systemic problems or exciting visions for change) and then undertake successful and significant change to address those priorities.

There are many approaches to guiding change — some planned, structured and explicit, while others are more organic, unfolding and implicit. Some approaches work from the future to the present, for example, involving visioning and then action planning about how to achieve that vision. Other approaches work from the present to the future, for example, identifying current priorities (issues and/or goals) and then action planning about to address those priorities (the action research approach is one example). Different people often have very different — and strong — opinions about how change should be conducted. Thus, it is likely that some will disagree with some of the content in this topic. That's what makes this topic so diverse, robust and vital for us all.

To really understand organizational change and begin guiding successful change efforts, the change agent should have at least a broad understanding of the context of the change effort. This includes understanding the basic systems and structures in organizations, including their typical terms and roles. This requirement applies to the understanding of leadership and management of the organizations, as well. That is why graduate courses in business often initially include a course or some discussion on organizational theory. This topic includes several links to help you gain this broad understanding. Organizational change should not be conducted for the sake of change. Organizational change efforts should be geared to improve the performance of organizations and the people in those organizations. Therefore, it's useful to have some understanding of what is meant by "performance" and the various methods to manage performance in organizations.

The past few decades have seen an explosion in the number of very useful tools to help change agents to effectively explore, understand and communicate about organizations, as well as to guide successful change in those organizations. Tools from systems theory and systems thinking especially are a major breakthrough. Even if the change agent is not an expert about systems theory and thinking, even a basic understanding can cultivate an entire new way of working.

## ORGANIZATIONAL CHANGE AND DEVELOPMENT

The field of Organization Development is focused on improving the effectiveness of organizations and the people in those organizations. OD has a rich history of research and practice regarding change in organizations.

Your nature and the way you choose to work has significant impact on your client's organization, whether you know it or not. You cannot separate yourself from your client's organization, as if you are some kind of detached observer. You quickly become part of your client's system – the way the people and processes in the organization work with each other on a recurring basis. Thus, it is critical that you have a good understanding of yourself, including your biases (we all have them), how you manage feedback and conflict, how you like to make decisions and solve problems, how you naturally view organizations, your skills as a consultant, etc.

Nowadays, with the complex challenges faced by organizations and the broad diversity of values, perspectives and opinions among the members of those organizations, it's vital that change agents work from a strong set of principles to ensure they operate in a highly effective and ethical manner.

There are several phrases regarding organizational change and development that look and sound a lot alike, but have different meanings. As a result of the prominence of the topic, there seems to be increasingly different interpretations of some of these phrases, while others are used interchangeably. Without at least some sense of the differences between these phrases, communications about organizational change and development can be increasingly vague, confusing and frustrating.

There are different overall types of organizational change, including planned versus unplanned, organization-wide versus change primarily to one part of the organization, incremental (slow, gradual change) versus transformational (radical, fundamental), etc.. Knowing which types of change you are doing helps all participants to retain scope and perspective during the many complexities and frequent frustrations during.

Successful change efforts often include several key roles, including the initiator, champion, change agent, sponsor and leaders. The following article describes each of these roles.

Organization-wide change in corporations should involve the Board of Directors. Whether their members are closely involved in the change or not, they should at least be aware of the change project and monitor if the results are being achieved or not.

How to Make Sure the Board of Directors Participates in the Project for Change.

As the change agent, you might be performing different roles during the project. The following article might help you decide which role to perform.

Appreciative Inquiry is a recent and powerful breakthrough in organizational change and development. It's based on the philosophy that "problems" are often caused as much by our perception of them as problems as by other influencing factors. The philosophy has spawned a strong movement that, in turn, has generated an increasing number of models, tools and tips, most of which seem to build from the positive perceptions (visions, fantasies, wishes and stories) of those involved in the change effort.

## VARIOUS MODELS FOR CHANGE MANAGEMENT

There are numerous well-organized approaches (or models) from which to manage a change effort. Some of the approaches have been around for many years — we just haven't thought of them as such. For example, many organizations undertake strategic planning. The implementation of strategic planning, when done in a systematic, cyclical and explicit approach, is strategic management. Strategic management is also one model for ensuring the success of a change effort. Many people would agree that traditional models of organizational performance management are also models for managing change.

A typical planned, systemic (and systematic) organizational development process often follows an overall action research approach. There are many variations of the action research approach, including by combining its various phases and/or splitting some into more phases. This section provides resources that are organized into one variation of the action research approach. Note that the more collaborative you are in working with members of the organization during the following process, the more likely the success of your overall change effort.

**Phase 1**

This phase is sometimes called the "Contracting" and/or "Entry" phase. This phase is usually where the relationship between you (the initial change agent) and your client starts, whether you are an external or internal consultant. Experts assert that this phase is one of the most - if not the most - important phases in the organizational change process. Activities during this stage form the foundation for successful organizational change. The quality of how this phase is carried out usually is a strong indicator of how the project will go.

**Phase 2**

The more collaborative the change agent is in working with members of the client's organization, the more likely that the change effort will be successful. Your client might not have the resources to fully participate in all aspects of this discovery activity — the more participation they can muster, the better off your project will be.

Whether you are an external or internal change agent in this project, you and your client will work together during this phase to understand more about the overall priority of the change effort and how you all can effectively address it. It might be a major problem in the organization or an exciting vision to achieve. Together, you will collect information, analyze it to identify findings and conclusions, and then make recommendations from that information. Sometimes the data-collection effort is very quick, for example, facilitating a large planning meeting. Other times, the effort is more extensive, for example, evaluating an entire organization and developing a complete plan for change. The nature of discovery also depends on the philosophy of the change agent and client. For example, subscribers to the philosophy of Appreciative Inquiry (referenced above) might conduct discovery, not by digging into the number and causes of problems in the organization, but by conducting interviews to disover the visions and wishes of people in the organization.

Sometimes, people minimize the importance of - or altogether skip - this critical discovery phase, and start change management by articulating an ambitious and comprehensive vision for change. Many would argue that it is unethical to initiate a project for organizational change without fully examining (or discovering) the current situation in the client's organization. Focusing most of the change efforts on achieving a robust vision, without at least some careful discovery, often can be harmful to your client's organization because your project can end up dealing with symptoms of any current issues, rather than the root causes. Also, the project could end up pushing an exciting vision that, while initially inspiring and motivating to many, could be completely unrealistic to achieve — especially if the organization already has many current, major issues to address. Therefore, when working to guide change in an organization that already is facing several significant issues, you are usually better off to start from where your client is at — that usually means conducting an effective discovery to identify priorities for change.

One of the most powerful means to cultivate collaboration is by working with a project team. Besides, no change agent sees all aspects of the situation in the organization — team members help to see more of those various aspects.

**Phase 3**

In the previous phase about discovery, you and your client conducted research, discovered various priorities that needed attention, generated recommendations to address those priorities, and shared your information with others, for example, in a feedback meeting. Part of that meeting included discussions - and, hopefully, decisions - about the overall mutual recommendations that your client should follow to in order address the priorities that were identified by you and your client during your discovery. This phase is focused on further clarifying those recommendations, along with developing them into various action plans. The various plans are sometimes integrated into an overall change management plan. Thus, the early activities in this phase often overlap with, and are a continuation of, the activities near the end of the earlier discovery phase. This is true whether you are an external or internal consultant. Action plans together can now provide a clear and realistic vision for change. They provide the "roadmap" for managing the transition from the present state to the desired future state.

Development of the various action plans is often an enlightening experience for your client as members of their organization begin to realize a more systematic approach to their planning and day-to-day activities. As with other activities during change management, plans can vary widely in how they are developed. Some plans are very comprehensive and systematic (often the best form used for successful change). Others are comprised of diverse sections that are expected to somehow integrate with each other. Subscribers to the philosophy of Appreciative Inquiry (referenced above) might do planning by building on past positive outcomes and on the strengths of members of the organization.

**Phase 4**

During this phase, emphasis is on sustaining and evaluating the change effort, including by addressing resistance that arises from members of the organization — and sometimes in the change agent, as well.

Evaluation occurs both to the quality of implementation of plans so far during the project and also regarding the extent of achievement of desired results from the project. Results might be whether certain indicators of success have been achieved, all issues have been addressed, a vision of success has been achieved, action plans have been implemented and/ or leaders in the organization agree the project has been successful.

As part of the final evaluation, you might redo some of the assessments that you used during the discovery phase in order to measure the difference made by the project.

## If the Project Gets Stuck

During this phase, if the implementation of the plans gets stalled for a long time, for example, many months, then you might cycle back to an earlier phase in the process in order to update and restart the change management project. Projects can get stuck for a variety of reasons, e.g., if the overall situation changes (there suddenly are new and other priorities in the client's organization), people succumb to burnout, key people leave the organization, the relationship between the consultant and client changes, or people refuse to implement action plans.

## Project Termination

These activities are very important to address, even if all participants agree that the project has been successful and no further activities are needed. Project termination activities recognize key learnings from the project, acknowledge the client's development, and identify next steps for you and your client. They also help to avoid "project creep" where the project never ends because the requirements for success keep expanding.

The field of Organization Development uses a variety of processes, approaches, methods, techniques, applications, etc., (these are often termed "interventions") to address organizational issues and goals in order to increase performance. The following partial list of interventions is organized generally in the order presented by Cummings and Worley in their "Organization Development and Change". The following types of interventions are often highly integrated with each other during a project for change.

There are no standard activities that always successfully address certain types of issues in organizations. Many times, the success of a project lies not with having selected the perfect choice of activities, but rather with how honest and participative people were during the project, how much they learned and how open they were to changing their plans for change.

However, there are some basic considerations that most people make when selecting from among the many choices for organizational development, or capacity building, activities. Considerations include:

1. First, does the change-management method (if one was used) suggest what organizational development activities to use now, for example, the method of strategic management might suggest that a SWOT analysis be done, strategic goals be established along with action plans for each goal, and then implementation of the action plans be closely monitored.
2. Is the activity most likely to address the findings from the discovery, that is, to solve the problems or achieve the goals? To find out, review any research about use of the activity, discuss the potential outcomes with experts and also with members of the organization. Consider posing your questions in online groups of experts about change.
3. Does the nature of the activity match the culture of the organization? The best way to find out is to discuss the activity with members of the organization.
4. Does the change agent and key members of the organization have the ability to conduct the activity? For example, technostructural and strategic interventions sometimes require technical skills that are not common to many people.
5. Does the activity require more time to conduct than the time available in which to address the problem or goal? For example, a cash crisis requires immediate attention, so while a comprehensive strategic planning process might ultimately be useful, the four to five months to do that planning is impractical.
6. Does the client's organization have the resources that are necessary to conduct the activity, considering resources such as funding, attention and time from people and facilities.

Before you and your client select types of interventions for the project, be aware of your strong biases about how you view organizations. Without recognizing those biases, you might favor certain types of interventions primarily because those are the only ones you can readily see and understand, even if other types of interventions might be much more effective in your project.

With today's strong emphasis on humanistic values, the following interventions are getting a great deal of attention and emphasis during efforts for change. They focus on helping members of the organization to enhance themselves, each other and the ways in which they work together in order to enhance their overall organization. Although the types of interventions selected for a project depend on a variety of considerations and the interventions in a project often are highly integrated with each other, the following human process interventions might be particularly helpful during change projects in organizations where there is some combination of the following: many new employees, different cultures working together, many complaints among organizational members, many conflicts, low morale, high turnover, ineffective teams, etc.

## HUMAN RESOURCE MANAGEMENT INTERVENTIONS

Performance is in regard to setting goals, monitoring progress to the goals, sharing feedback, reinforcing activities to achieve goals and dissuading those that don't. Performance also is in regard to developing employees, including by enhancing their overall sense of well-being. Although the types of interventions selected for a project depend on a variety of considerations and the interventions in a project often are highly integrated, the following human resource interventions might be particularly helpful in the following kinds of situations: new organizational goals have been established, a major new system or technology must be implemented in a timely fashion, many new employees, plans don't seem to get implemented, productivity is low, ineffective teams, etc.

The following activities focus especially on the organization and its interactions with its external environment, and often involve changes to many aspects of the organization, including employees, groups, technologies, products and services, etc. Although the types of interventions selected for a project depend on a variety of considerations and the interventions in a project often are highly integrated, the following strategic interventions might be particularly helpful in the following kinds of situations: rapid changes in the external environment, rapid or stagnant sales, significantly increased competition, rapid expansion of markets, mergers and acquisitions, the need for quick and comprehensive change throughout the organization, etc.

Significant organizational change occurs, for example, when an organization changes its overall strategy for success, adds or removes a major section or practice, and/or wants to change the very nature by which it operates. It also occurs when an organization evolves through various life cycles, just like people must successfully evolve through life cycles. For organizations to develop, they often must undergo significant change at various points in their development. That's why the topic of organizational change and development has become widespread in communications about business, organizations, leadership and management.

Leaders and managers continually make efforts to accomplish successful and significant change — it's inherent in their jobs. Some are very good at this effort (probably more than we realize), while others continually struggle and fail. That's often the difference between people who thrive in their roles and those that get shuttled around from job to job, ultimately settling into a role where they're frustrated and ineffective. There are many schools with educational programs about organizations, business, leadership and management. Unfortunately, there still are not enough schools with programs about how to analyze organizations, identify critically important priorities to address (such as systemic problems or exciting visions for change) and then undertake successful and significant change to address those priorities. This Library topic aims to improve that situation.

Successful organizational change can be quite difficult to accomplish — it can be like trying to change a person's habits. Fortunately, there is an increasing body of research, practice and tools from which we all can learn. A major goal of this Library topic is to make this body of information much more accessible to many — to give the reader more clear perspective on overall organizational change and development, along with sufficient understanding to begin applying principles and practices for successful change in their roles and organizations. The following resources are not sufficient to guide a large, comprehensive and detailed organizational change effort — that amount of resources comprises a significantly sized book — and besides, there is no standard procedure for guiding change. However, the following resources might be sufficient to provide the reader at least a framework that takes him or her from which to begin guiding change in smaller efforts for organizational change — and then to begin to learn more.

There are many approaches to guiding change — some planned, structured and explicit, while others are more organic, unfolding and implicit. Some approaches work from the future to the present, for example, involving visioning and then action planning about how to achieve that vision. Other approaches work from the present to the future, for example, identifying current priorities (issues and/or goals) and then action planning about to address those priorities (the action research approach is one example). Different people often have very different — and strong — opinions about how change should be conducted. Thus, it is likely that some will disagree with some of the content in this topic. That's what makes this topic so diverse, robust and vital for us all.

## UNDERSTANDING ORGANIZATIONS, LEADERSHIP AND MANAGEMENT

To really understand organizational change and begin guiding successful change efforts, the change agent should have at least a broad understanding of the context of the change effort. This includes understanding the basic systems and structures in organizations, including their typical terms and roles. This requirement applies to the understanding of leadership and management of the organizations, as well. That is why graduate courses in business often initially include a course or some discussion on organizational theory. Organizational change should not be conducted for the sake of change. Organizational change efforts should be geared to improve the performance of organizations and the people in those organizations. Therefore, it's useful to have some understanding of what is meant by "performance" and the various methods to manage performance in organizations.

## SYSTEMS THINKING

The past few decades have seen an explosion in the number of very useful tools to help change agents to effectively explore, understand and communicate about organizations, as well as to guide successful change in those organizations. Tools from systems theory and systems thinking especially are a major breakthrough. Even if the change agent is not an expert about systems theory and thinking, even a basic understanding can cultivate an entire new way of working.

The field of Organization Development is focused on improving the effectiveness of organizations and the people in those organizations. OD has a rich history of research and practice regarding change in organizations. Why not learn from that history? Your nature and the way you choose to work has significant impact on your client's organization, whether you know it or not. You cannot separate yourself from your client's organization, as if you are some kind of detached observer. You quickly become part of your client's system — the way the people and processes in the organization work with each other on a recurring basis. Thus, it is critical that you have a good understanding of yourself, including your biases (we all have them), how you manage feedback and conflict, how you like to make decisions and solve problems, how you naturally view organizations, your skills as a consultant, etc.

Nowadays, with the complex challenges faced by organizations and the broad diversity of values, perspectives and opinions among the members of those organizations, it's vital that change agents work from a strong set of principles to ensure they operate in a highly effective and ethical manner.

## CHANGE MANAGEMENT

There are several phrases regarding organizational change and development that look and sound a lot alike, but have different meanings. As a result of the prominence of the topic, there seems to be increasingly different interpretations of some of these phrases, while others are used interchangeably. Without at least some sense of the differences between these phrases, communications about organizational change and development can be increasingly vague, confusing and frustrating.

There are different overall types of organizational change, including planned versus unplanned, organization-wide versus change primarily to one part of the organization, incremental (slow, gradual change) versus transformational (radical, fundamental), etc.. Knowing which types of change you are doing helps all participants to retain scope and perspective during the many complexities and frequent frustrations during change.

Successful change efforts often include several key roles, including the initiator, champion, change agent, sponsor and leaders. Organization-wide change in corporations should involve the Board of Directors. Whether their members are closely involved in the change or not, they should at least be aware of the change project and monitor if the results are being achieved or not.

As the change agent, you might be performing different roles during the project.

Appreciative Inquiry is a recent and powerful breakthrough in organizational change and development. It's based on the philosophy that "problems" are often caused as much by our perception of them as problems as by other influencing factors. The philosophy has spawned a strong movement that, in turn, has generated an increasing number of models, tools and tips, most of which seem to build from the positive perceptions (visions, fantasies, wishes and stories) of those involved in the change effort.

There are numerous well-organized approaches (or models) from which to manage a change effort. Some of the approaches have been around for many years – we just haven't thought of them as such. For example, many organizations undertake strategic planning. The implementation of strategic planning, when done in a systematic, cyclical and explicit approach, is strategic management. Strategic management is also one model for ensuring the success of a change effort. There are numerous, major methods and movements to regularly increase the performance of organizations. Each includes regular recurring activities to establish organizational goals, monitor progress toward the goals, and make adjustments to achieve those goals more effectively and efficiently.

Any or all of the following approaches will improve organizational performance depending on if they are implemented comprehensively and remain focused on organizational results. Some of the following, e.g., organizational learning and knowledge management, might be interpreted more as movements than organization performance strategies because there are wide interpretations of the concepts, not all of which include focusing on achieving top-level organizational results. However, if these two concepts are instilled across the organization and focus on organizational results, they contribute strongly to organizational performance. On the other hand, the Balanced Scorecard, which is deliberately designed to be comprehensive and focused on organizational results, will not improve performance if not implemented from a strong design.

## P



## Q



## R



## S



## T



## U



## V